MACK FC-FCSW-NW 1936 THROUGH 1947

PHOTO ARCHIVE

MACK FC-FCSW-NW 1936 THROUGH 1947

PHOTO ARCHIVE

Photographs from the
Mack Trucks Historical Museum Archives

Edited with introduction by
Thomas E. Warth

Iconografix
Photo Archive Series

Iconografix
P.O. Box 18433
Minneapolis, Minnesota 55418 USA

Library of Congress Card Number 94-74209

ISBN 1-882256-28-X

95 96 97 98 99 00 5 4 3 2 1

Book design and digital imaging by Pixelperfect, Madison, Wisconsin

Printed in the United States of America

Book trade distribution by Voyageur Press, Inc. (800) 888-9653

PREFACE

The histories of machines and mechanical gadgets are contained in the books, journals, correspondence and personal papers stored in libraries and archives throughout the world. Written in tens of languages, covering thousands of subjects, the stories are recorded in millions of words.

Words are powerful. Yet, the impact of a single image, a photograph or an illustration, often relates more than dozens of pages of text. Fortunately, many of the libraries and archives that house the words also preserve the images.

In the *Photo Archive Series*, Iconografix reproduces photographs and illustrations selected from public and private collections. The images are chosen to tell a story—to capture the character of their subject. Reproduced as found, they are accompanied by the captions made available by the archive.

The Iconografix *Photo Archive Series* is dedicated to young and old alike, the enthusiast, the collector and anyone who, like us, is fascinated by "things" mechanical.

ACKNOWLEDGMENTS

The photographs appearing in this book were made available by the Mack Trucks Historical Museum. We are grateful to Colin Chisholm, Curator, for his assistance.

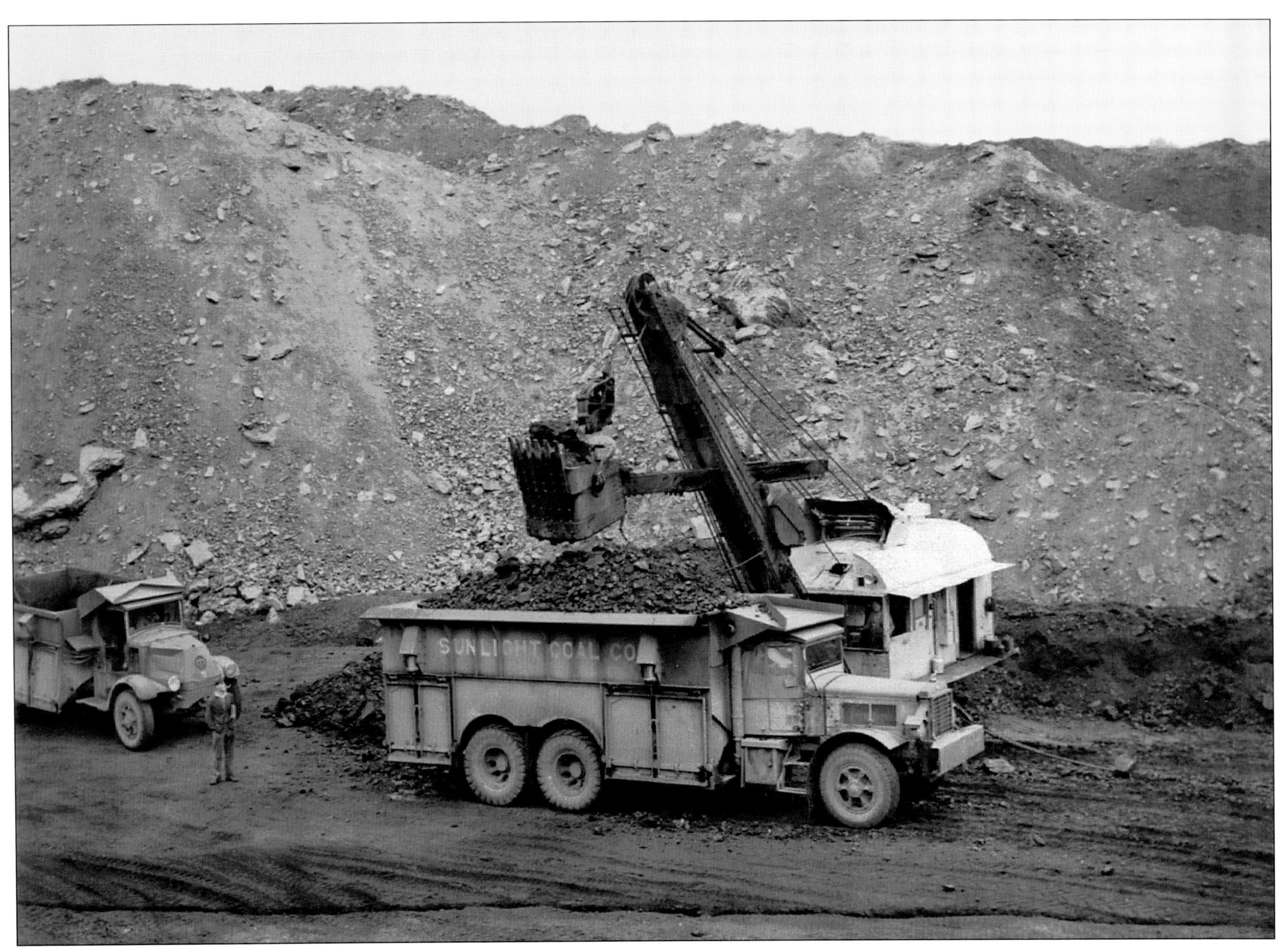

A 1937 Mack FCSW, the largest truck ever built to that time. (M2819)

Introduction

"Built like a Mack Truck." What a wonderful statement—one of the best descriptions you can give to a piece of equipment designed to stand up to tough conditions. Since just after the turn of the century, Mack has been turning out trucks of such a quality that the phrase has become part of our language. The first truck placed in the Smithsonian Collection was a Model AC—the venerable "Bulldog."

The Mack brothers made their name as horse drawn wagon builders in Brooklyn, New York in the 1800s. About 1902 they produced their first motor vehicle, and by 1911 Mack produced over 500 trucks a year. The outbreak of World War I proved a boon to their business, which by then was established in its present headquarters in Allentown, Pennsylvania.

The Model FC was introduced in 1936. It was the largest of the F-Series Super-Duty Mack trucks, a heavy-duty truck for off-highway use in the construction and mining industries. The FC, its successor the FCSW, and the limited-production NW were formidable pieces of engineering, as this book well illustrates. With gross vehicle weights as much as 50 tons, they would be impressive even today.

The photographs in this book were chosen from the Mack Trucks Historical Museum. They appear in a roughly chronological order, although photos of the same chassis have been kept together. In some cases, the captions indentify the chassis number; in other cases the General Sales Order or General Works Order number. All of these trucks were custom-built, generally in twos or threes, and model identifications seem to have varied; apparently different departments used different identifiers. The designation "2C", indicated two chain driven axles, and was used interchangeably with the designations "SW" (six wheel) and "6". The designation "2" indicated two driven axles; "1C" indicated one chain driven axle; "8" indicated all-wheel drive; "D" following the model number indicated dual reduction drive; "D" following the chassis number indicated a diesel engine; "X" and "H" both indicated heavy-duty.

Negative numbers are included when known. Captions furnished with the photographs were sometimes sparse, but we hope that by presenting these fascinating images the reader will be encouraged into further research.

MACK MODEL FC

The FC was a chain driven, single axle truck designed for off-highway use. Its gross vehicle weight was rated at 60,000 pounds. The FC wheelbase measured 170 inches, with overall width at the rear tires of 115 inches. Engine options included: Mack EY, a 706.5 cubic inch, 166 horsepower 6-cylinder gas model; Cummins HBD, a 672 cubic inch, 150 horsepower 6-cylinder diesel model; Waukesha WAK and WAKH, 1,199 cubic inch, 225 and 200 horsepower 6-cylinder gas models, respectively; and a Hercules 6-cylinder gasoline model.

The first FC was produced in 1936. Only 22 units were built, however, as the heavier duty FCSW proved more appealing to the customers.

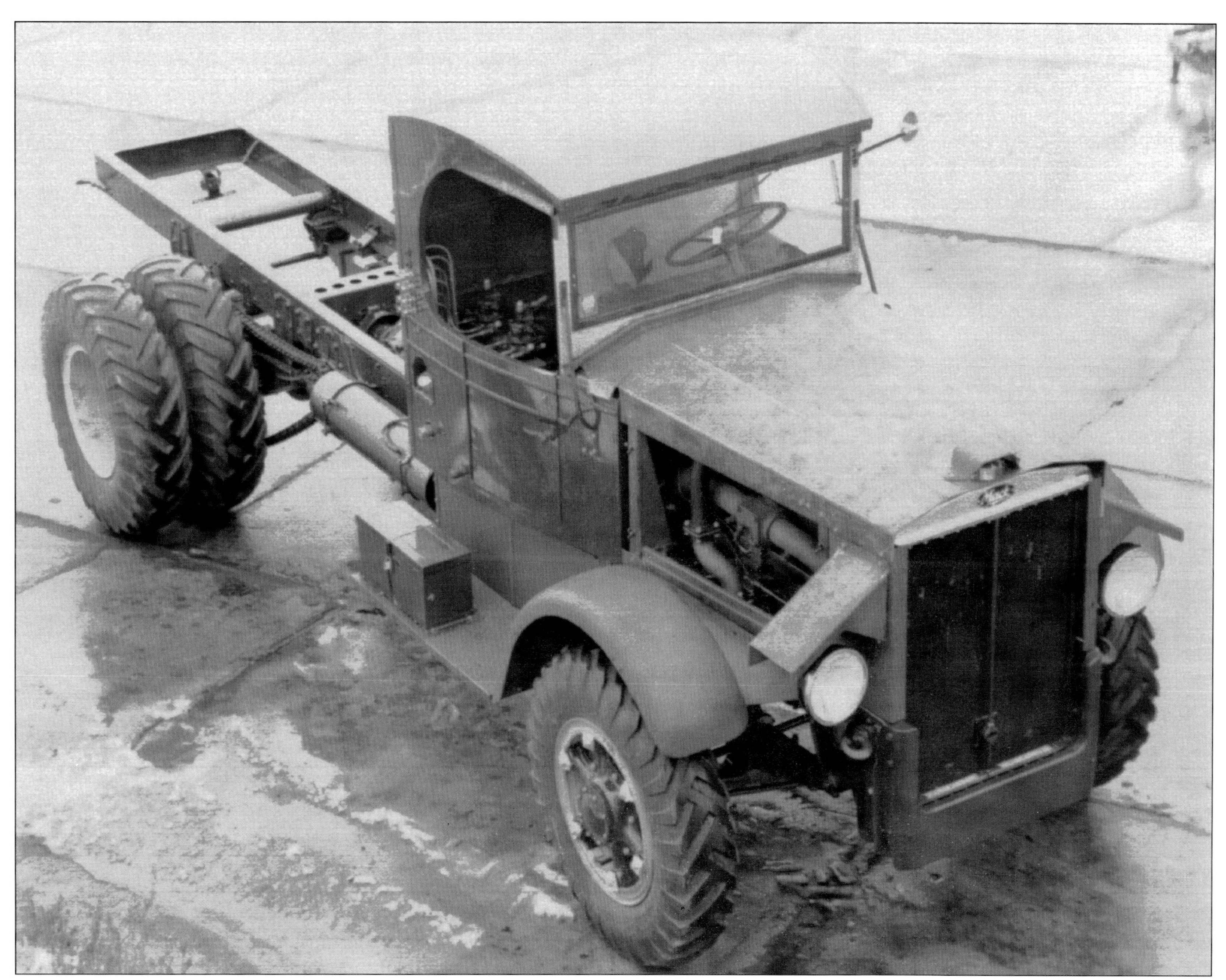

FC1C, chassis #1002, built for Southwestern Illinois Coal Co. November 1936. (A7508)

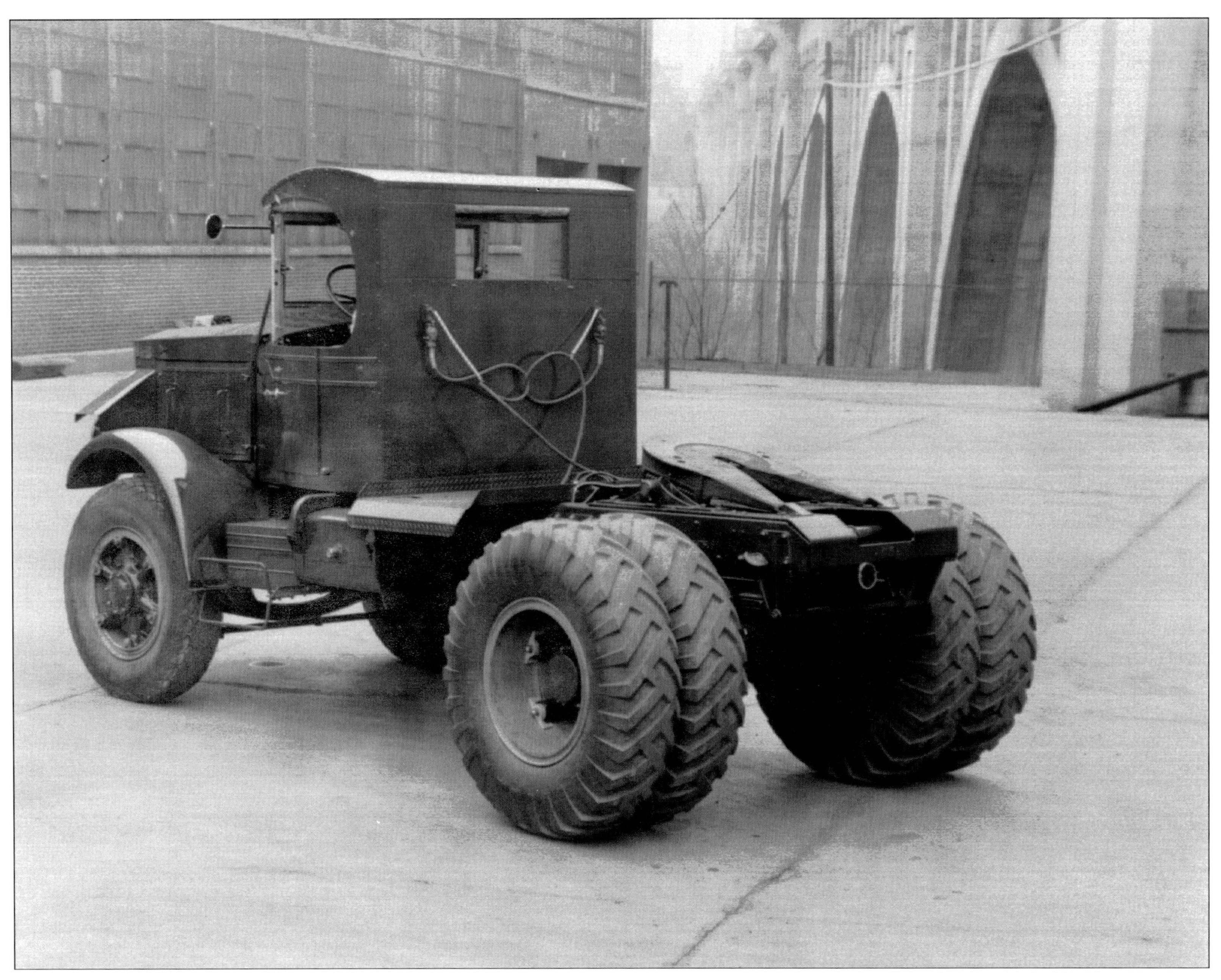

Rear view of chassis #1002 showing the fifth wheel, beveled rear of frame, and diamondette decking behind the cab. Rear tires were 13.50-24 duals with ground-grip treads. November 1936. (A7569)

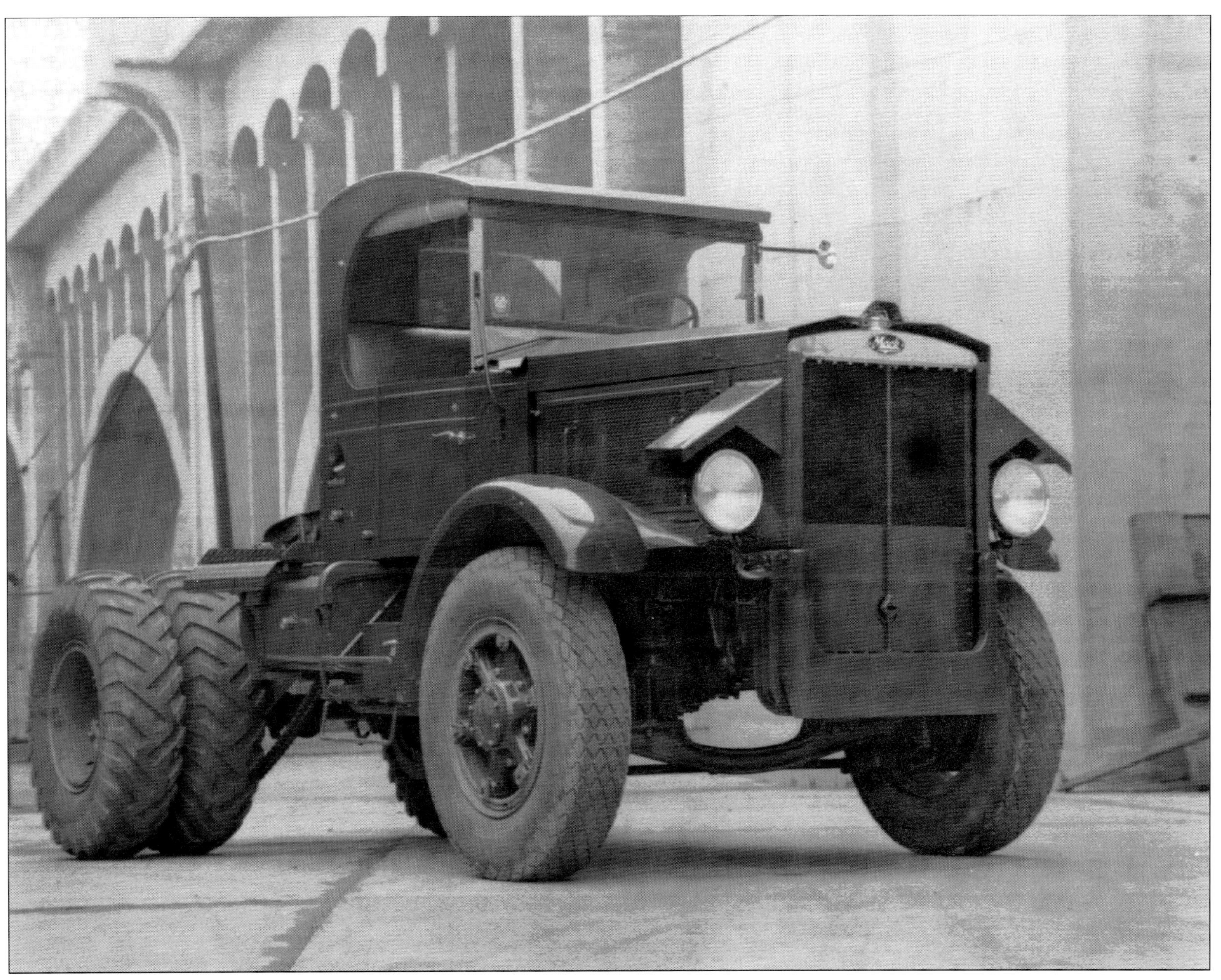

Chassis #1002 featured a cab with armored hood and lamp protection, runged mounting steps, and two auxiliary gasoline tanks. Note that the lower portion of the radiator was blanked off for winter service.

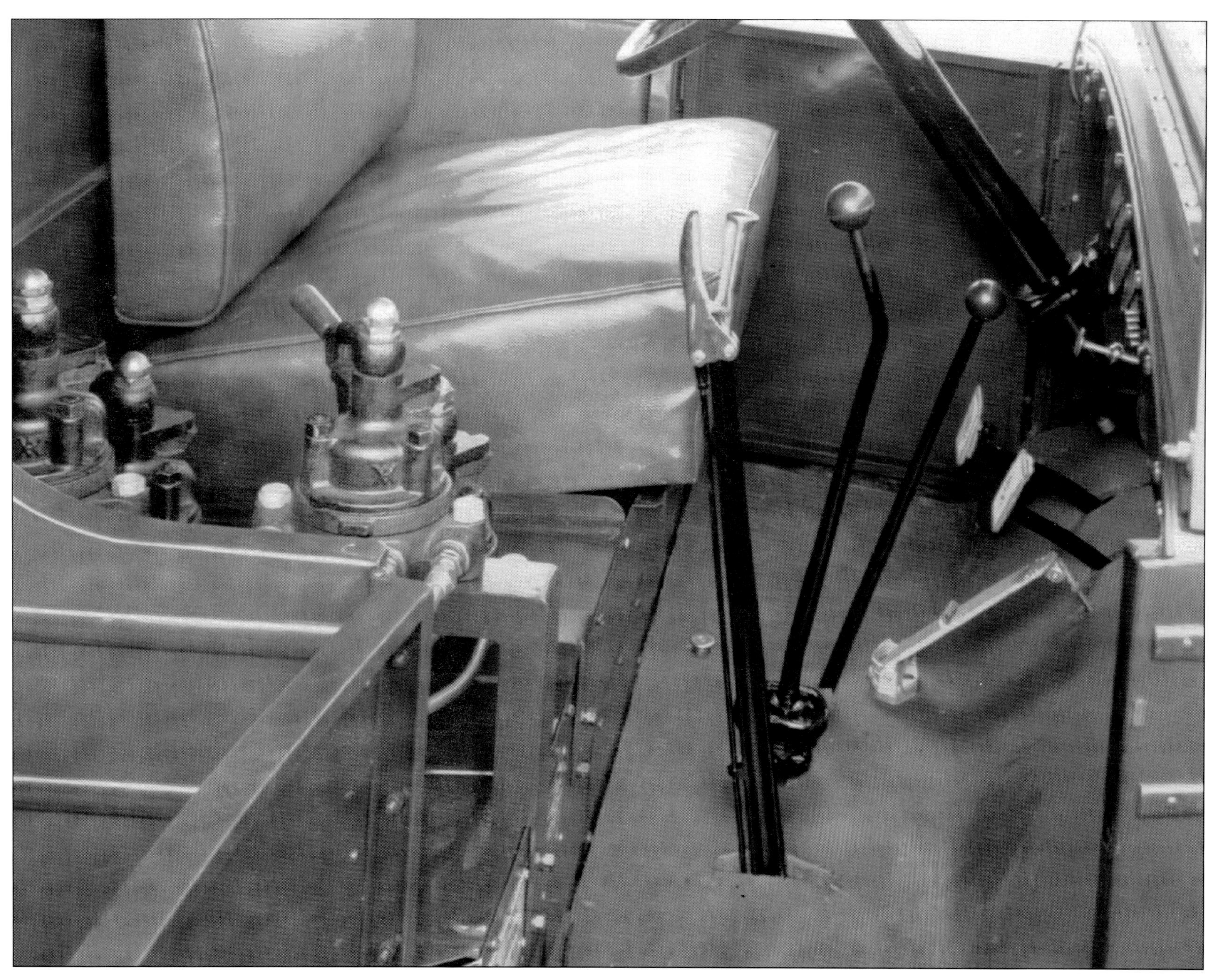

FC1C cab detail. The standard fuel tank was placed beneath the front seat. (A7492)

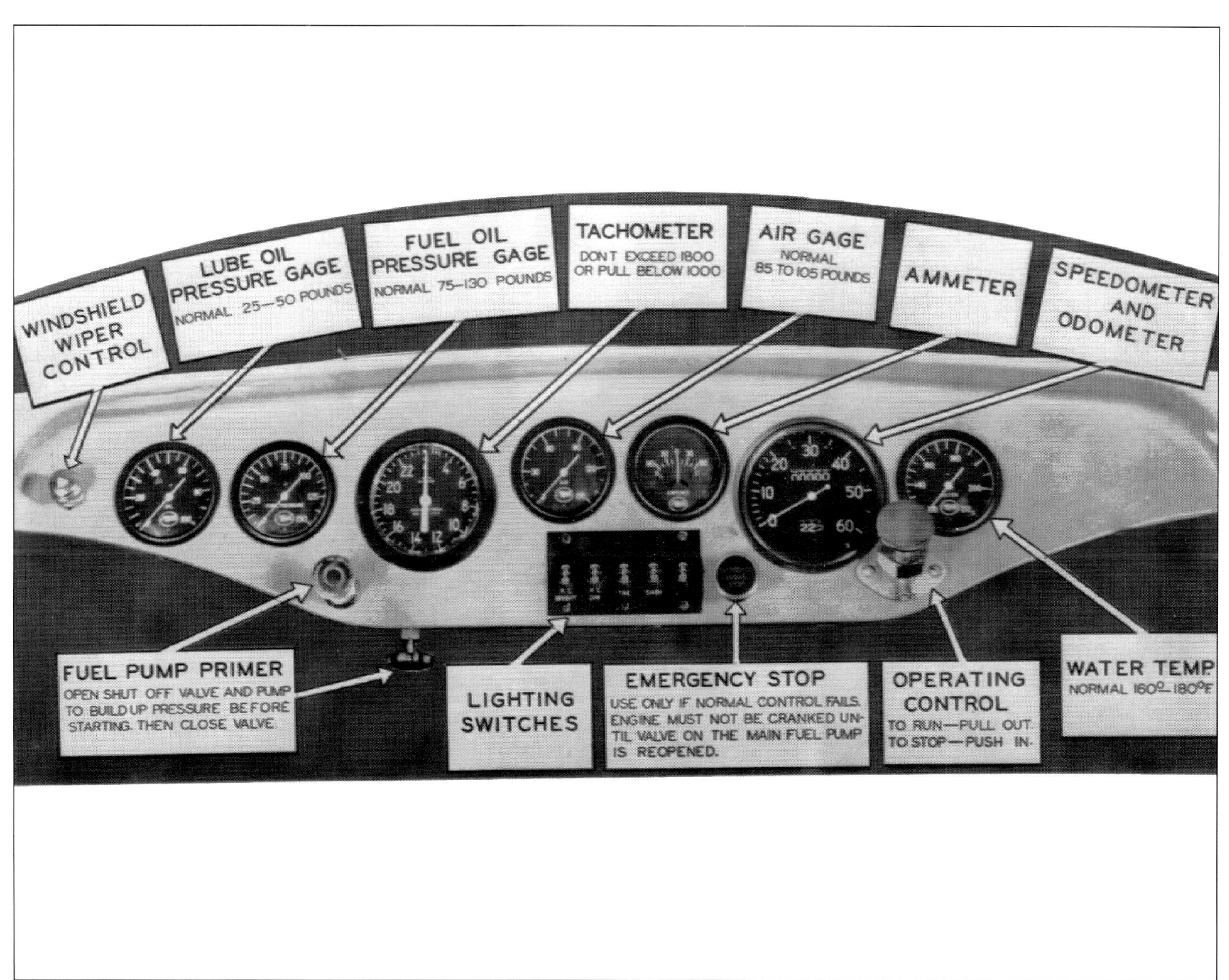

FC instrument panel. (M3163)

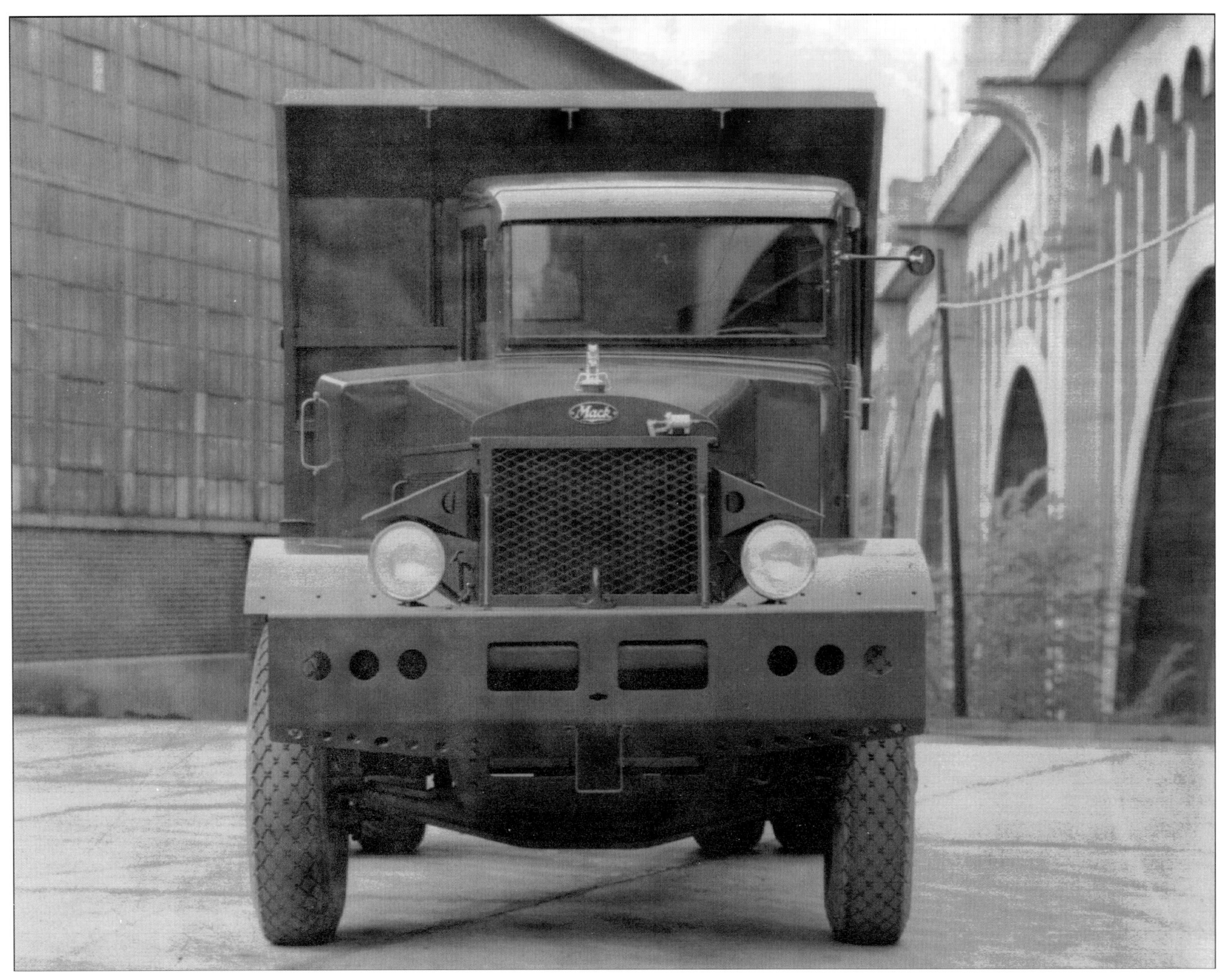

Front and side views of an FC1C with dump body, one of three built bearing chassis #1012 through #1014. May 1938. (A8670)

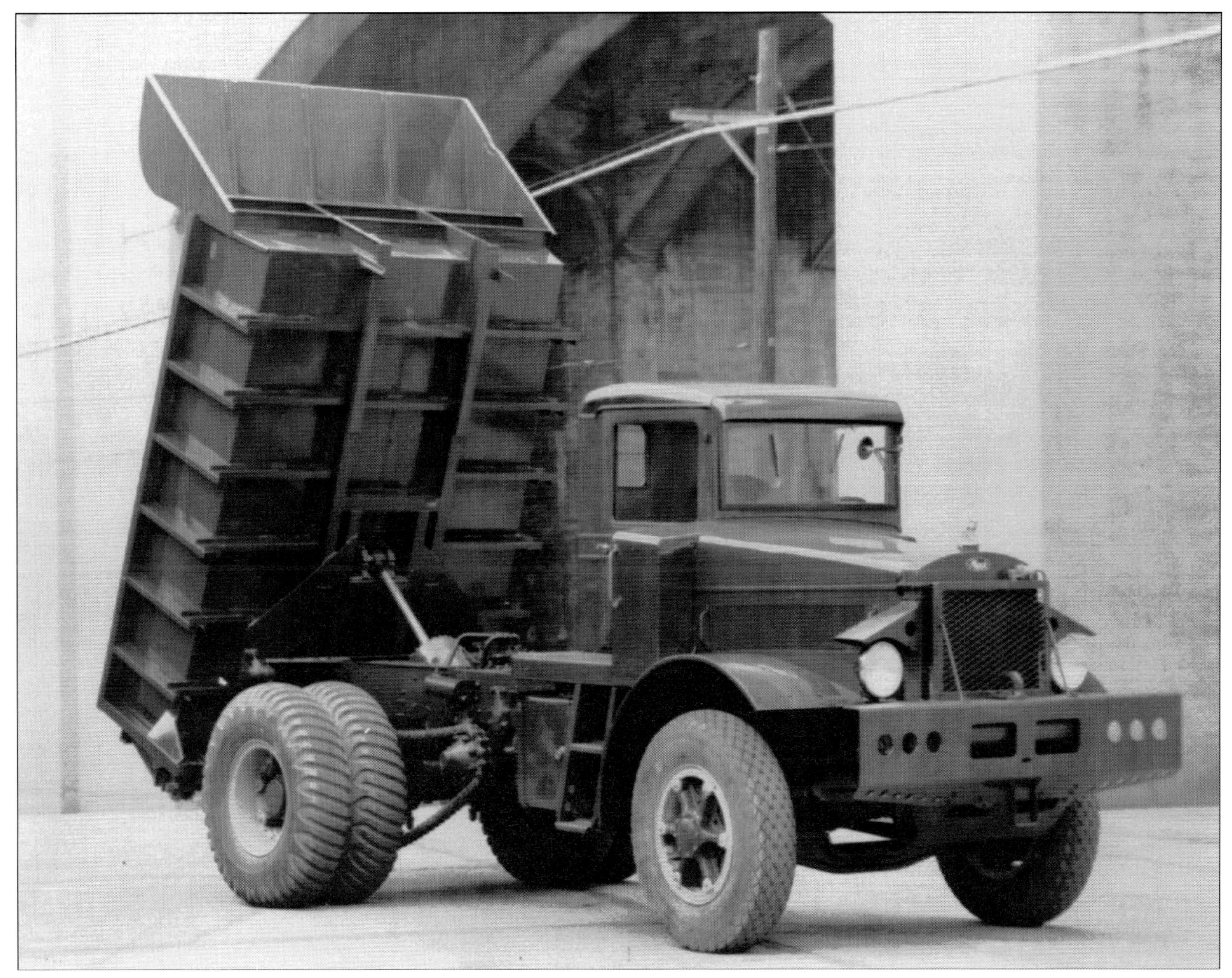

(A8668)

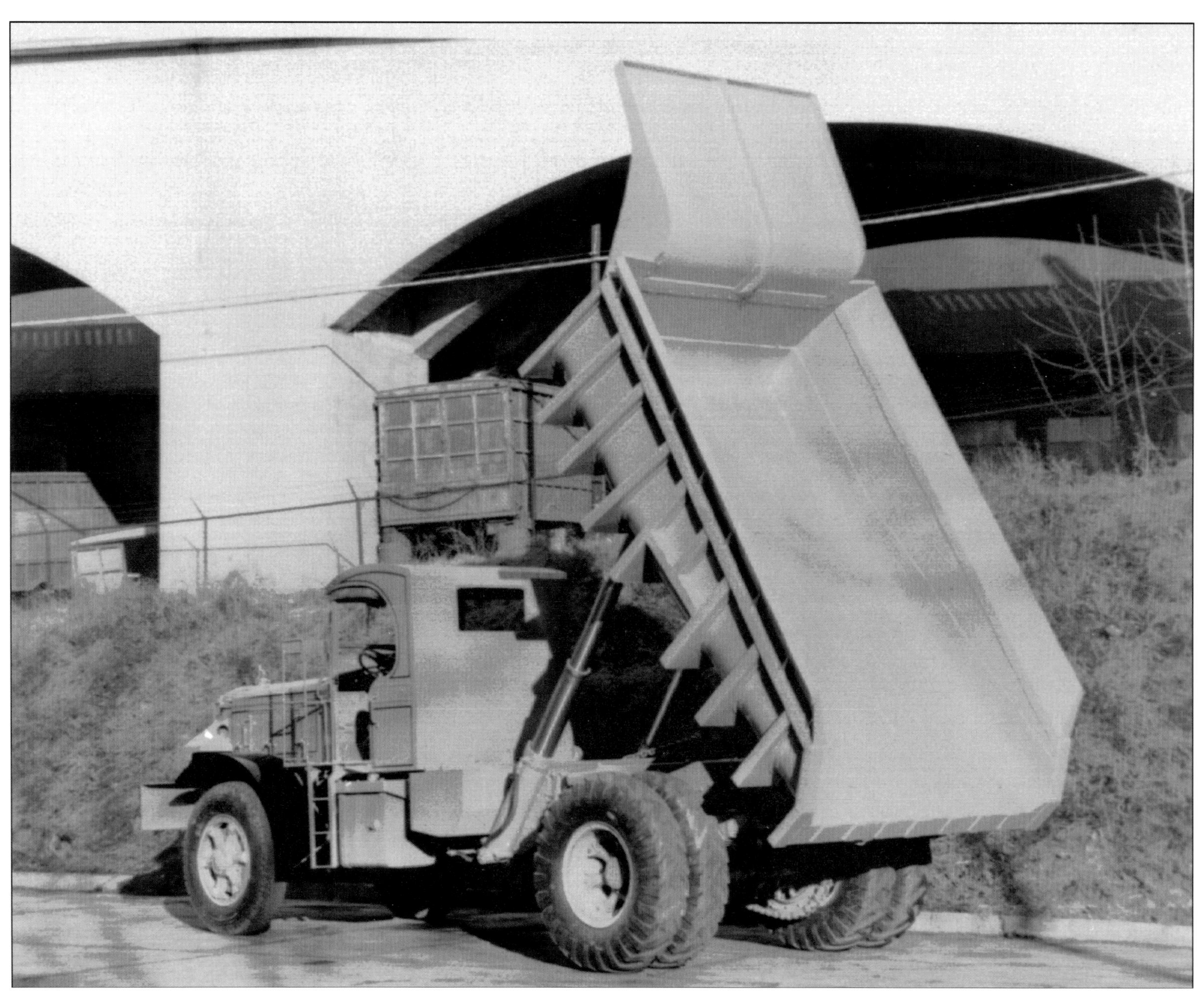

Rear and side views of an FC1C with dump body, one of three bearing chassis #1015 through #1017. January 1938. (A8670)

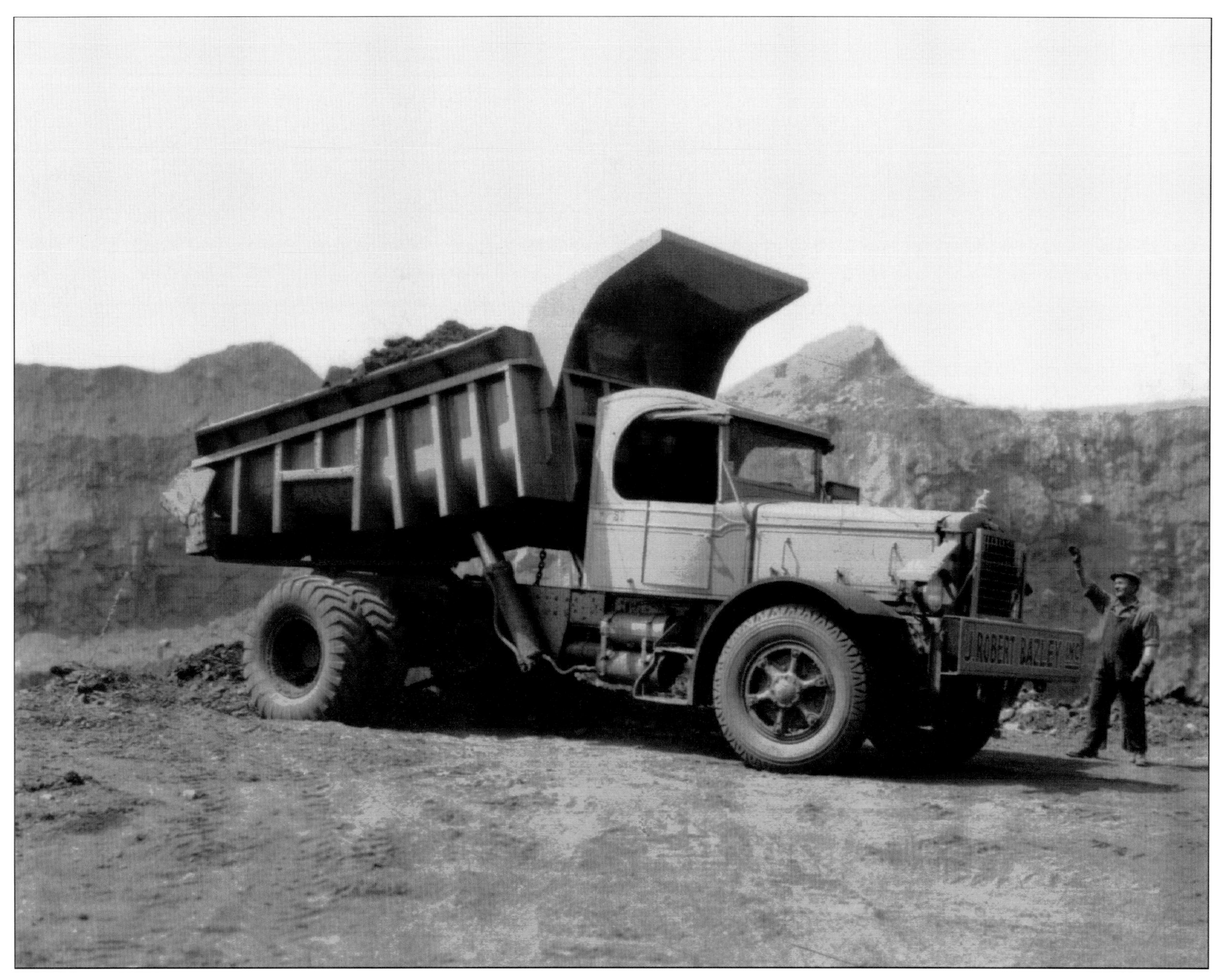

(A8397)

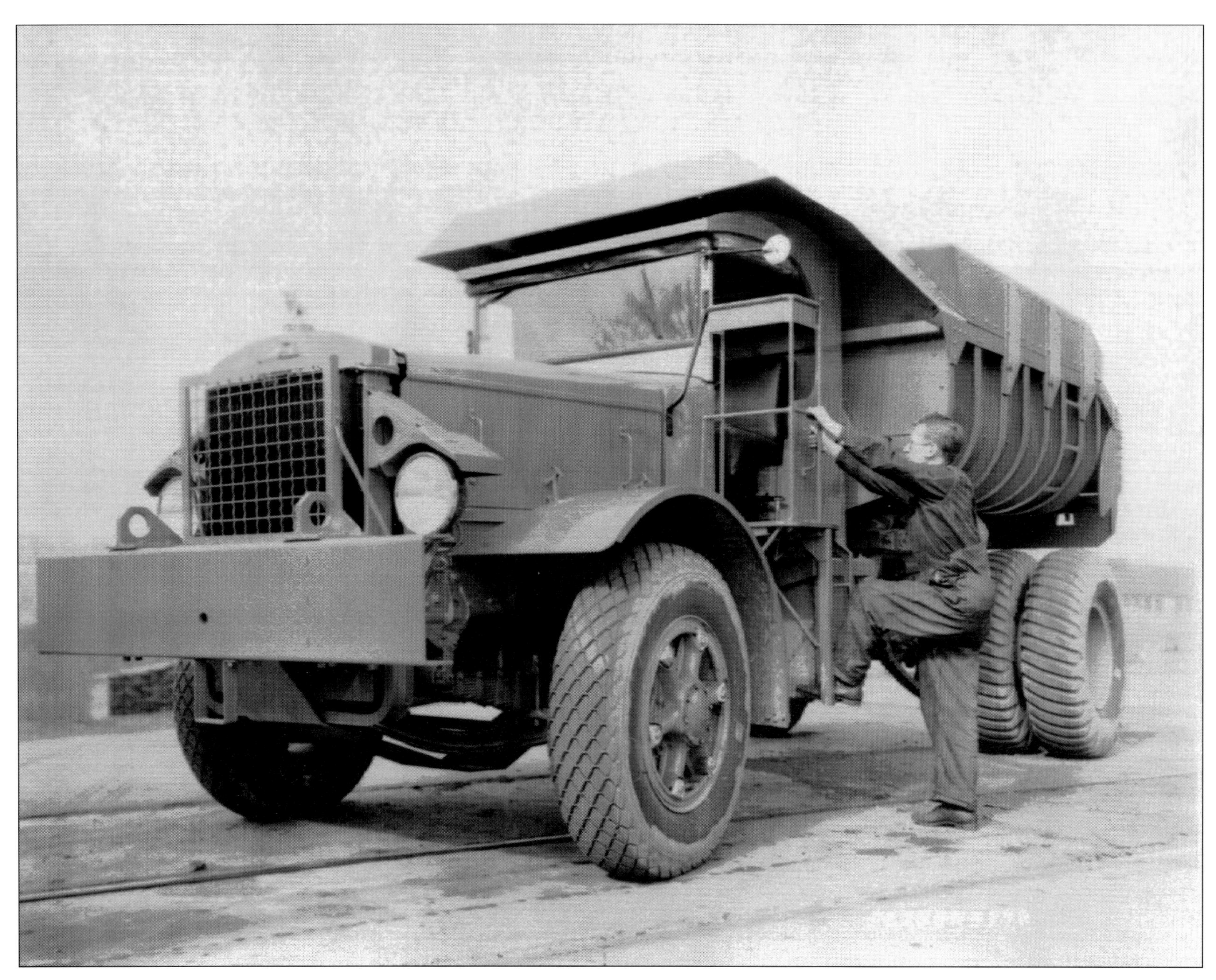

Front and side views of an FC1C with dump body, one of two bearing chassis #1018 and #1019. (A8398)

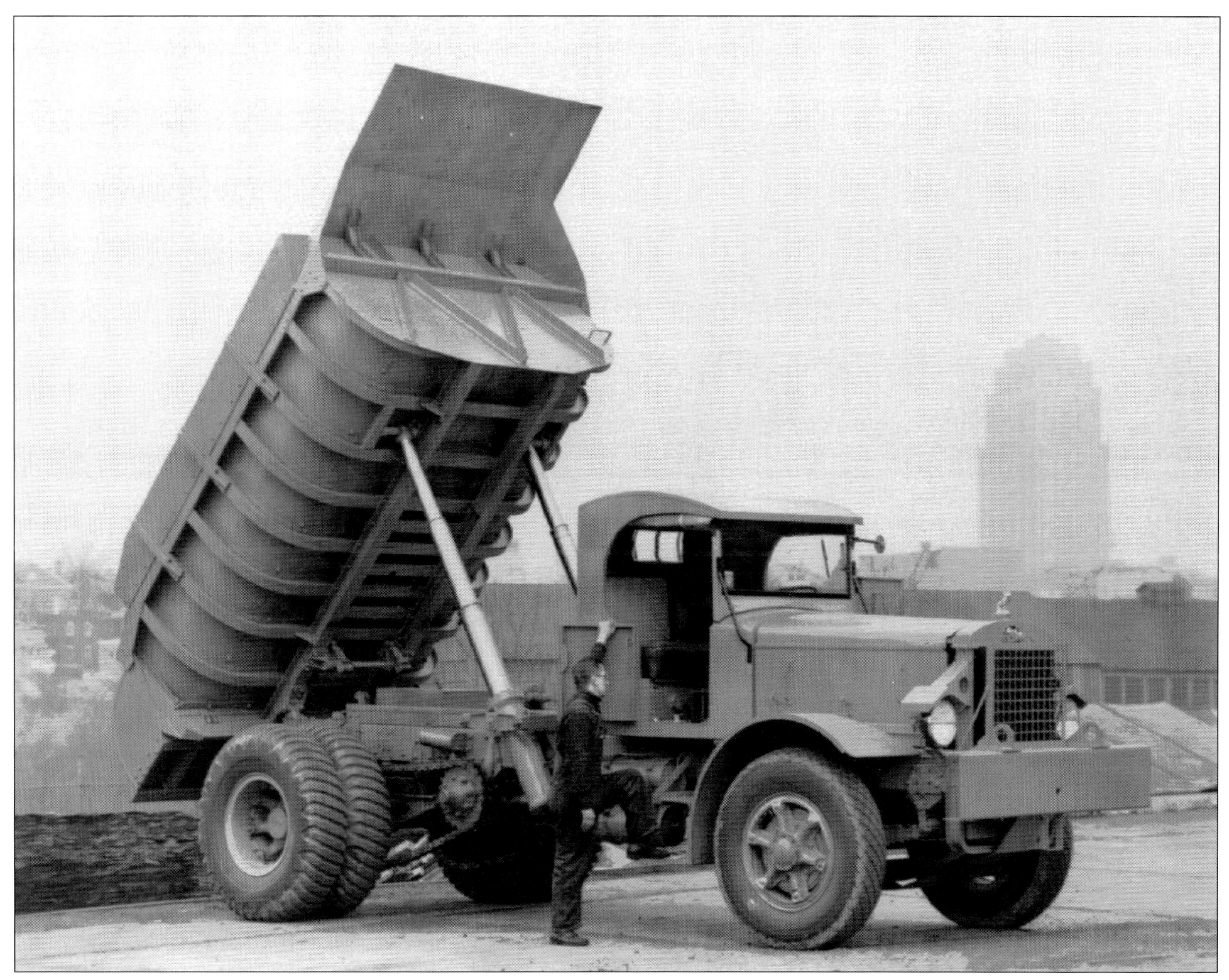

(A8397)

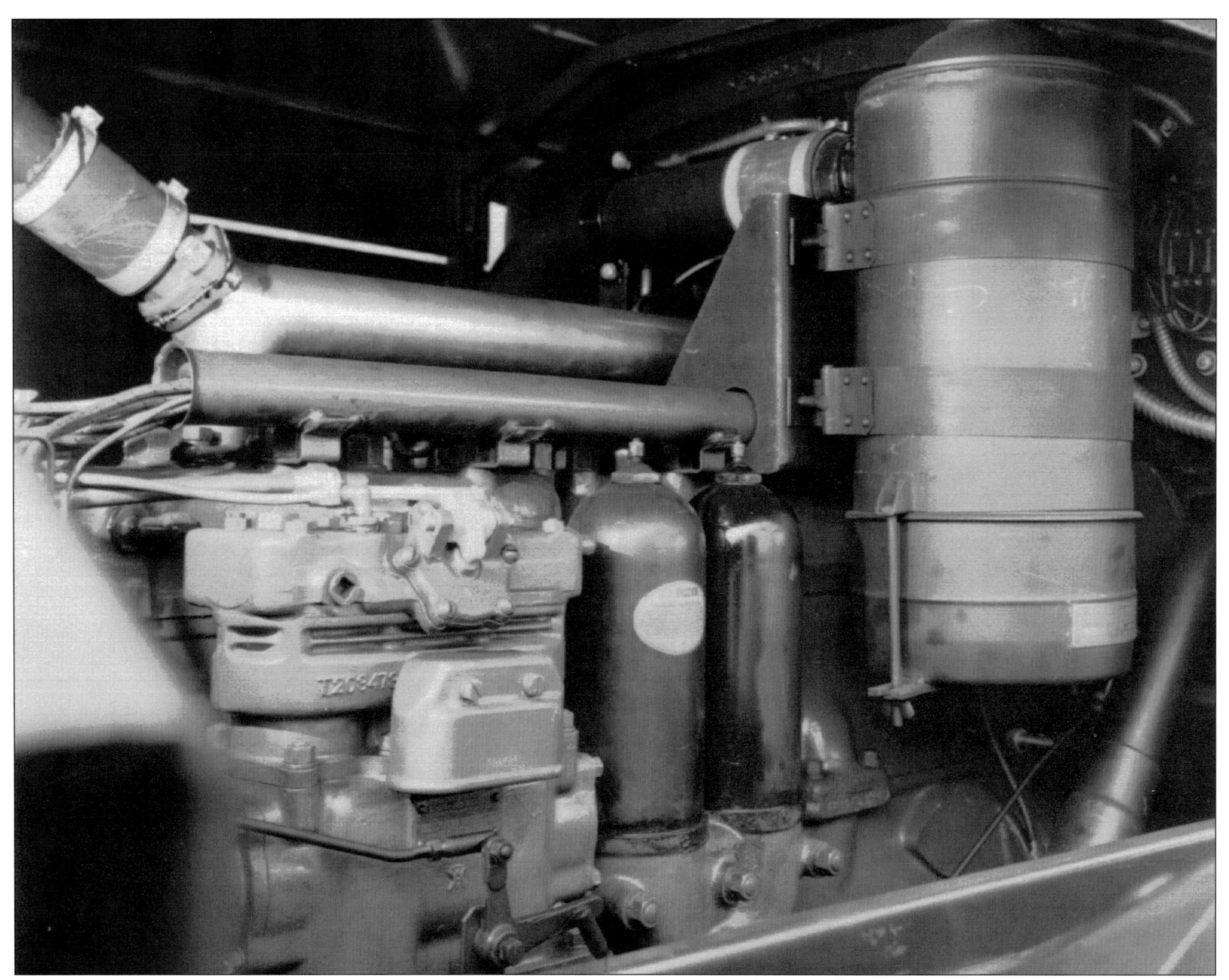

Hercules engine fitted to FC1C chassis #1002. (A7491)

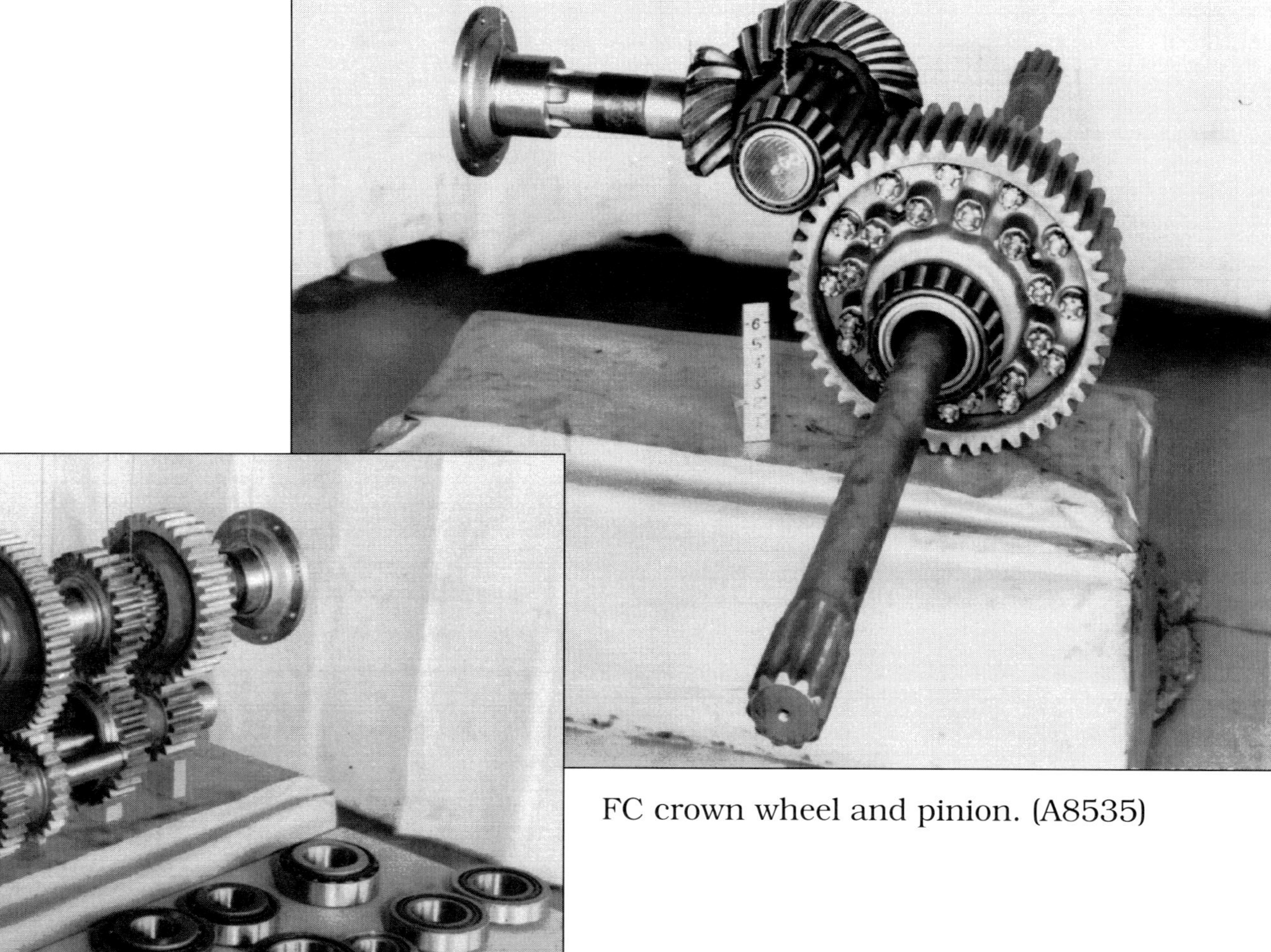

FC crown wheel and pinion. (A8535)

FC transmission gears. (A8473)

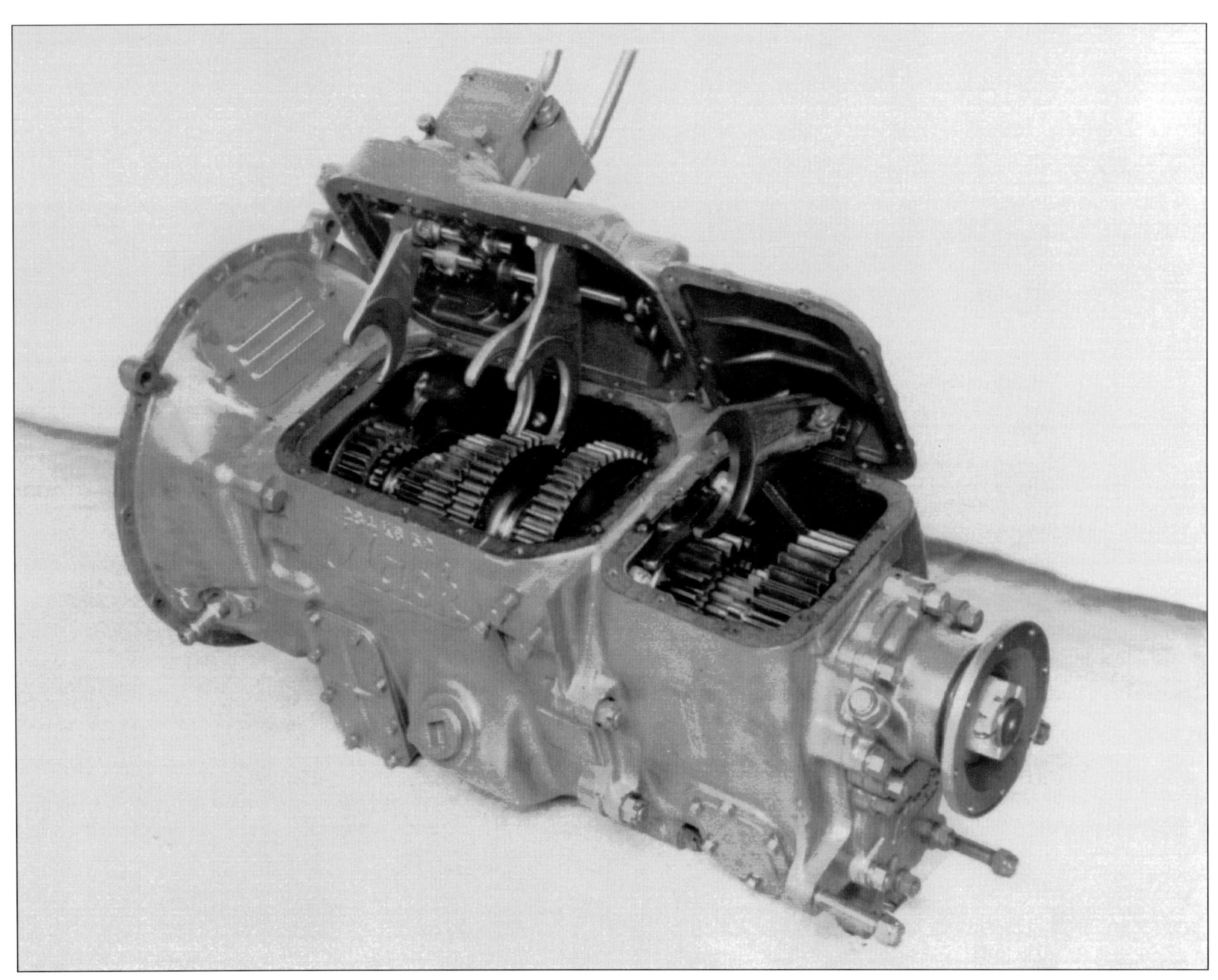

FC transmission. (A8610)

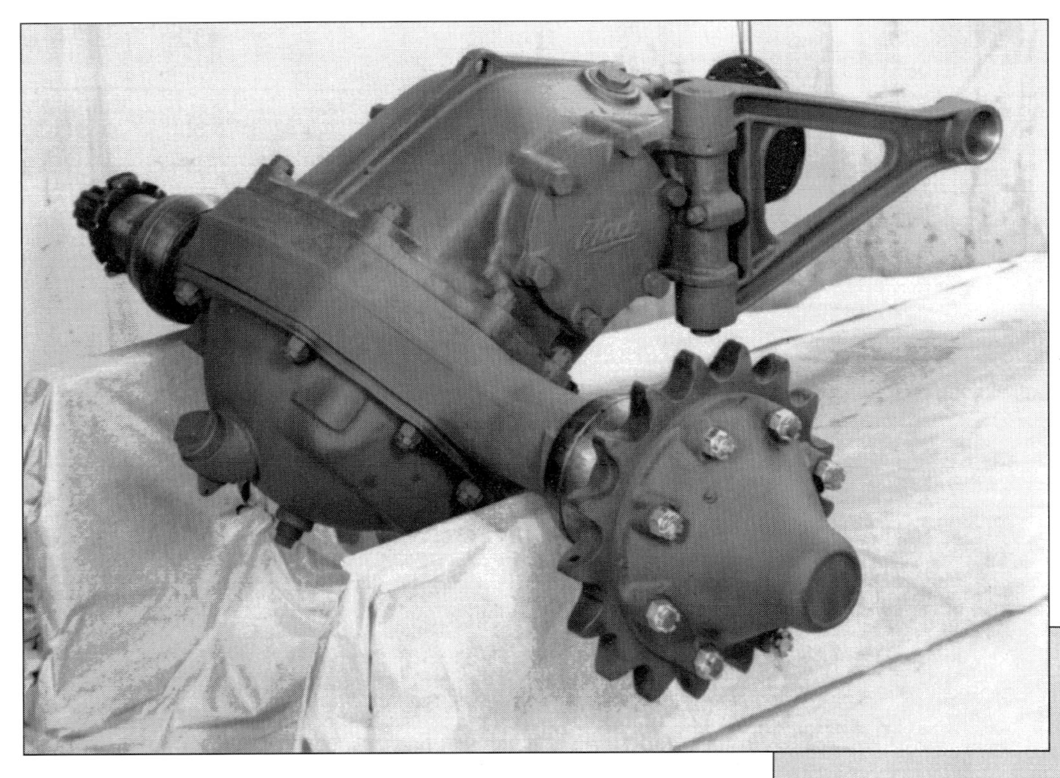

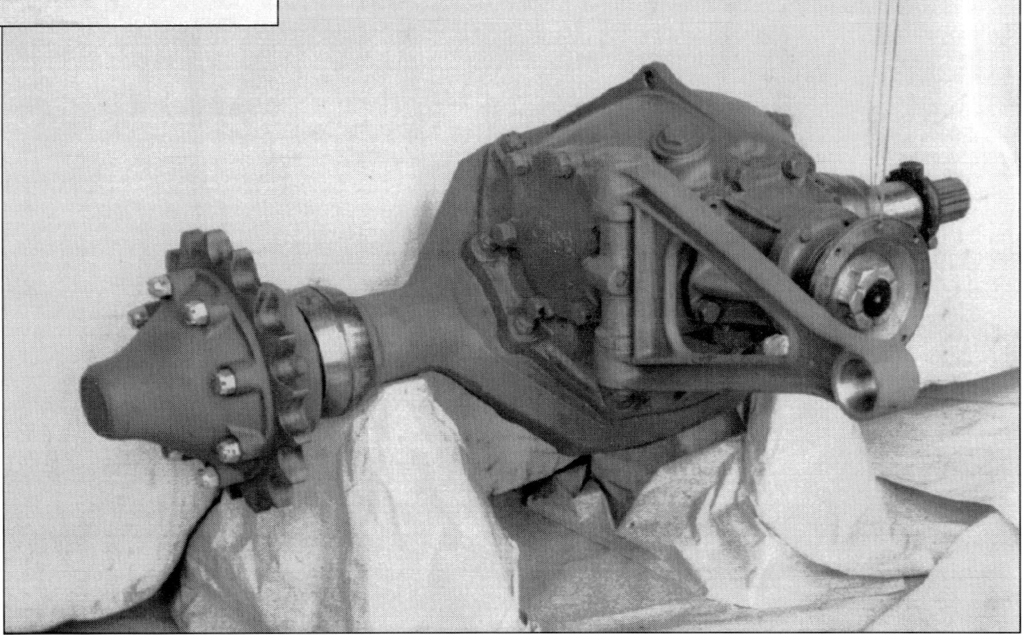

FC jackshaft with gear case. (A8680)

MACK MODEL FCSW

The FCSW was a chain driven, twin axle truck designed for off-highway use. Its gross vehicle weight was rated at 100,000 pounds. The FCSW wheelbase measured 170.5 inches, with overall width at the rear tires of 124.12 inches. Engine options included: Mack EY, a 706.5 cubic inch, 166 horsepower 6-cylinder gas model; Cummins HBD, a 672 cubic inch, 150 horsepower 6-cylinder diesel model; Waukesha WAK and WAKH, 1,199 cubic inch, 225 and 200 horsepower 6-cylinder gas models, respectively; and a Hercules 6-cylinder gasoline model.

A total of 251 FCSWs were produced between 1937 and 1947.

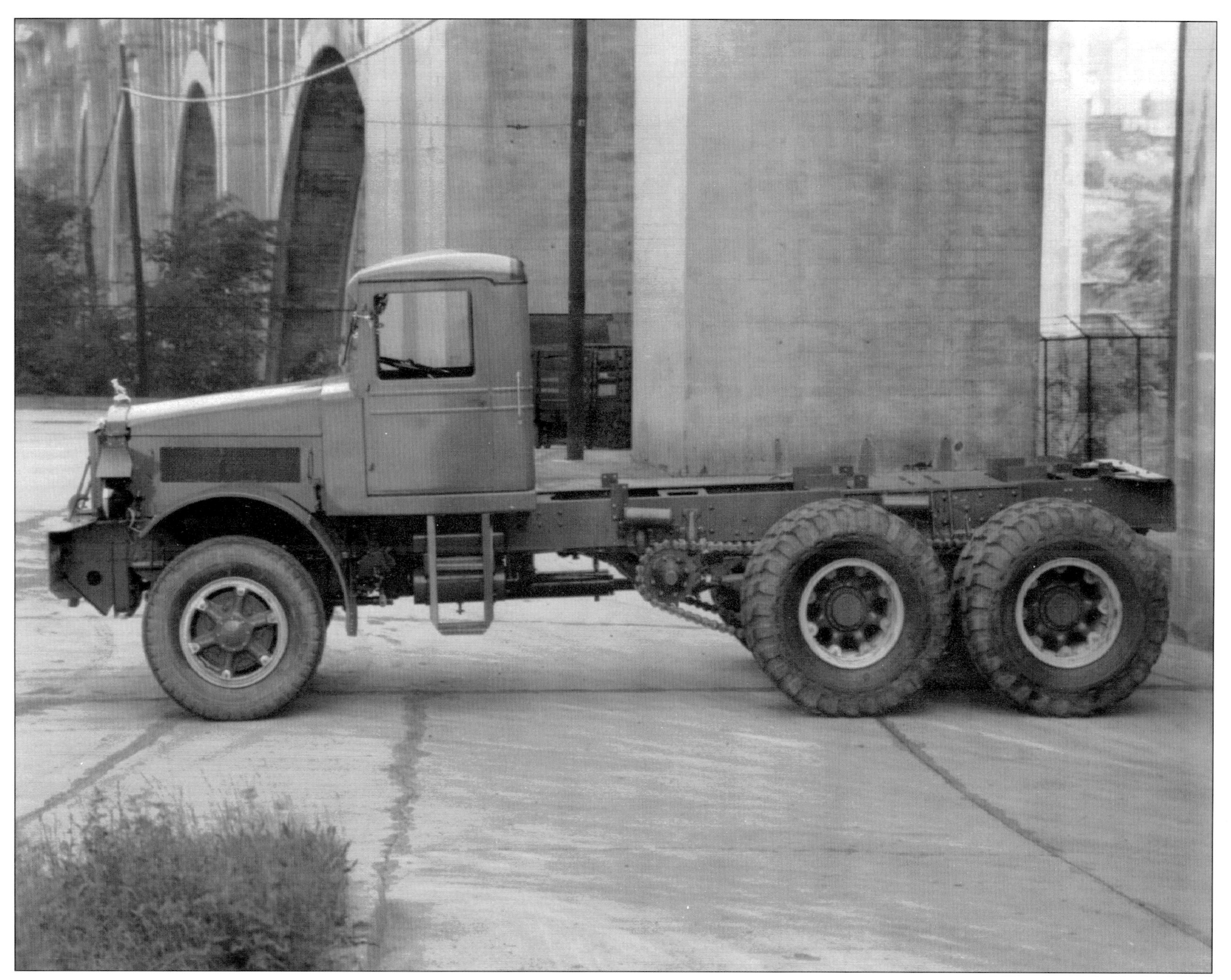

FCSW. July 1938. (A8762)

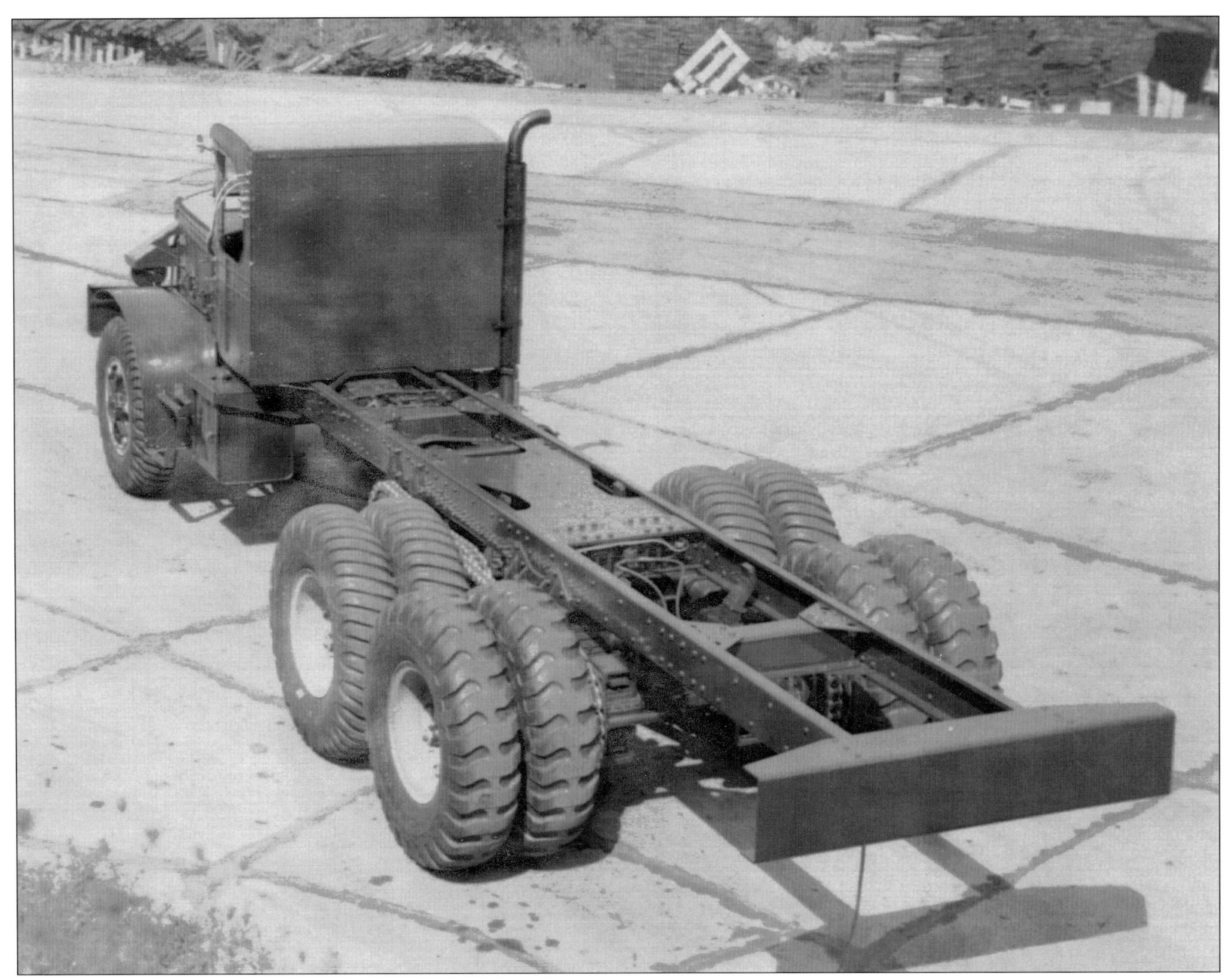

FCSW chassis #1001. September 1937. (A8066)

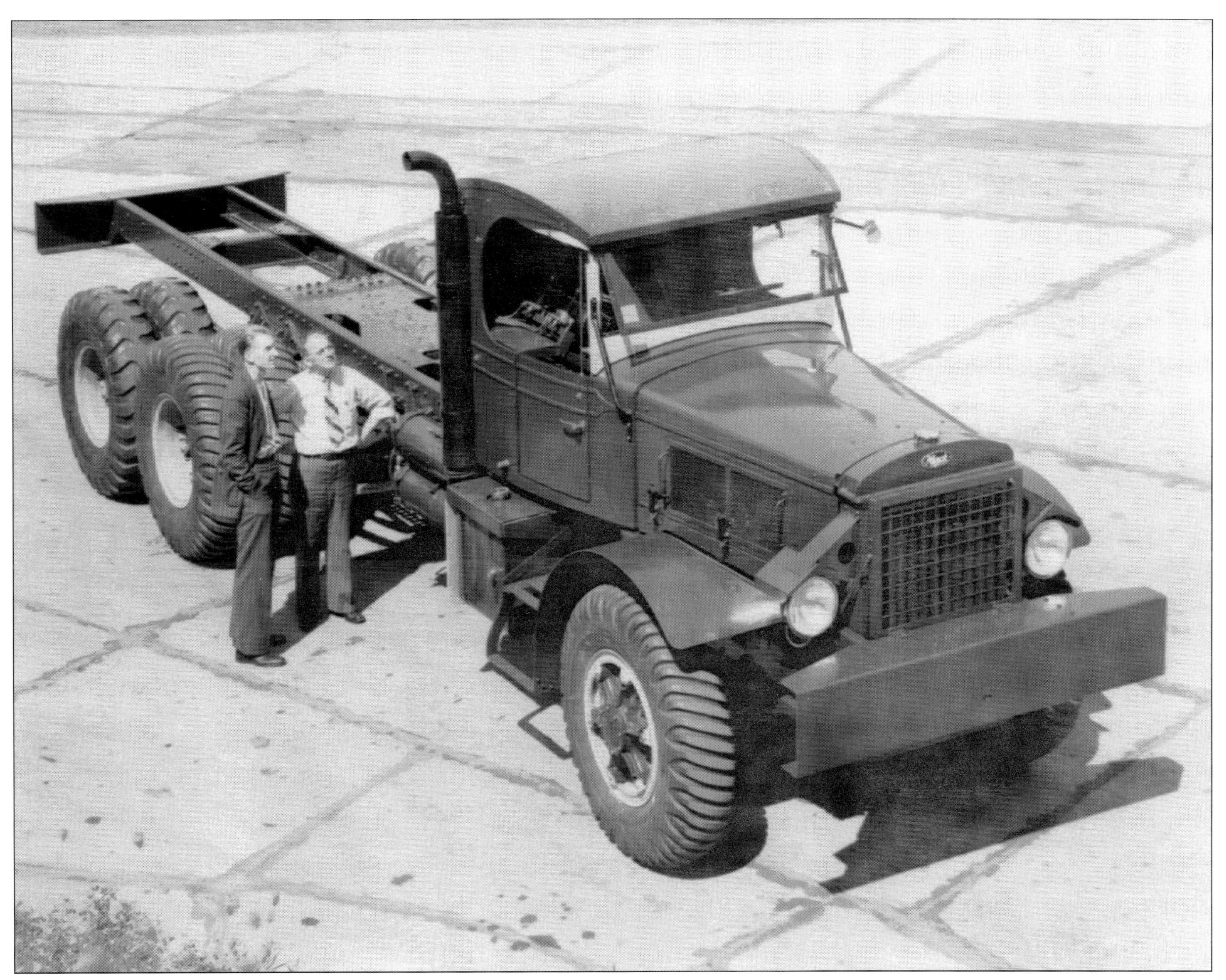

Larry Burgess, Chief Engineer Off-Highway trucks, at left, and FCSW chassis #1001. (A8068)

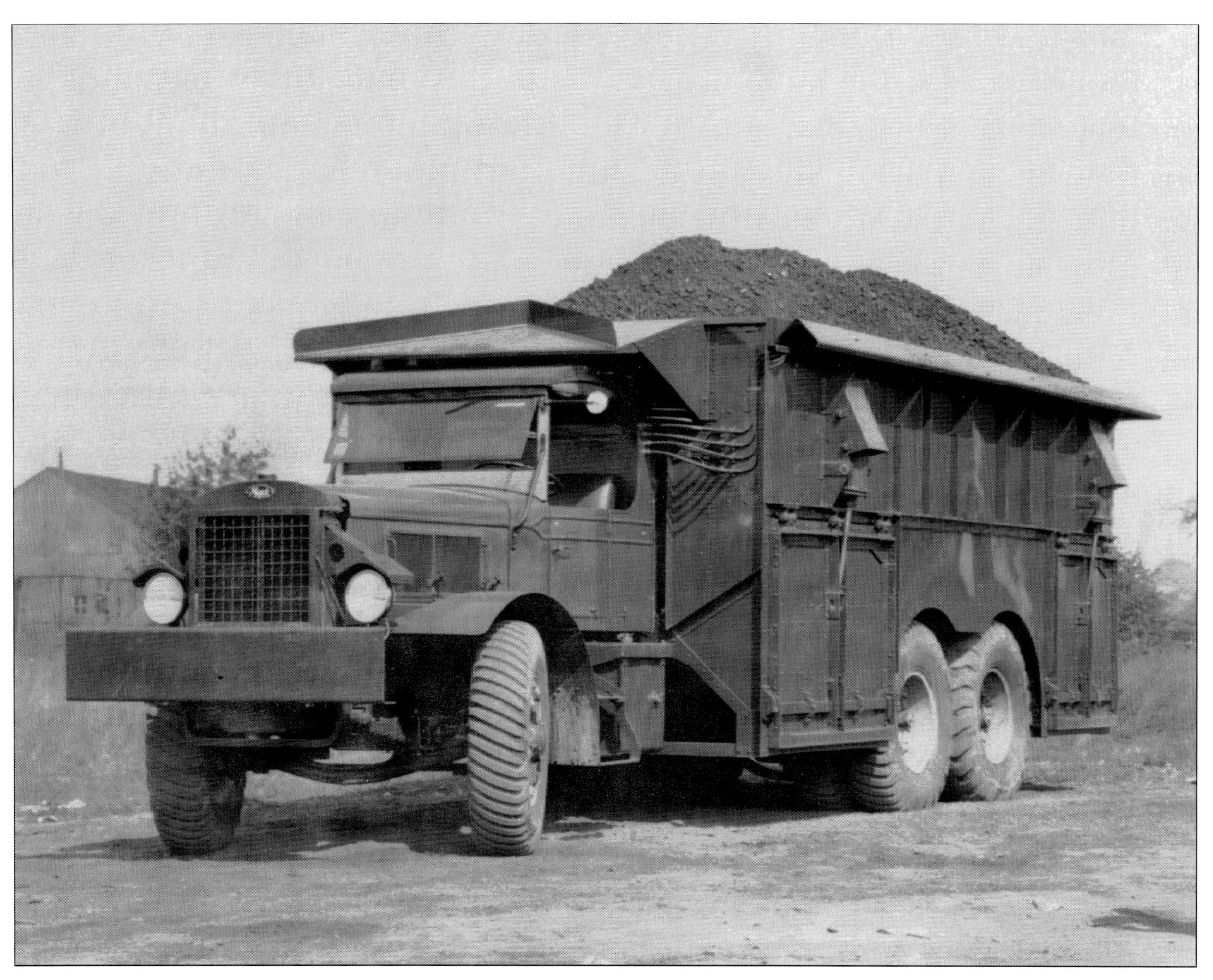

FCSW chassis #1001 with custom body built for Sunlight Coal Co., and used in a coal stripping operation. (A8095)

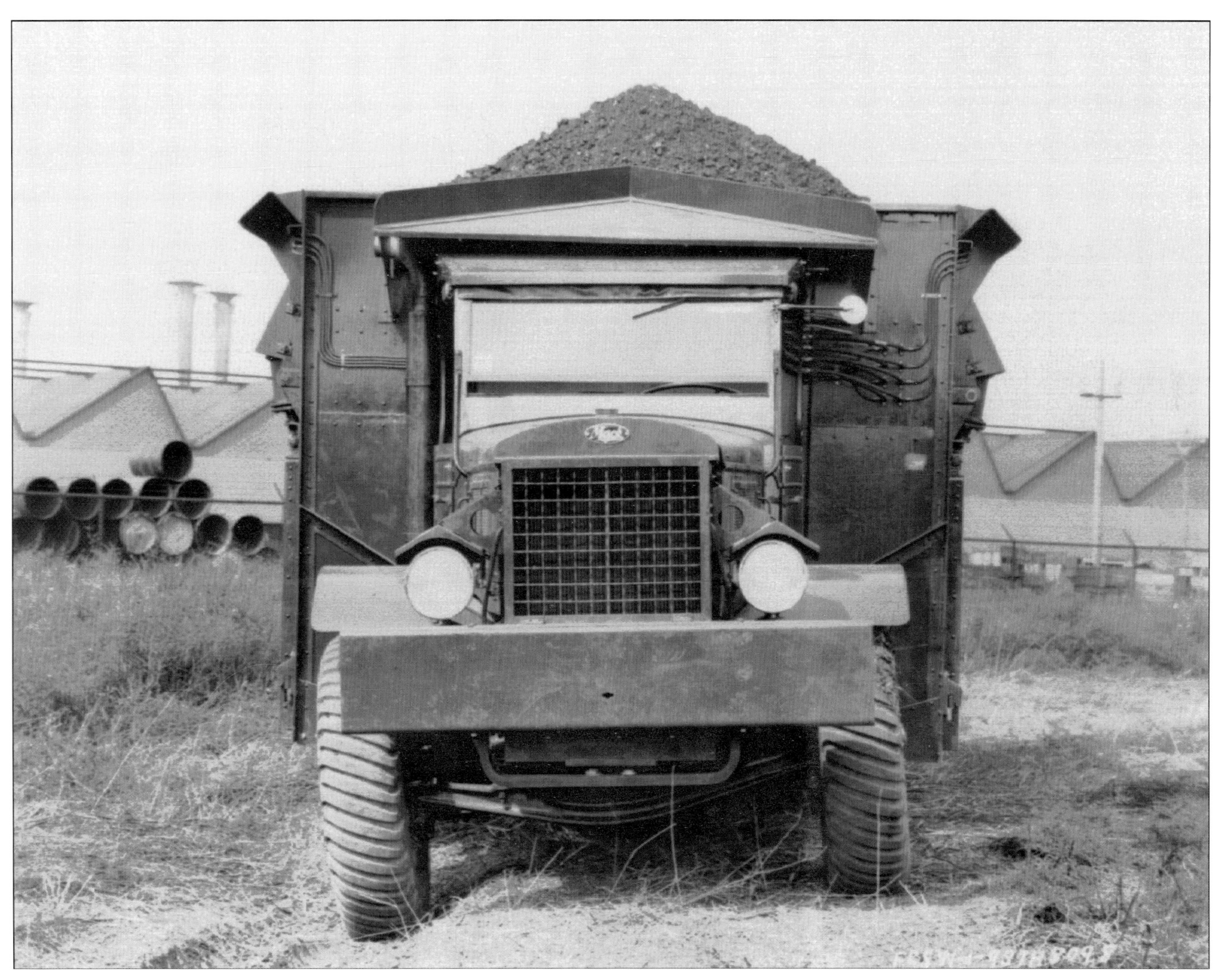

FCSW chassis #1001 featured a Hercules gas engine. The chassis and cab weighed 20,000 pounds; the body 17,000 pounds. (A8098)

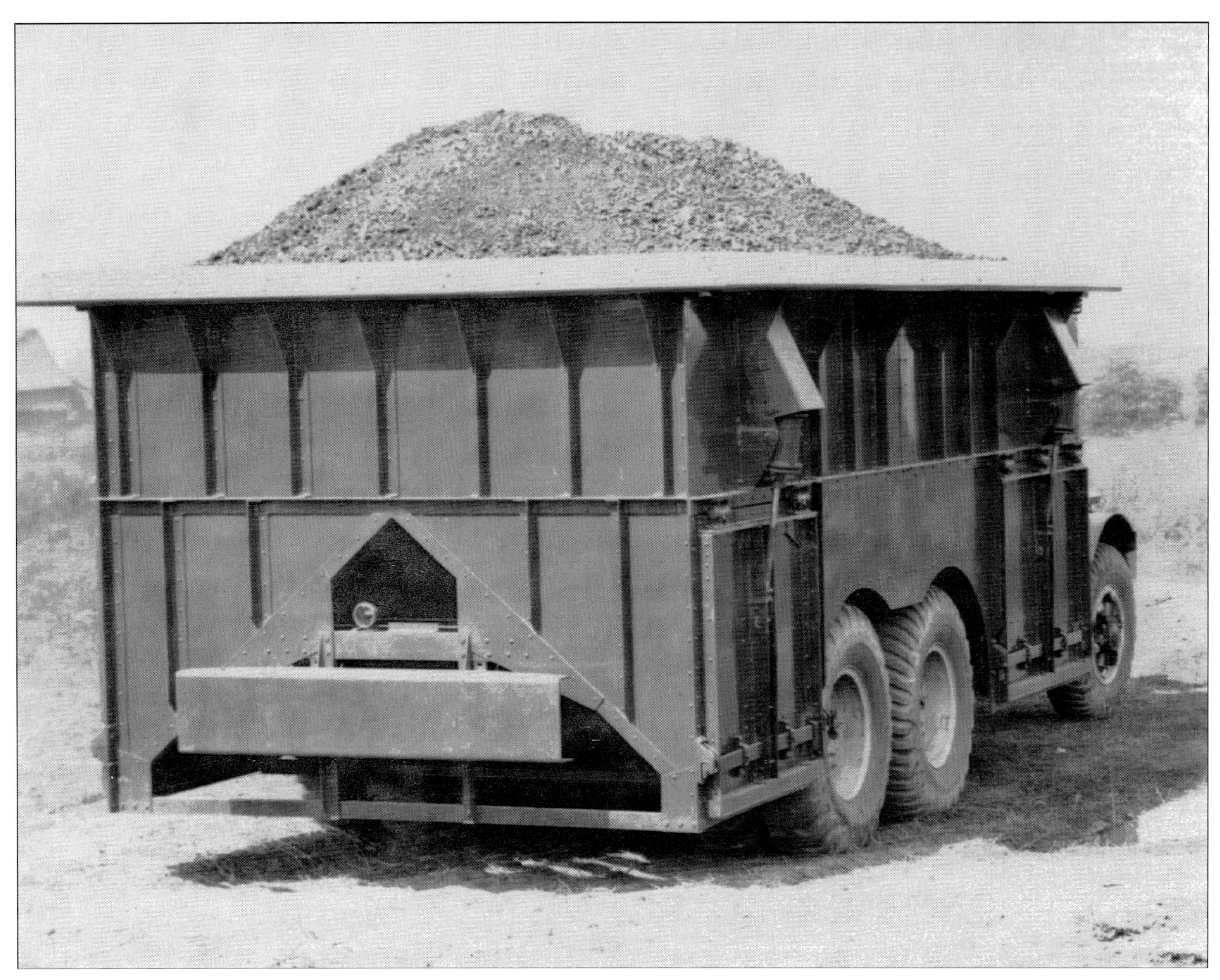

FCSW chassis #1001 with a full load. The gross vehicle weight was rated at 97,000 pounds. The dump doors were pneumatically operated from the cab. (A8099)

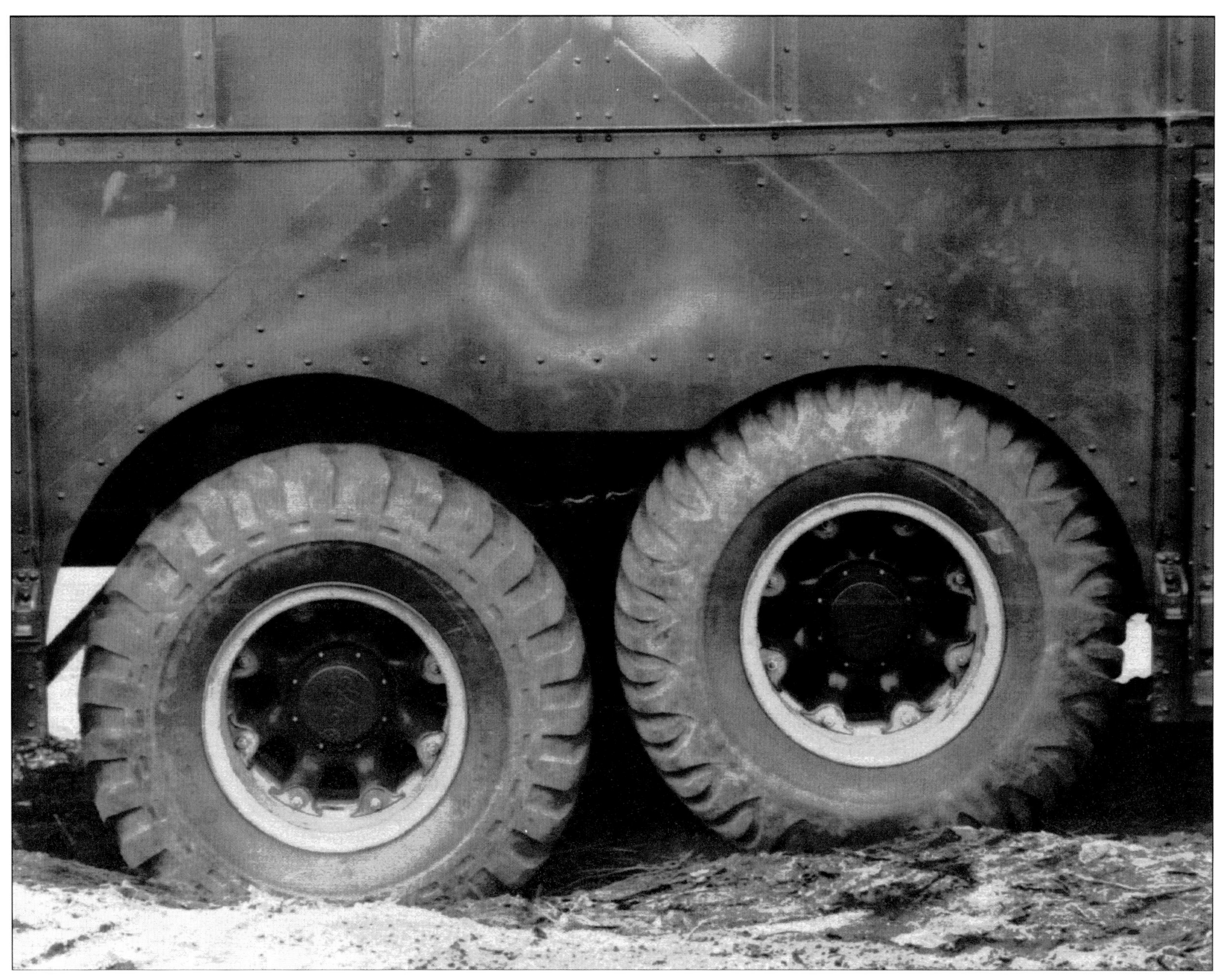

FCSW chassis #1001 equipped with chain drive and 13.50-24 rear duals. (A8100)

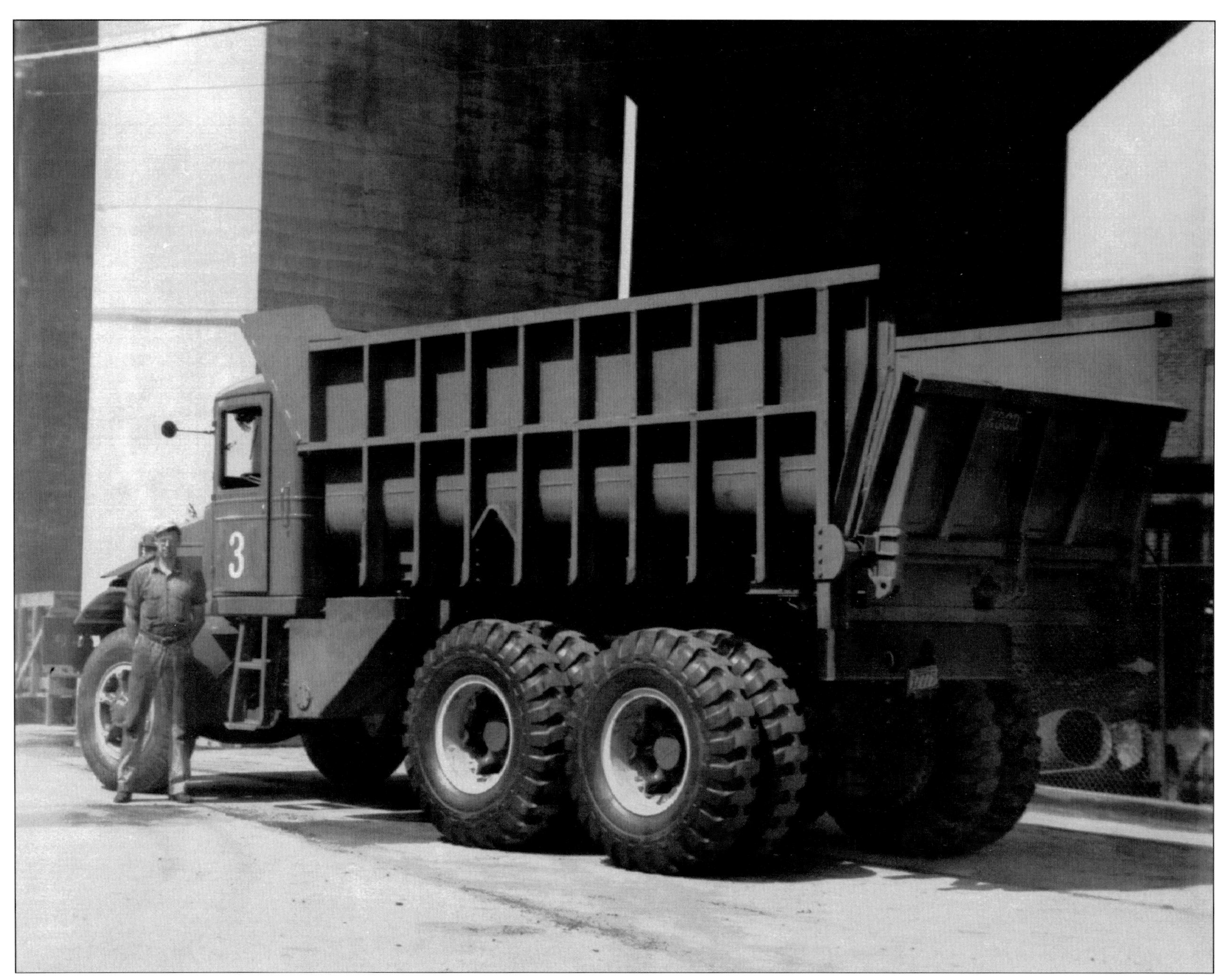

Two views of an FCSW dump truck. July 1938. (A8773)

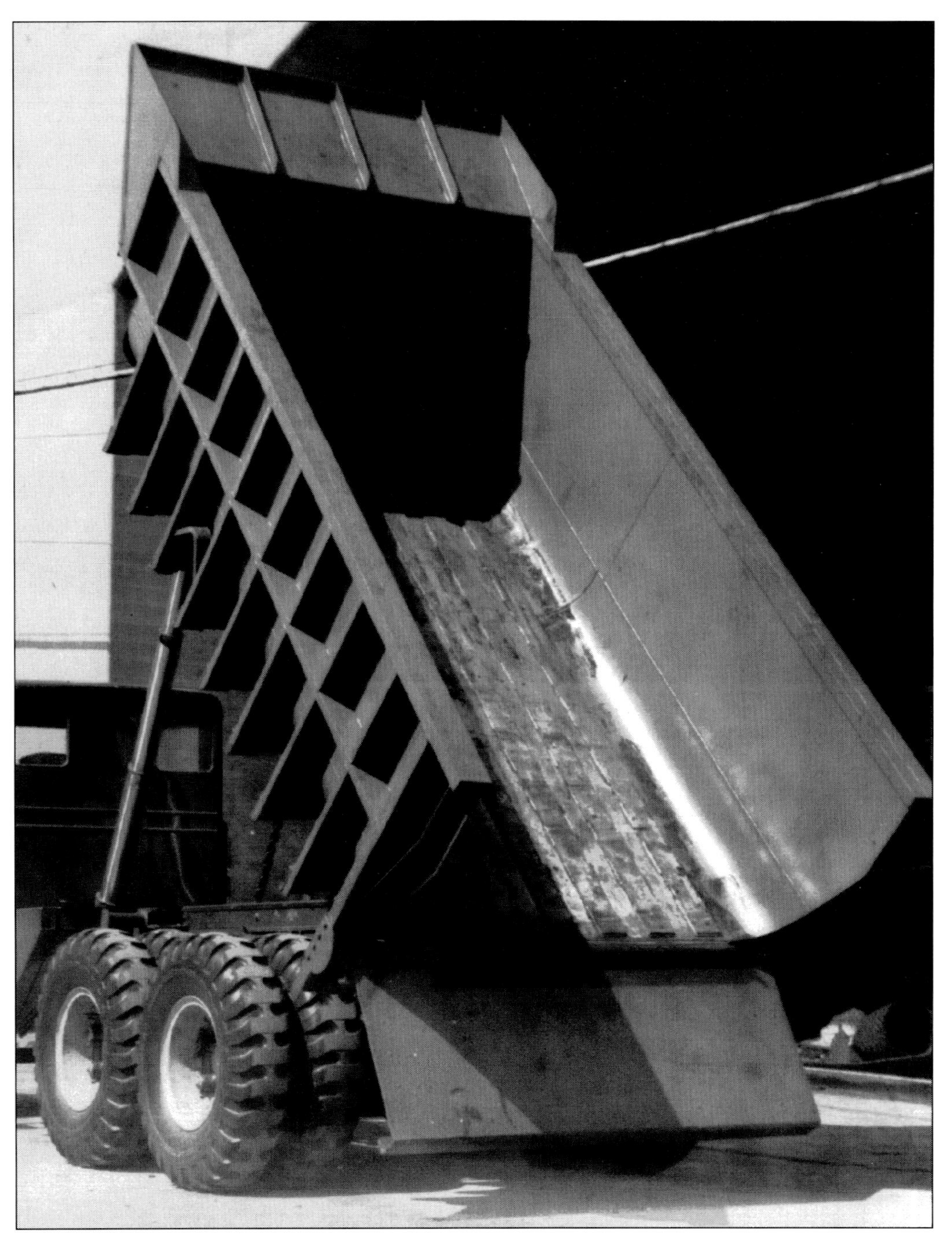

(A8774)

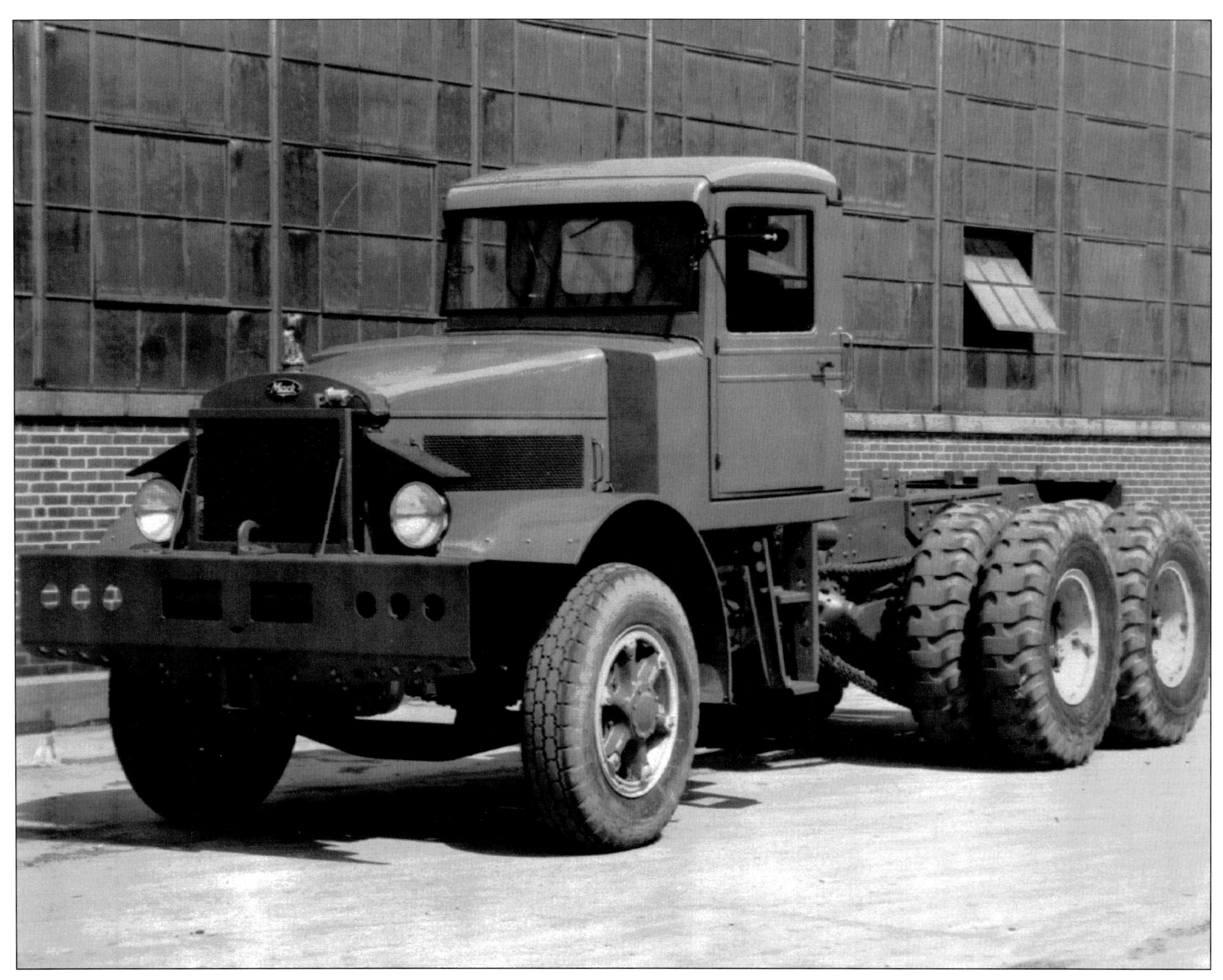

Front and rear views of an FCSW. July 1938. (A8763)

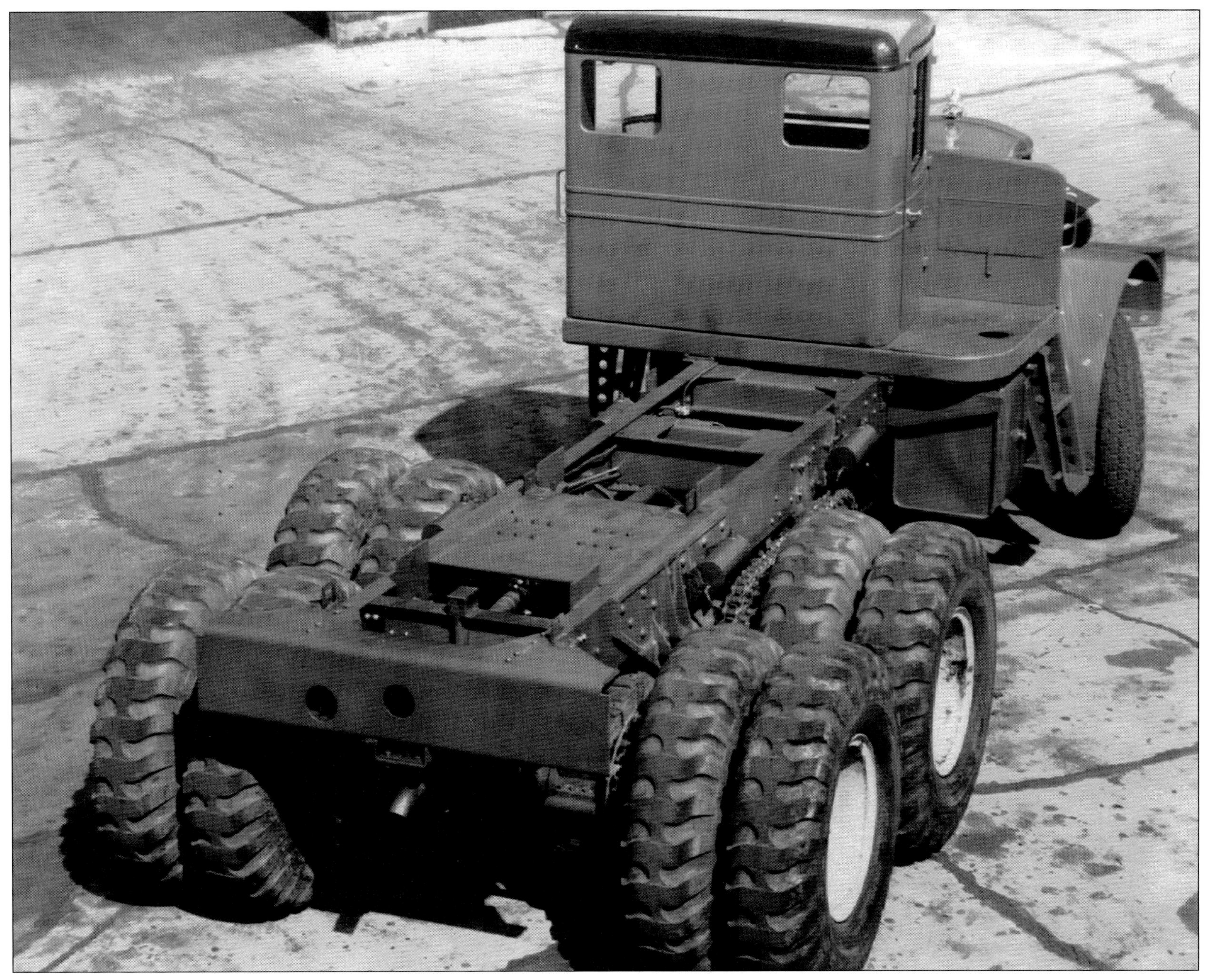

(A8760)

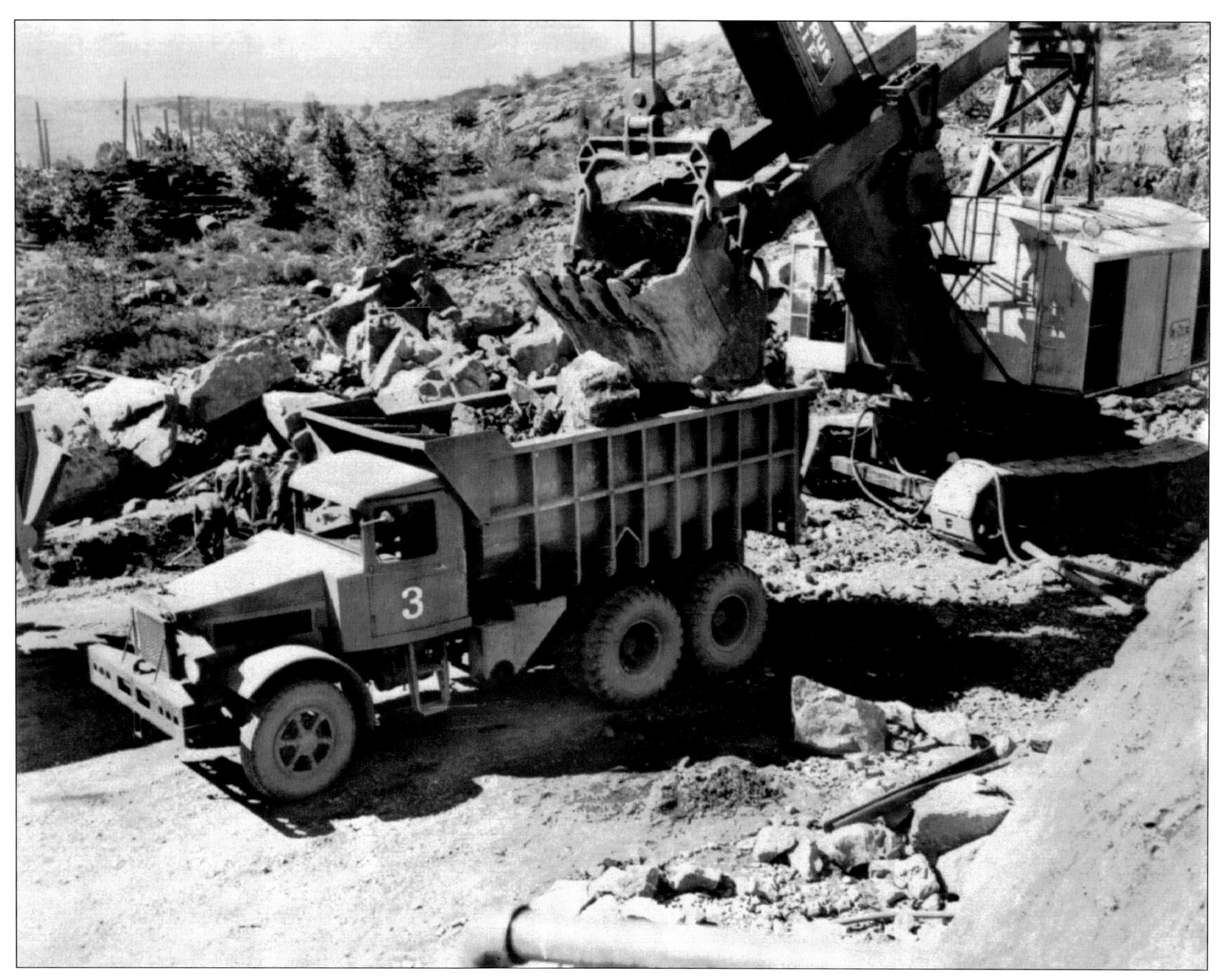

Loading an FC6 dump truck with a Bucyrus Erie120B shovel. November 1939. (A9900)

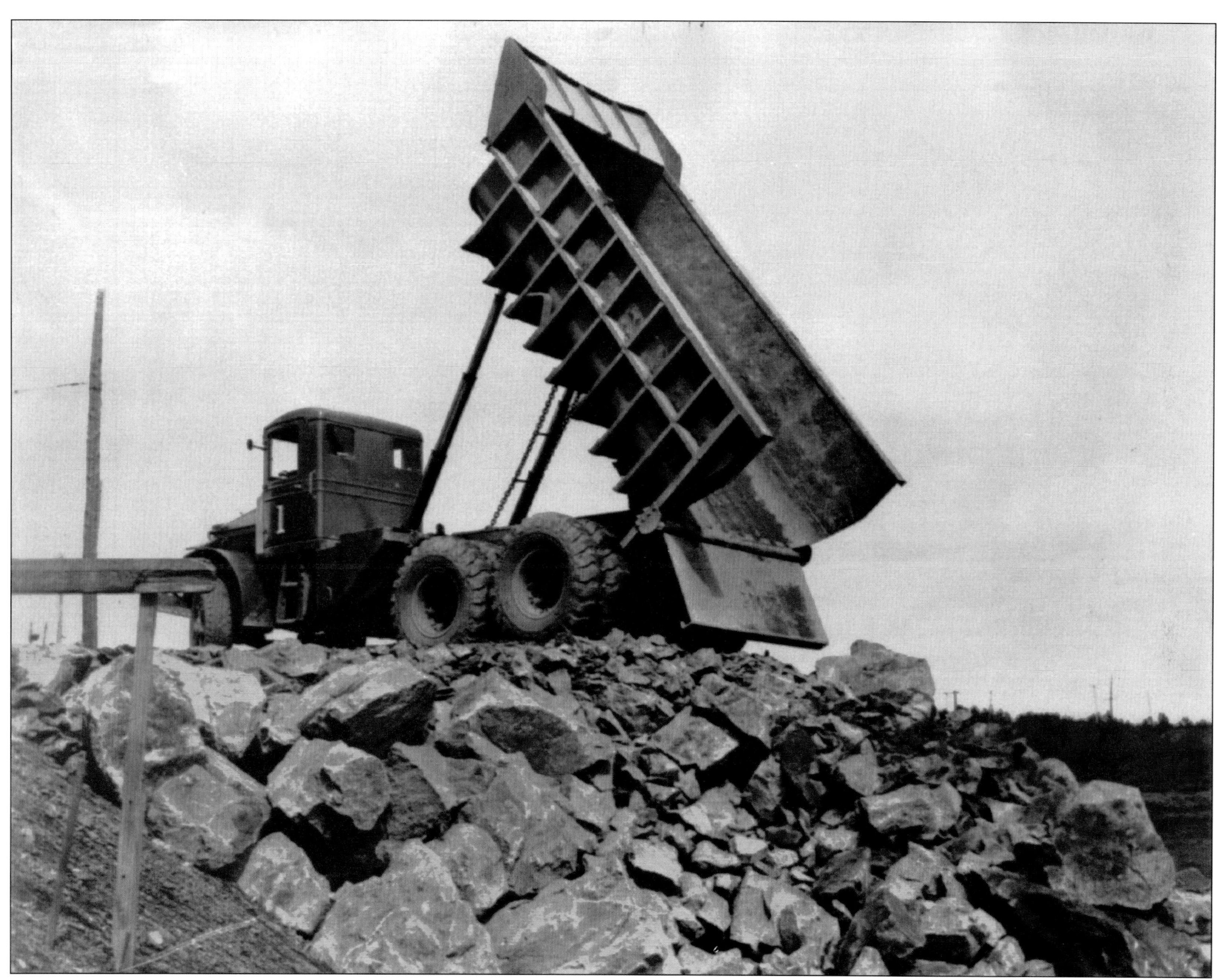
An FC6 dumps its load. November 1939. (A9903)

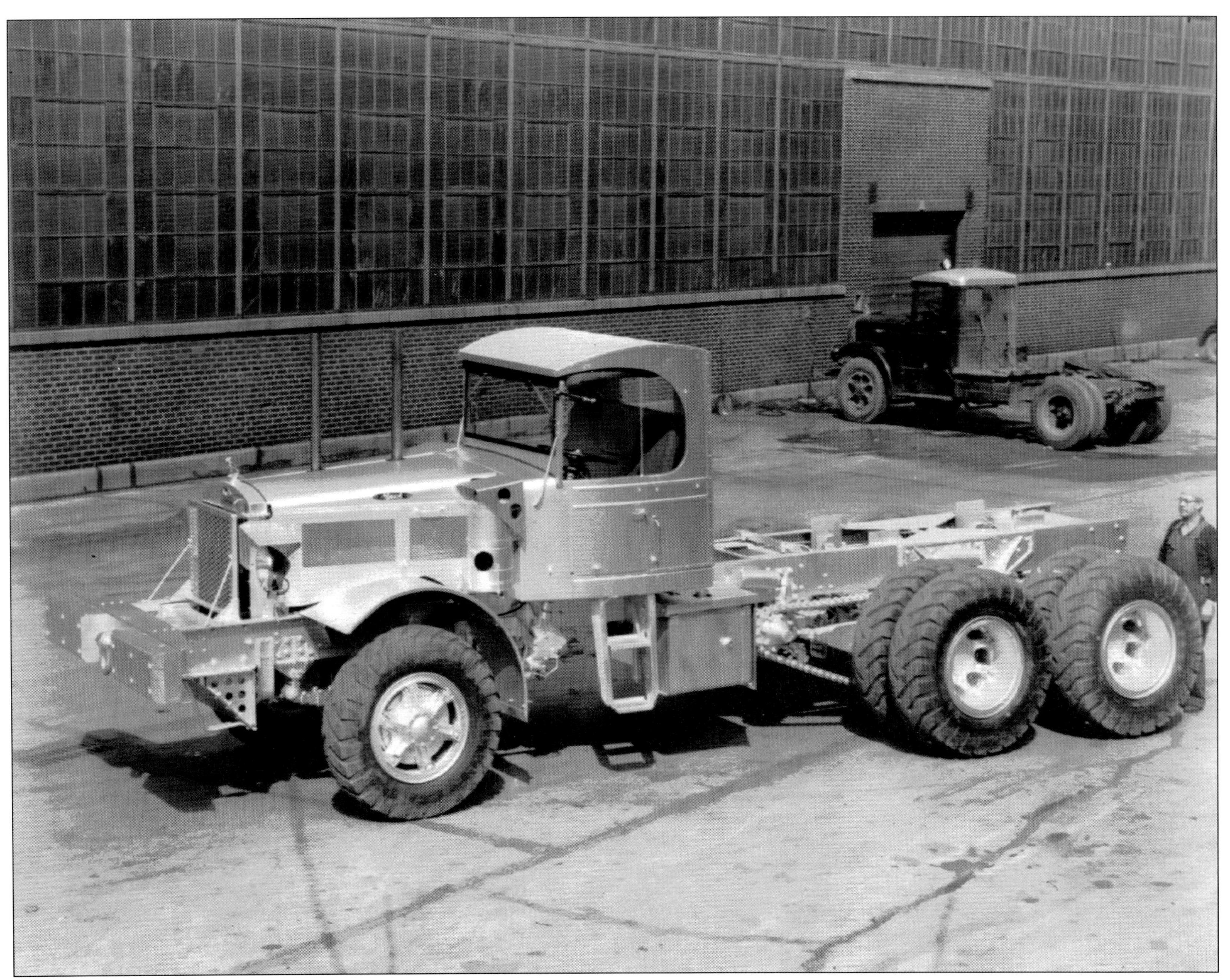

An FCSW built for Tecumseh Coal Corp. March 1940. (V1289)

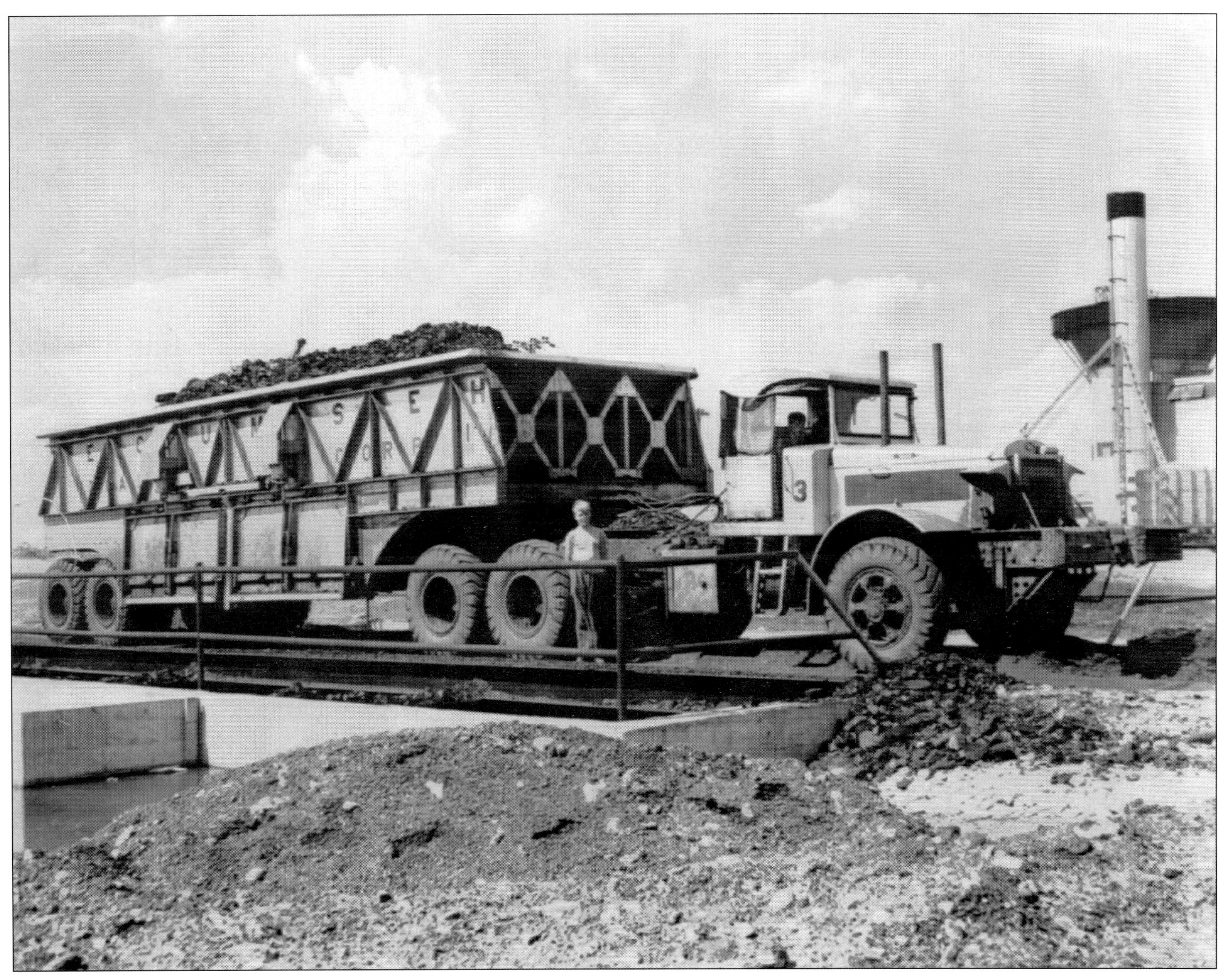

(M4947)

Mack Truck Press Release of September 1941:

PANAMA HATTIE SHOW GIRLS SEND GREETINGS BY PANAMA-BOUND MACK SUPER-DUMPER

The largest truck in the world, the gigantic 50-ton Mack Super-Dumper, takes greetings from chorines of the Broadway hit "Panama Hattie" to workers on the Panama Canal Third Locks System before shipment to this vital defense project. Left to right, the girls are: Xenia Bank, Audrey Westphal, handing note to driver, Doris Dowling, Kathryn Coulter, Mary McDonnell, and Ruth Rogue. A total of 69 of these monster Mack Super-Dumpers, costing more than one million dollars, will be used in this tremendous excavation job which involves the moving of over 35 million cubic yards of rock and earth.

B. G. DE SYLVA
Ethel Merman
PANAMA HATTIE
TREACHER
BARRETT
DUNN
FIELD
HYERS
LYNN
Cole Porter Songs
AIR-CONDITION
PANAMA CANAL
THIRD LOCKS PROJECT
17

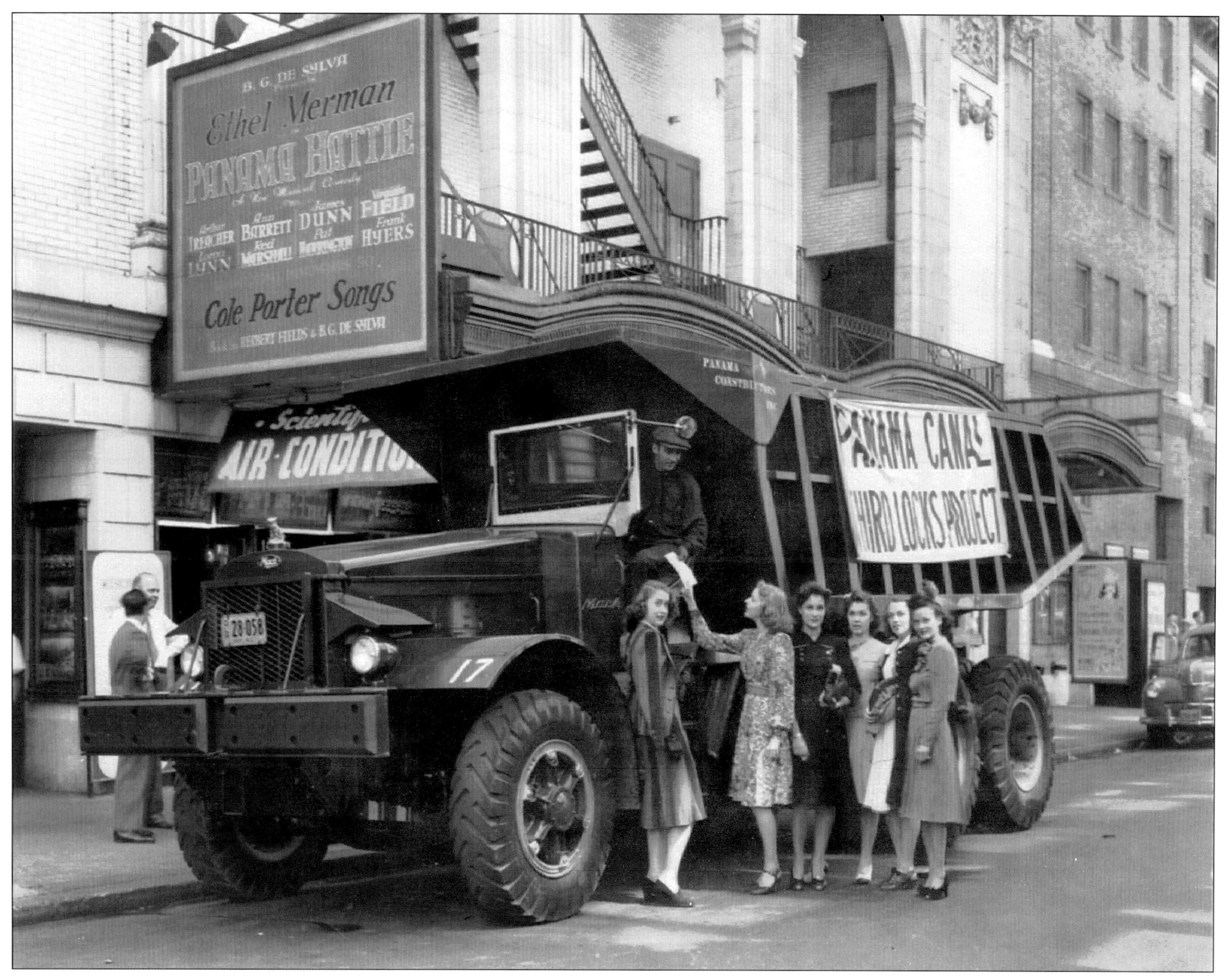

(M6019)

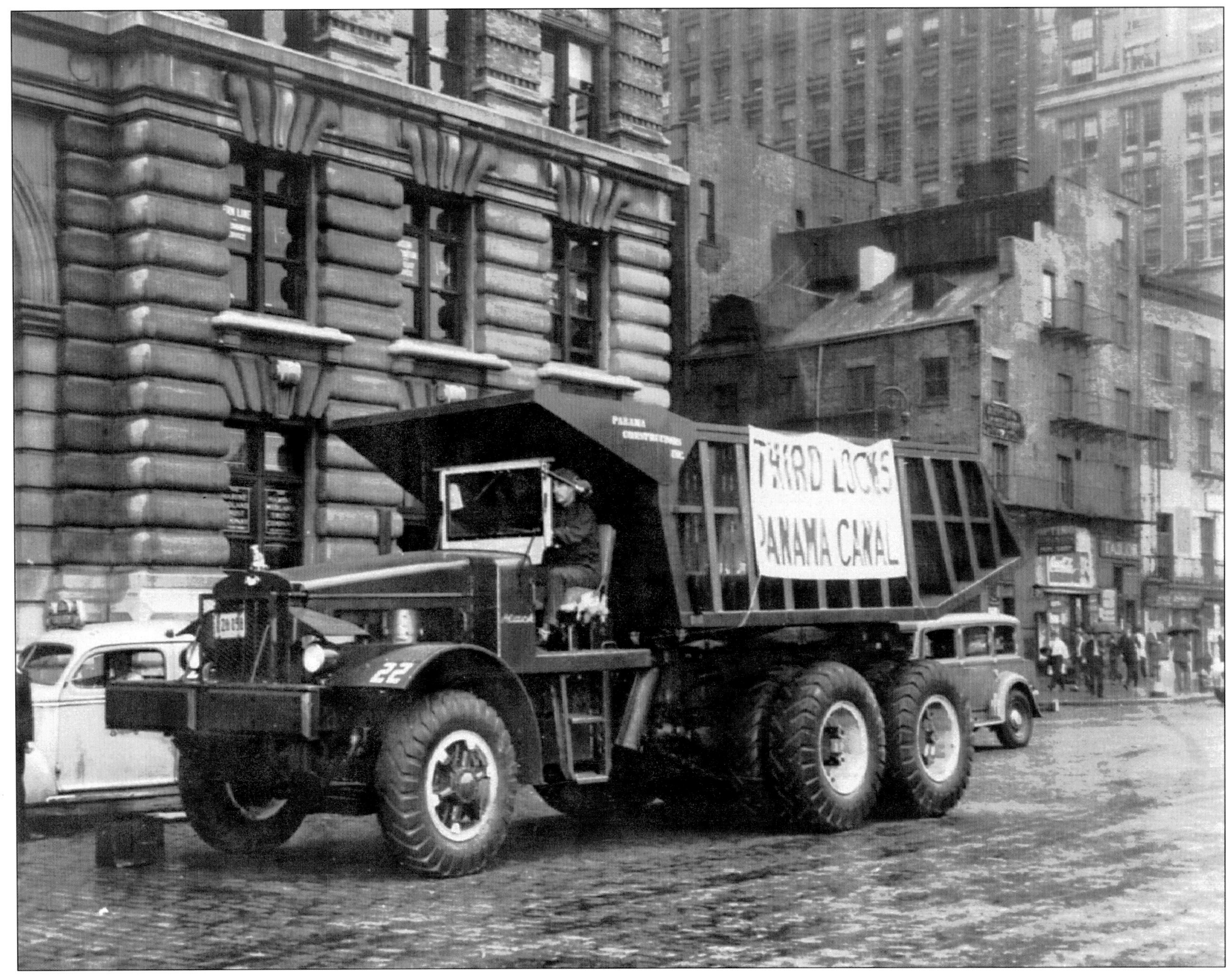

(M5995)

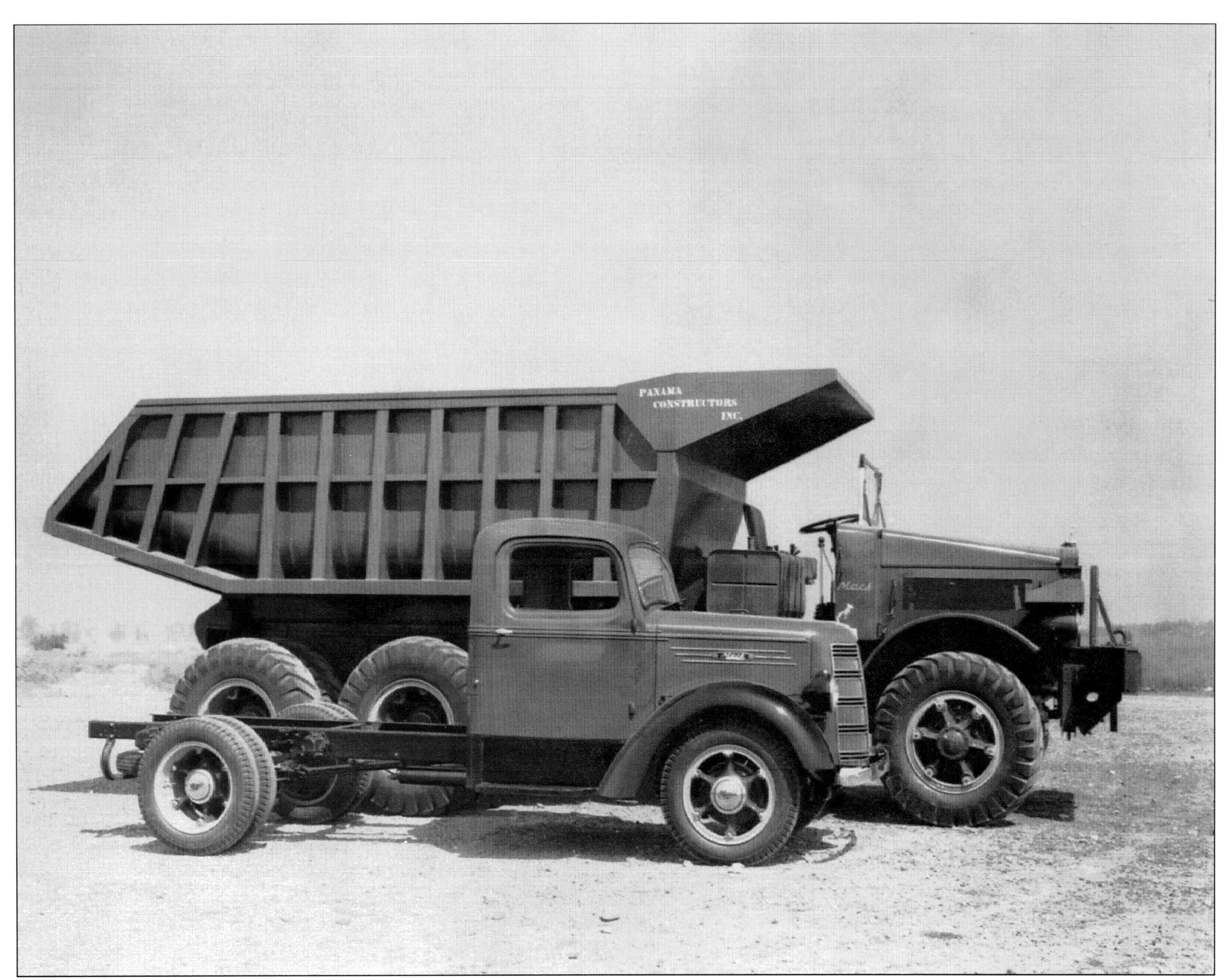

The FCSW and a Mack DE, the largest and the smallest Mack trucks. September 1941. (M6022)

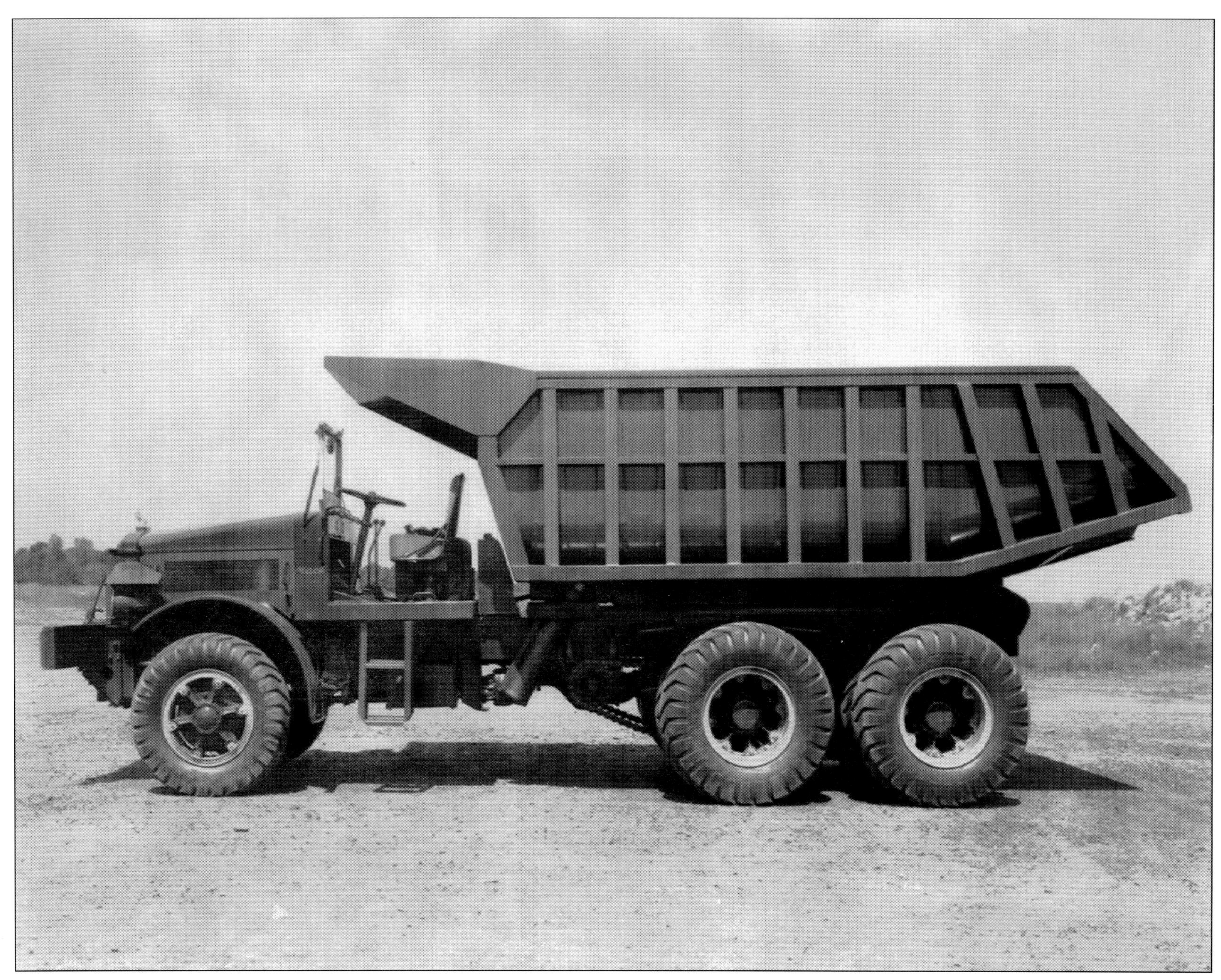

(M5947)

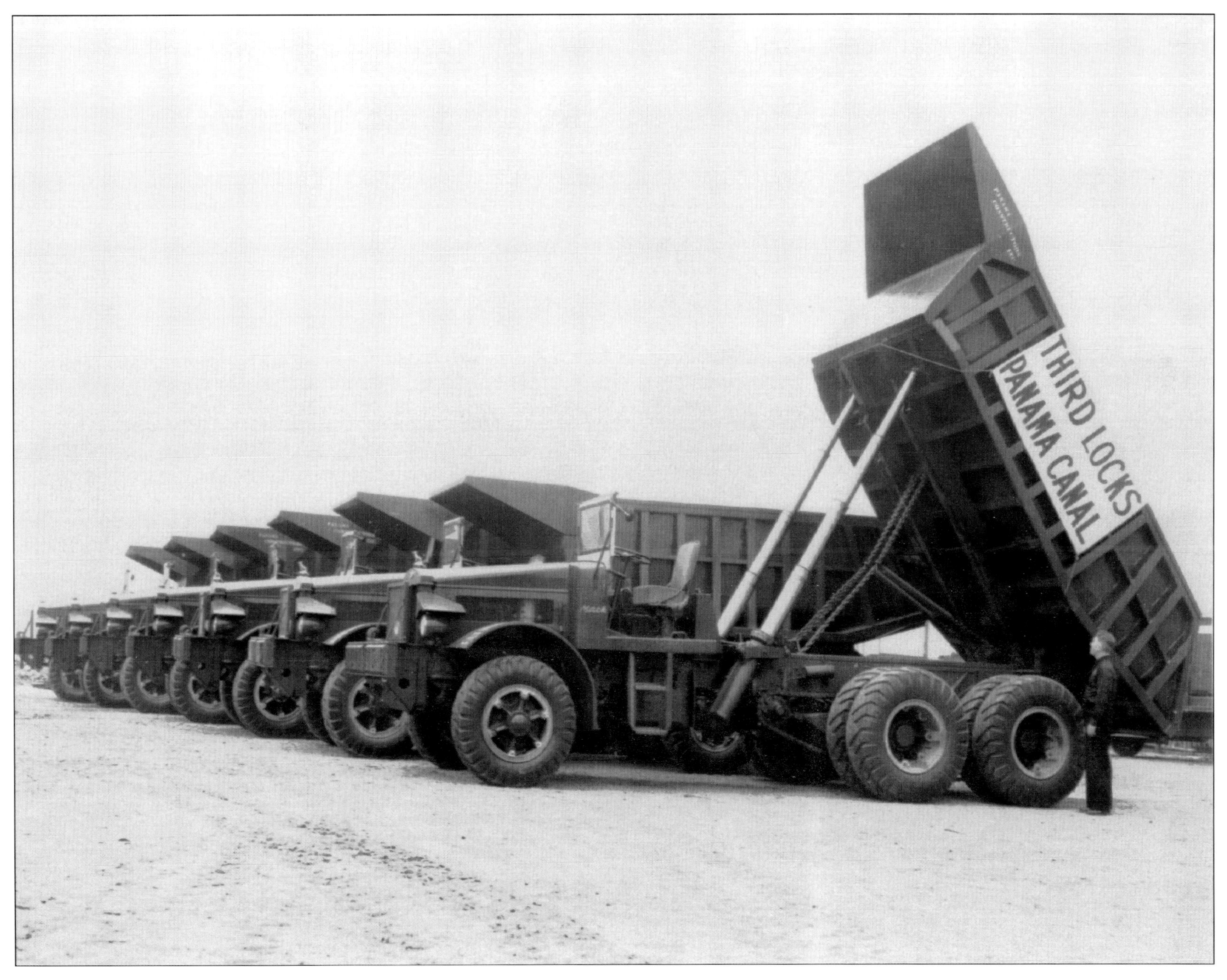

(M5984)

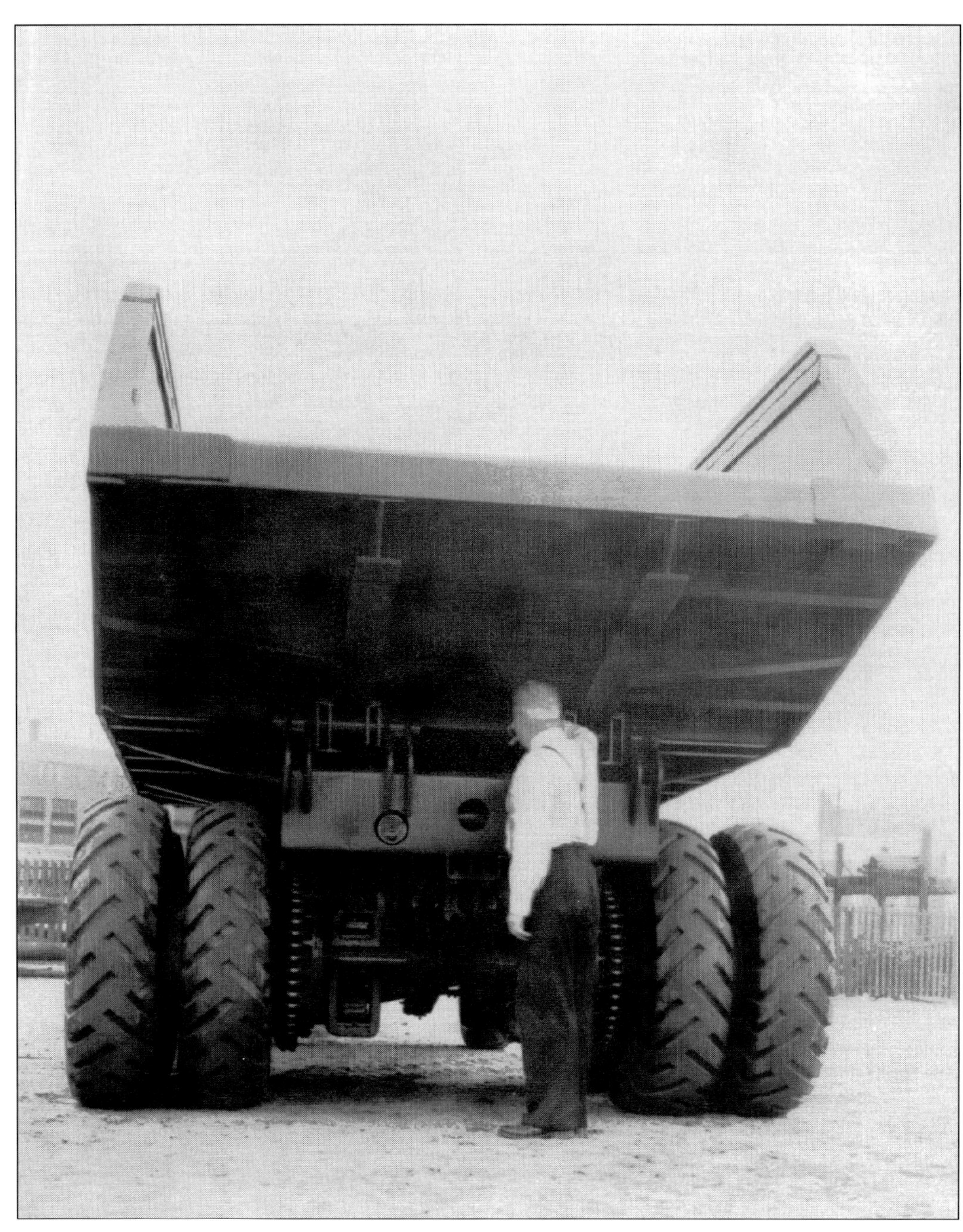

Two views of one of the 69 Panama-bound Super-Dumpers. (M5983)

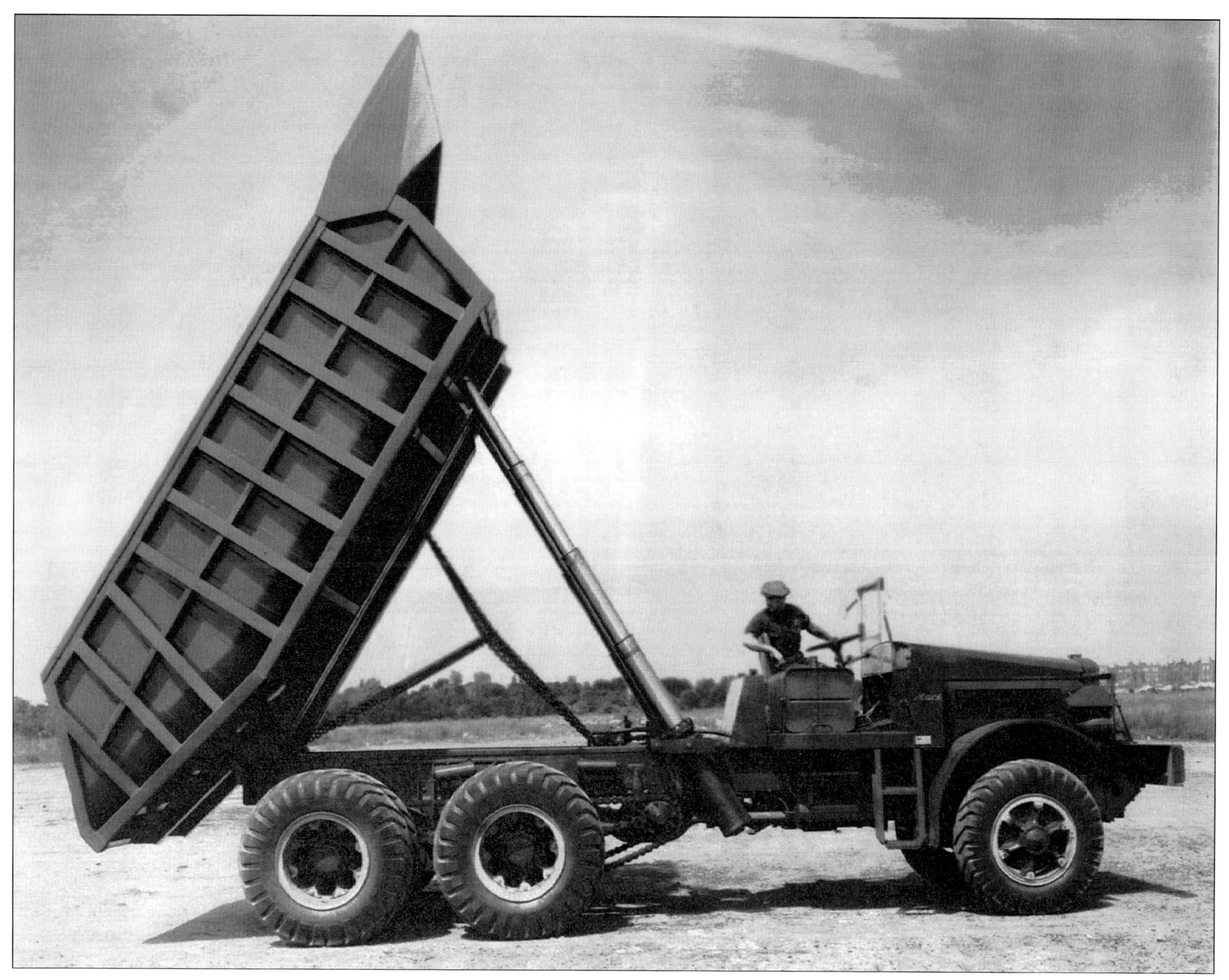

(M5946)

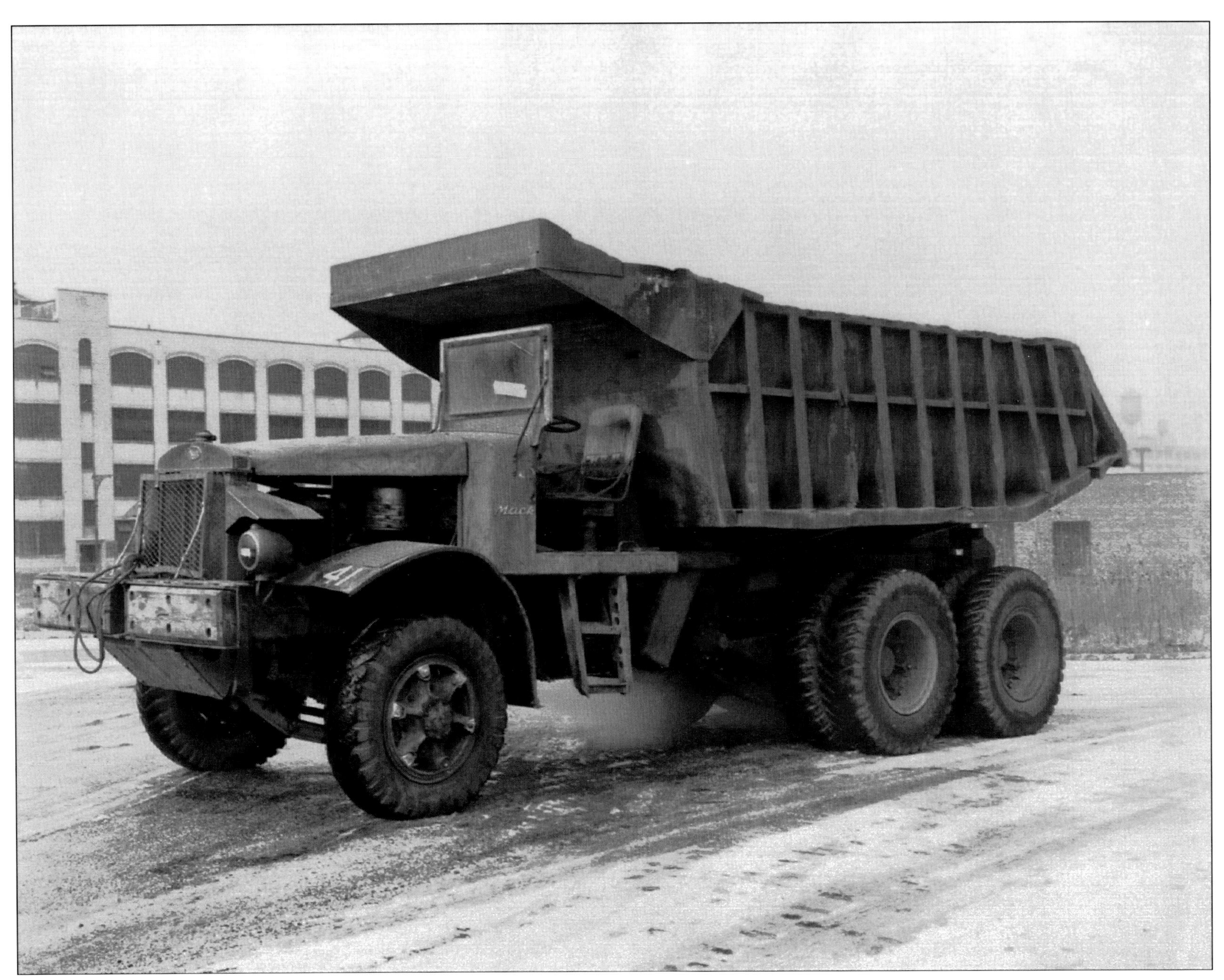

Two views of one of the Panama Canal Super-Dumpers on return to the U.S. in January 1944. (M7799)

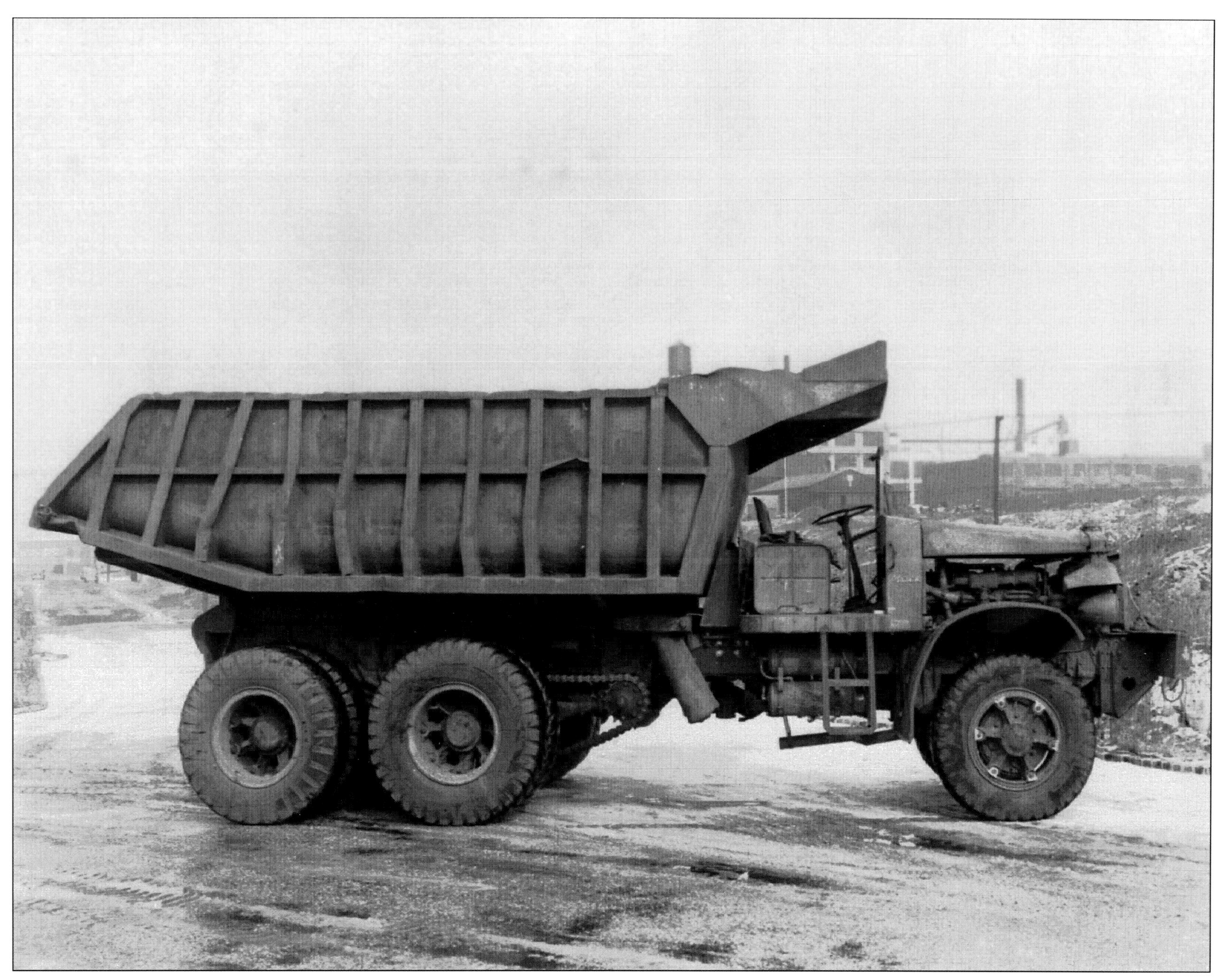

(M7797)

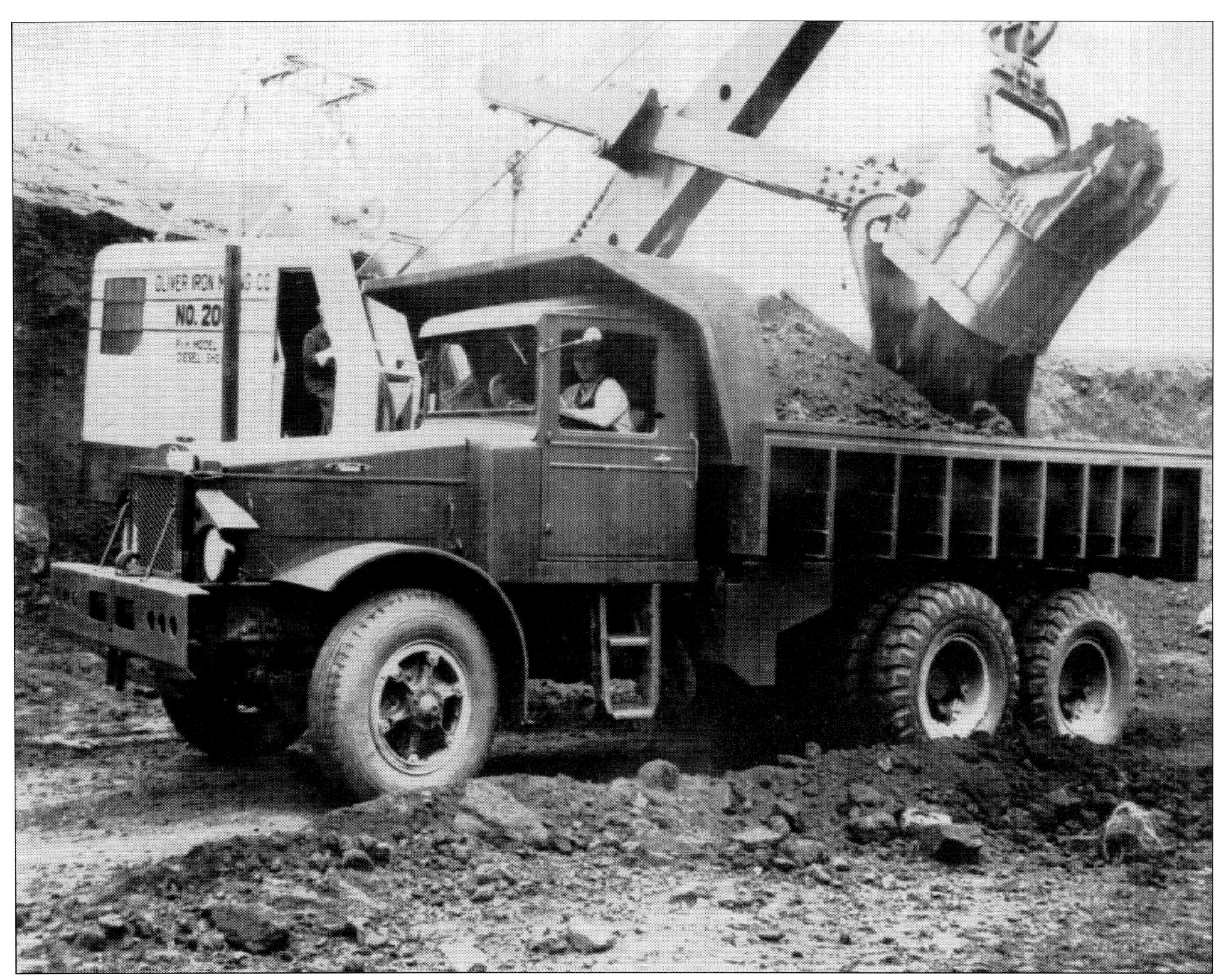

A Mack FCSW owned by Oliver Iron Mining Co. December 1941. (M6214)

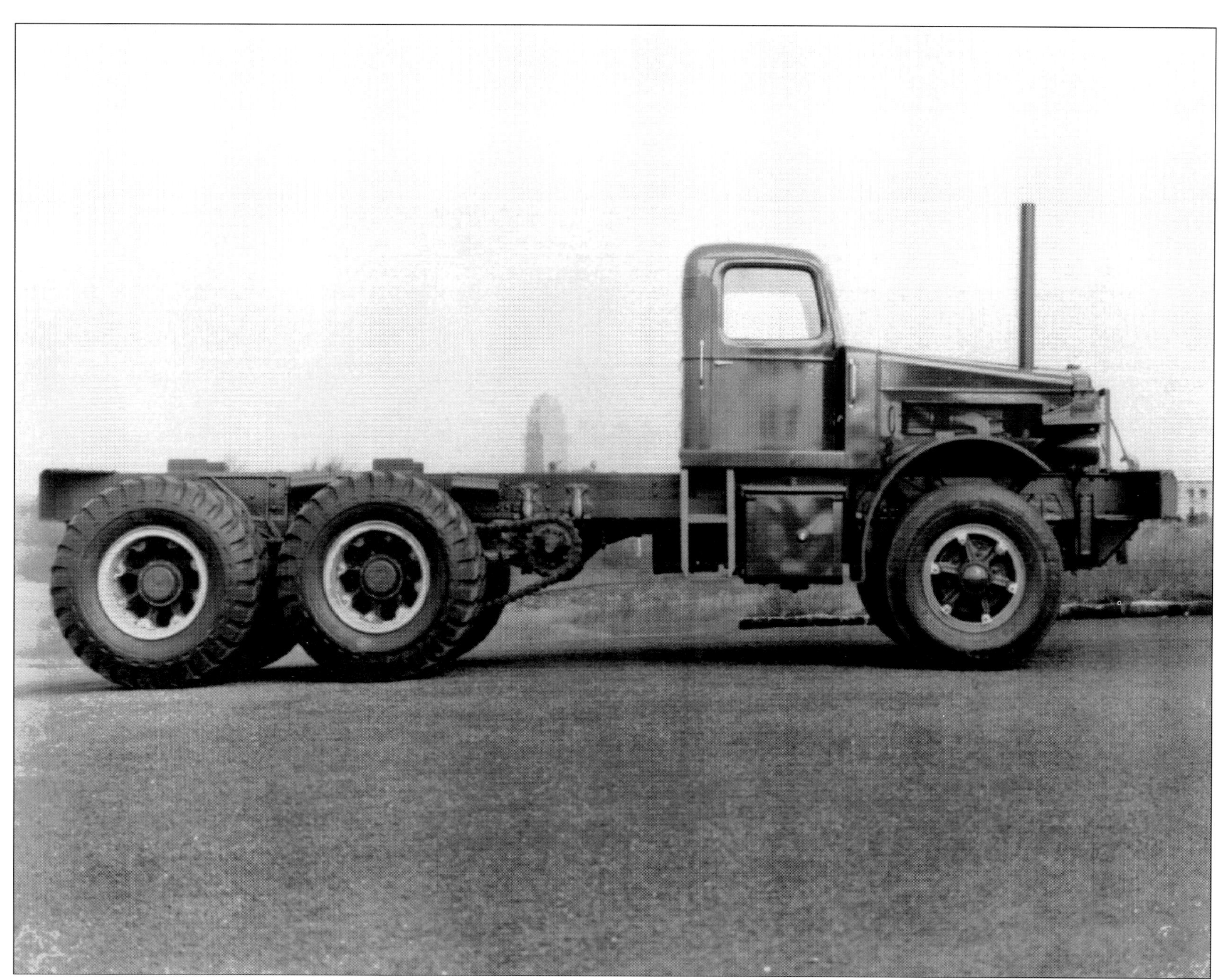

FC2C chassis #1080D built for Oliver Iron Mining Co. February 1942. (V3864)

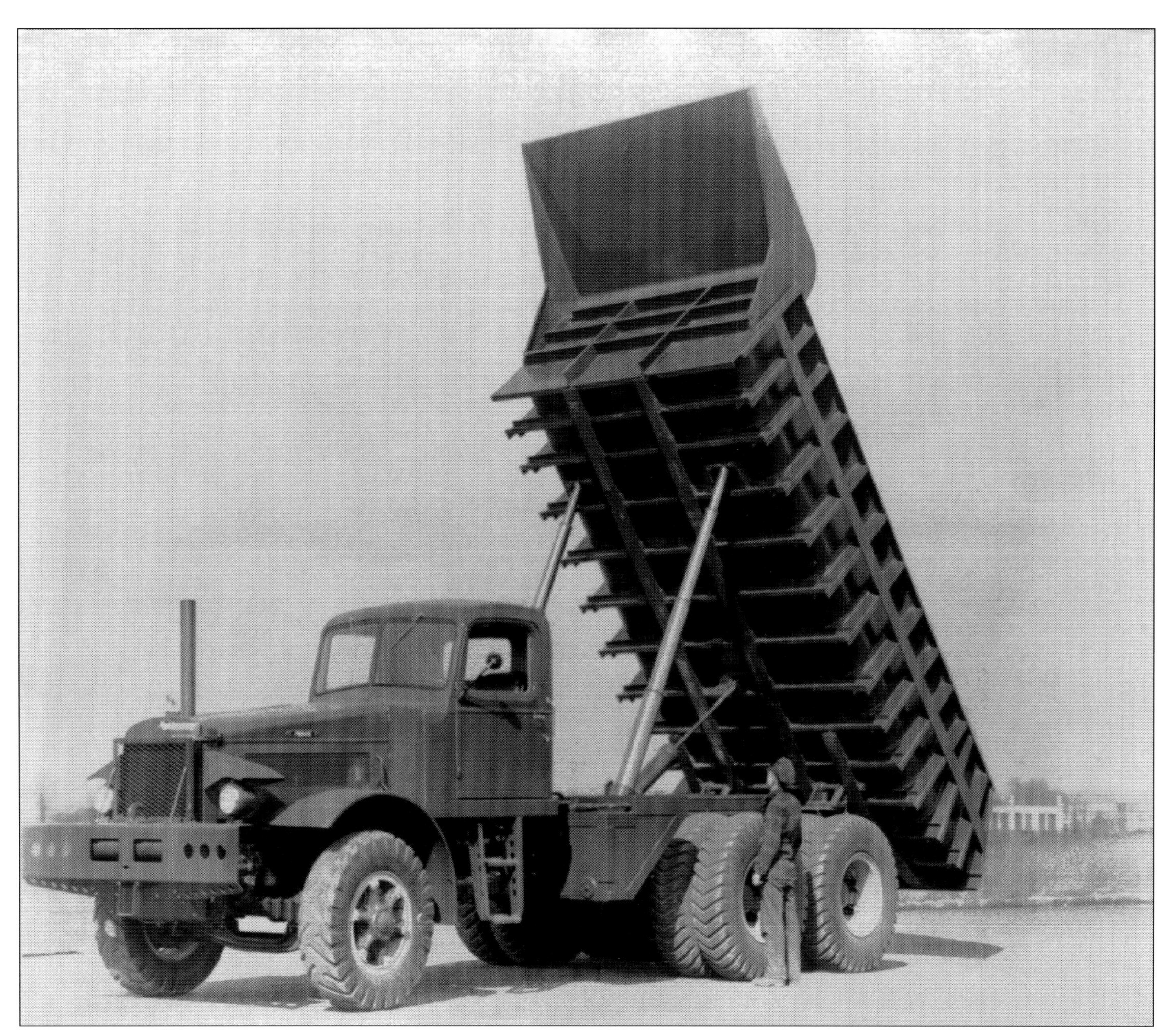

FC2C chassis #1069D built for Dick Construction Co., Hazleton, Pennsylvania, and used in a coal stripping operation. February 1942. (V3679)

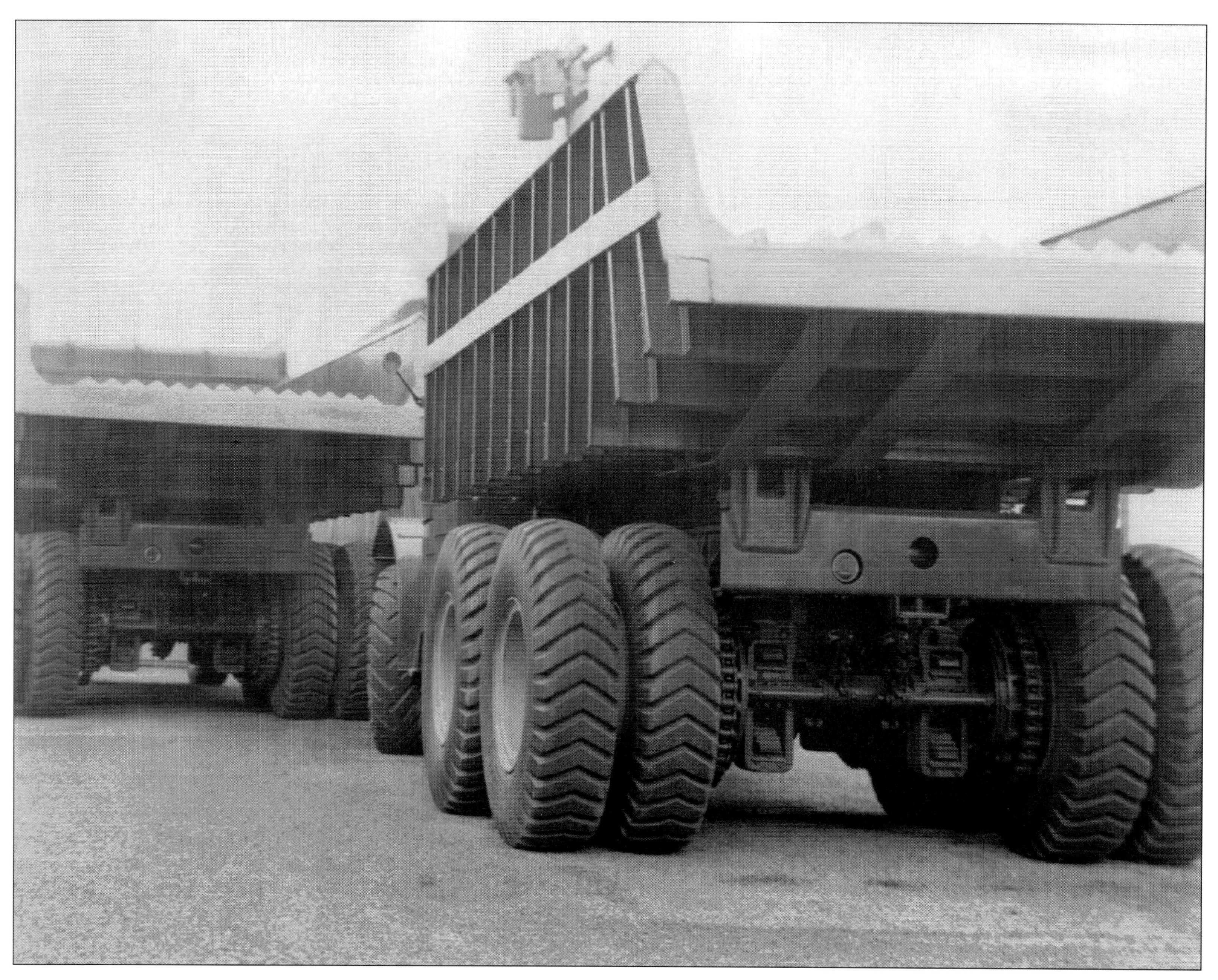

Two FCSW dump trucks, built under General Sales Order #11 for Dick Construction Co. March 1942. (V4983)

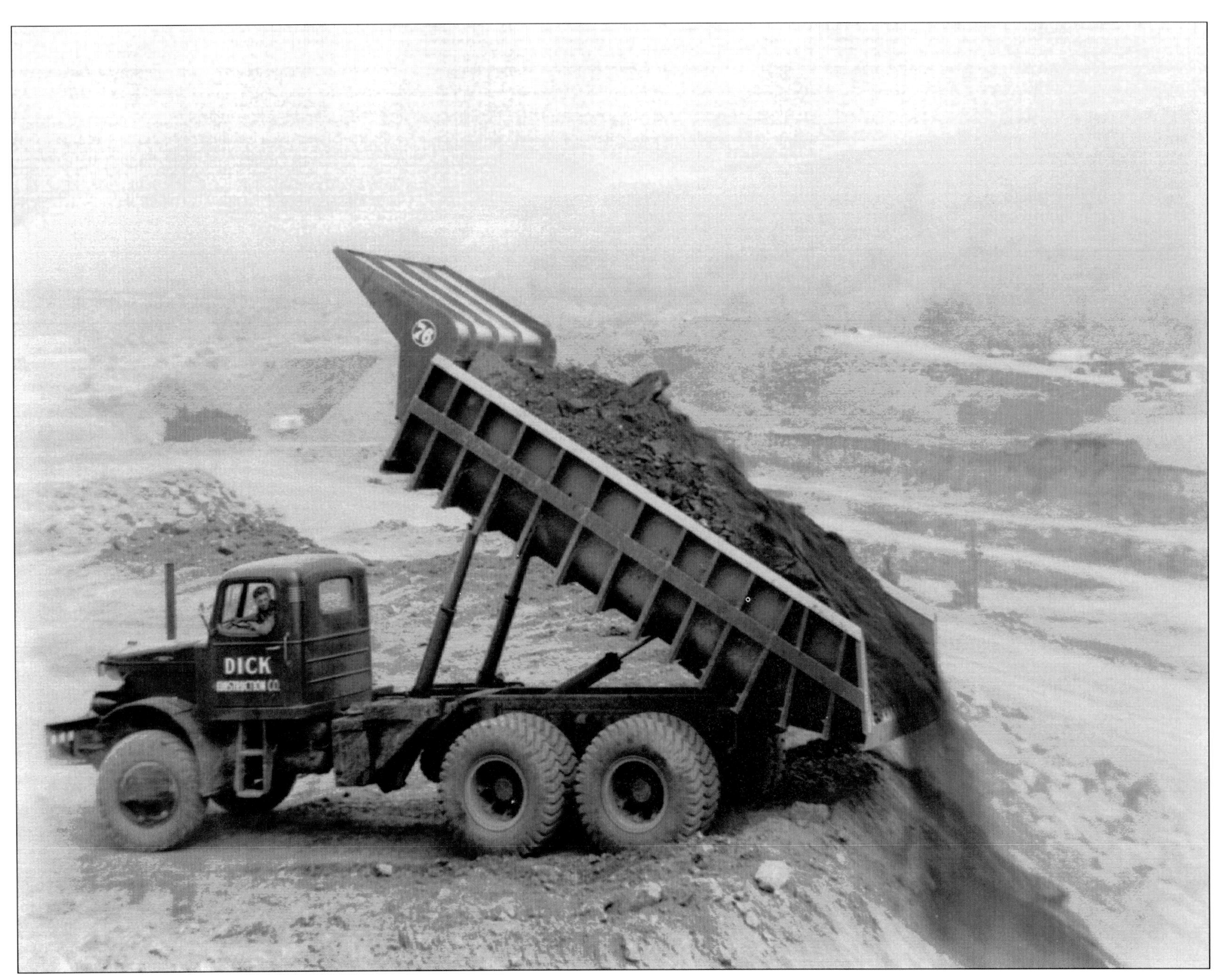

Three views of one of the two FCSW dump trucks built for Dick Construction Co. (V4983)

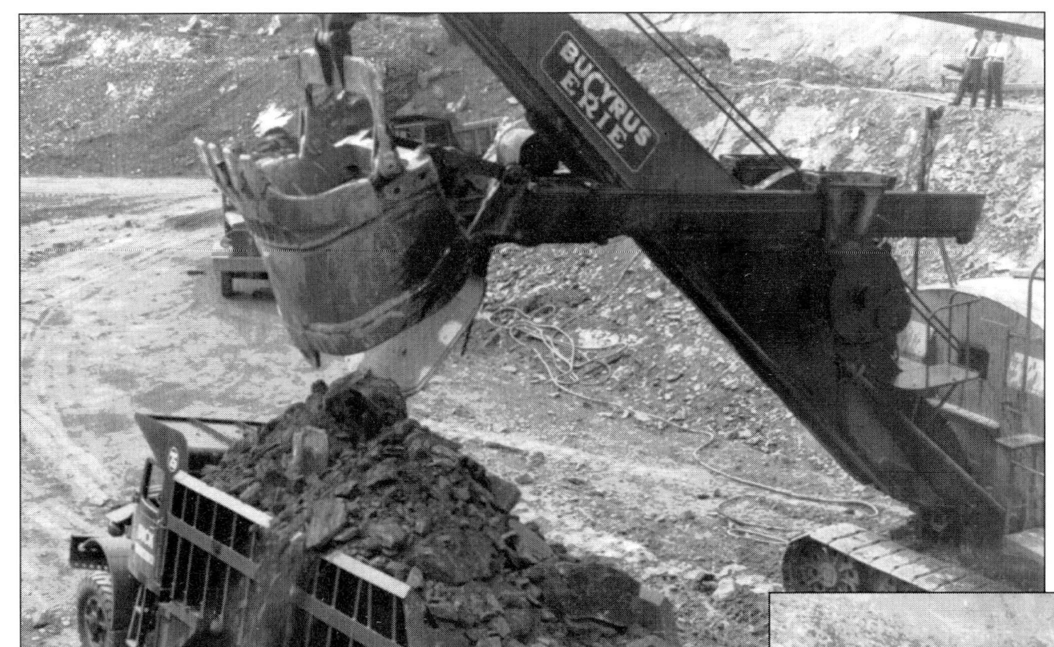

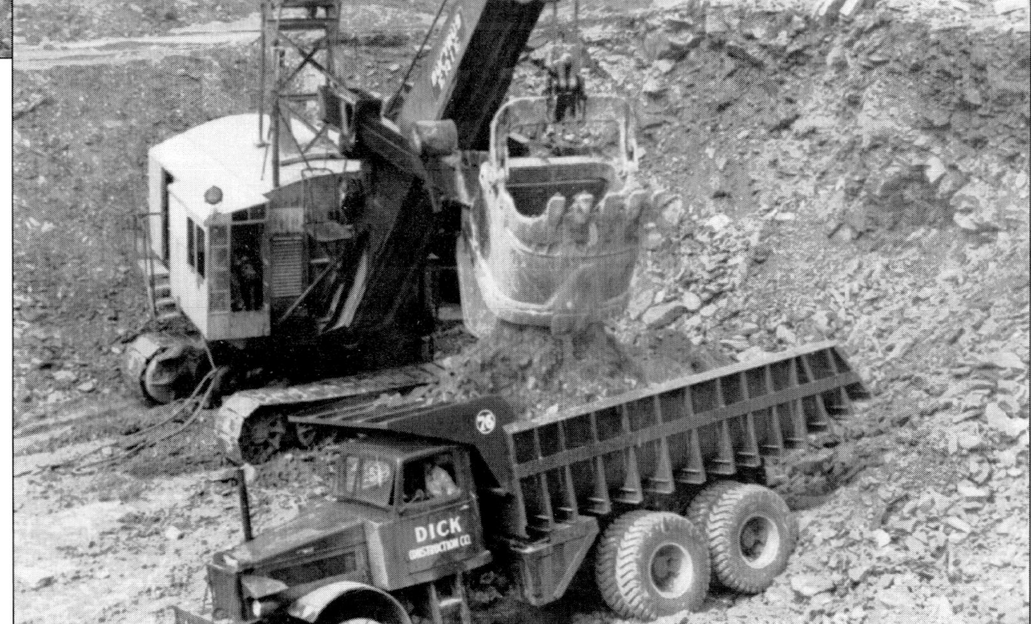

(M6820)

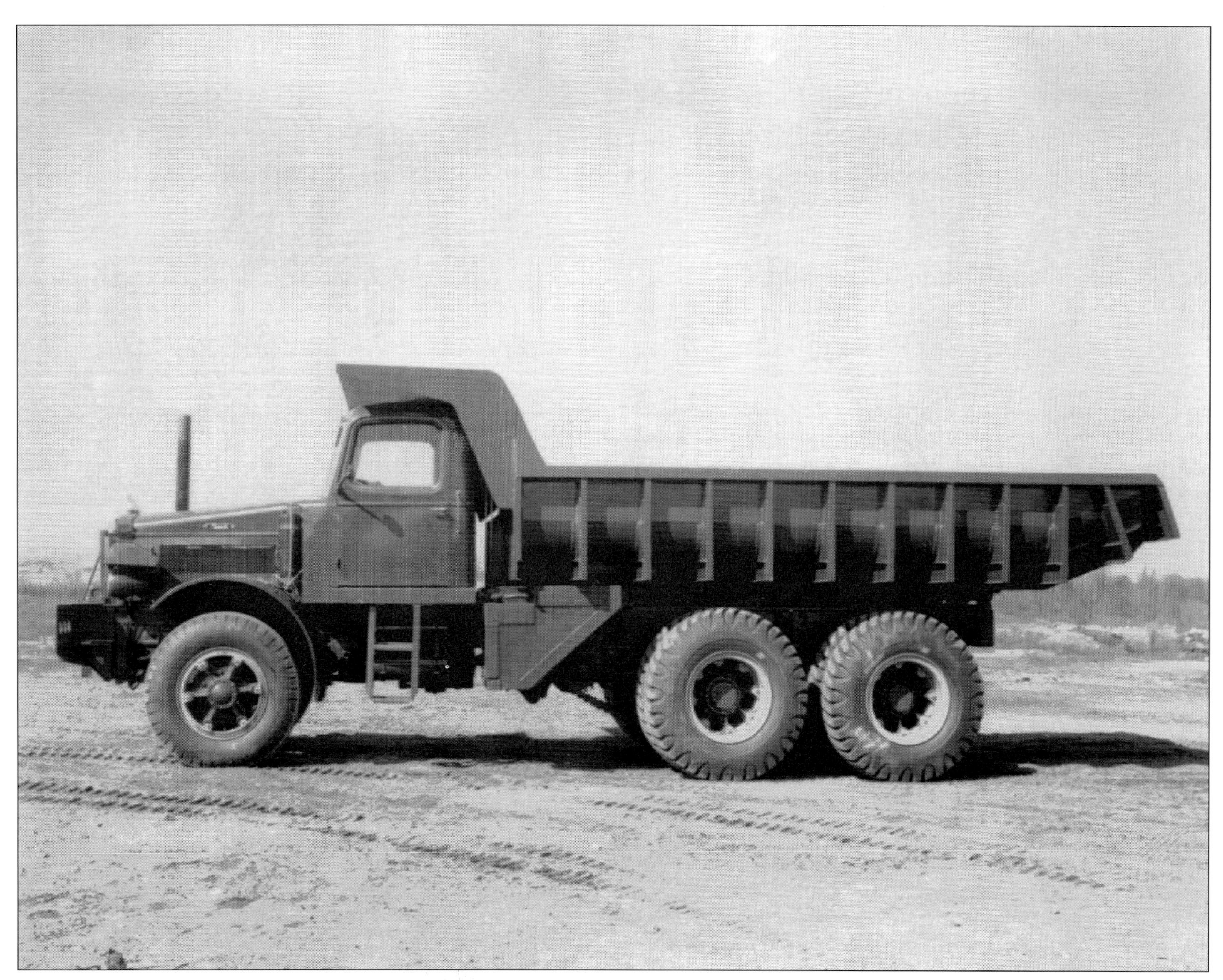

FCSW built for National Lead. March 1942. (V6387)

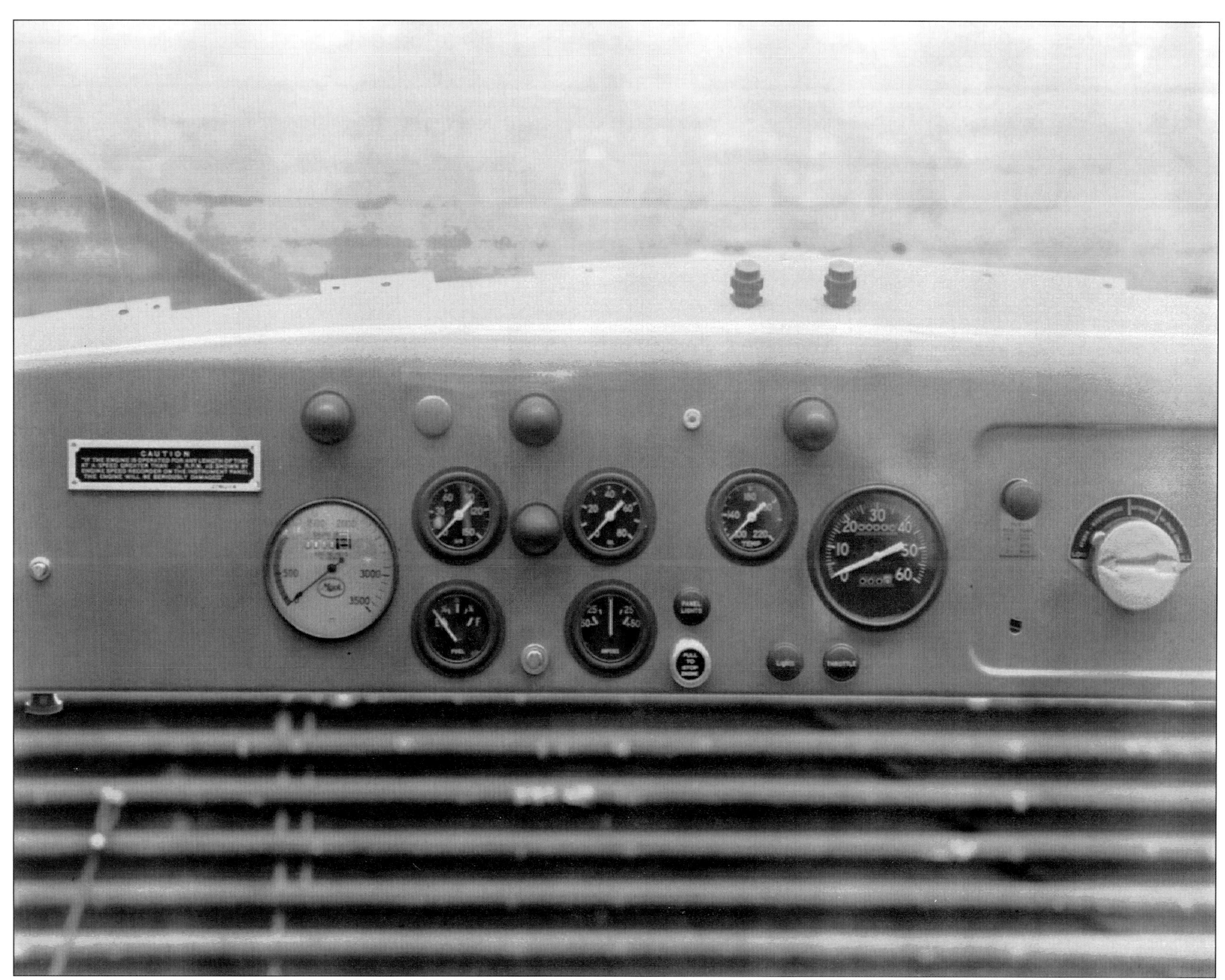

FCSW instrument board assembly. (V6543)

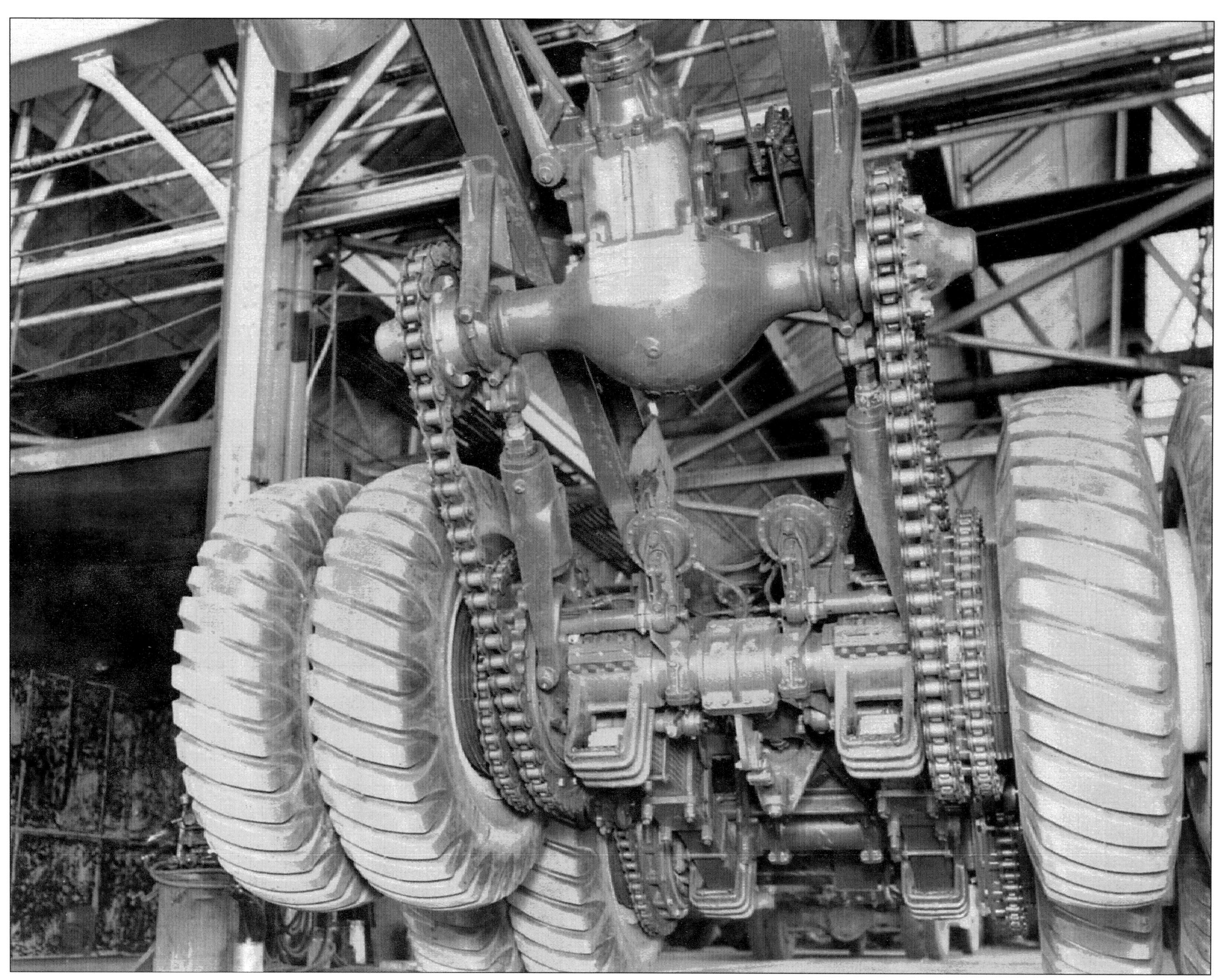

Views of the rear drive chain and front axle assemblies on FC2C chassis #1144. April 1943. (V6573)

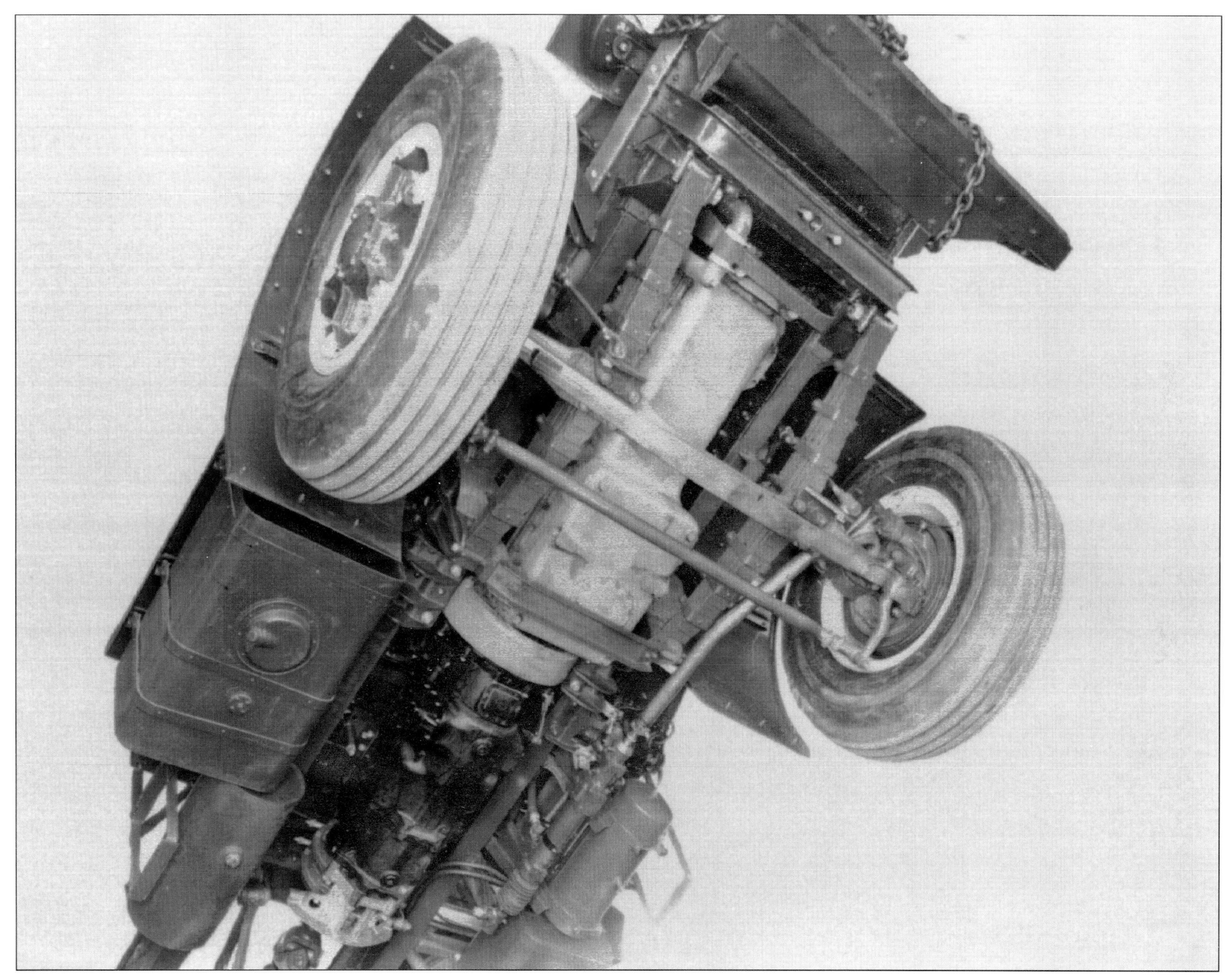

(V6574)

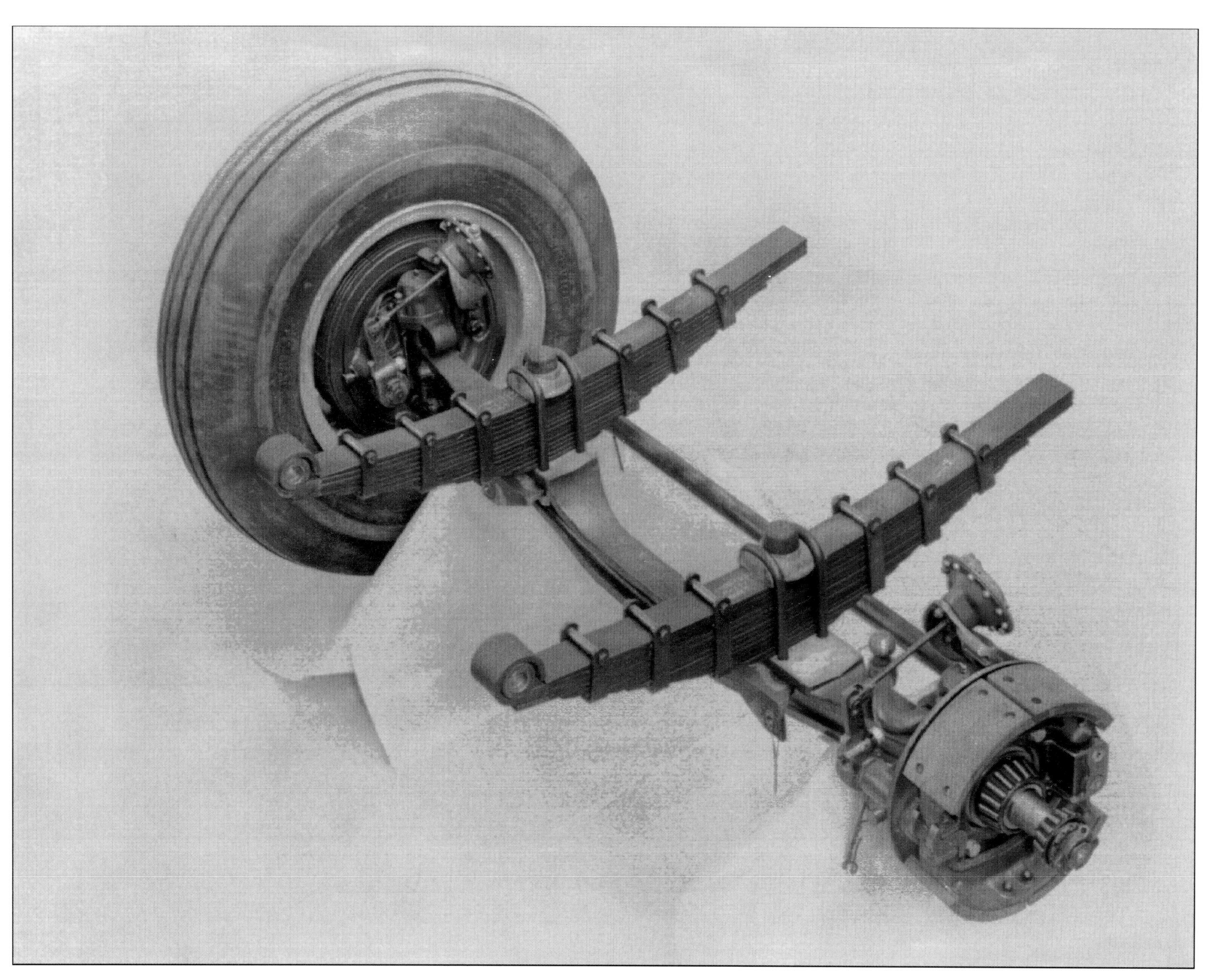

Front axle and suspension assembly from one of the FCSW chassis built under General Sales Order #16 through #21. April 1943. (V6612)

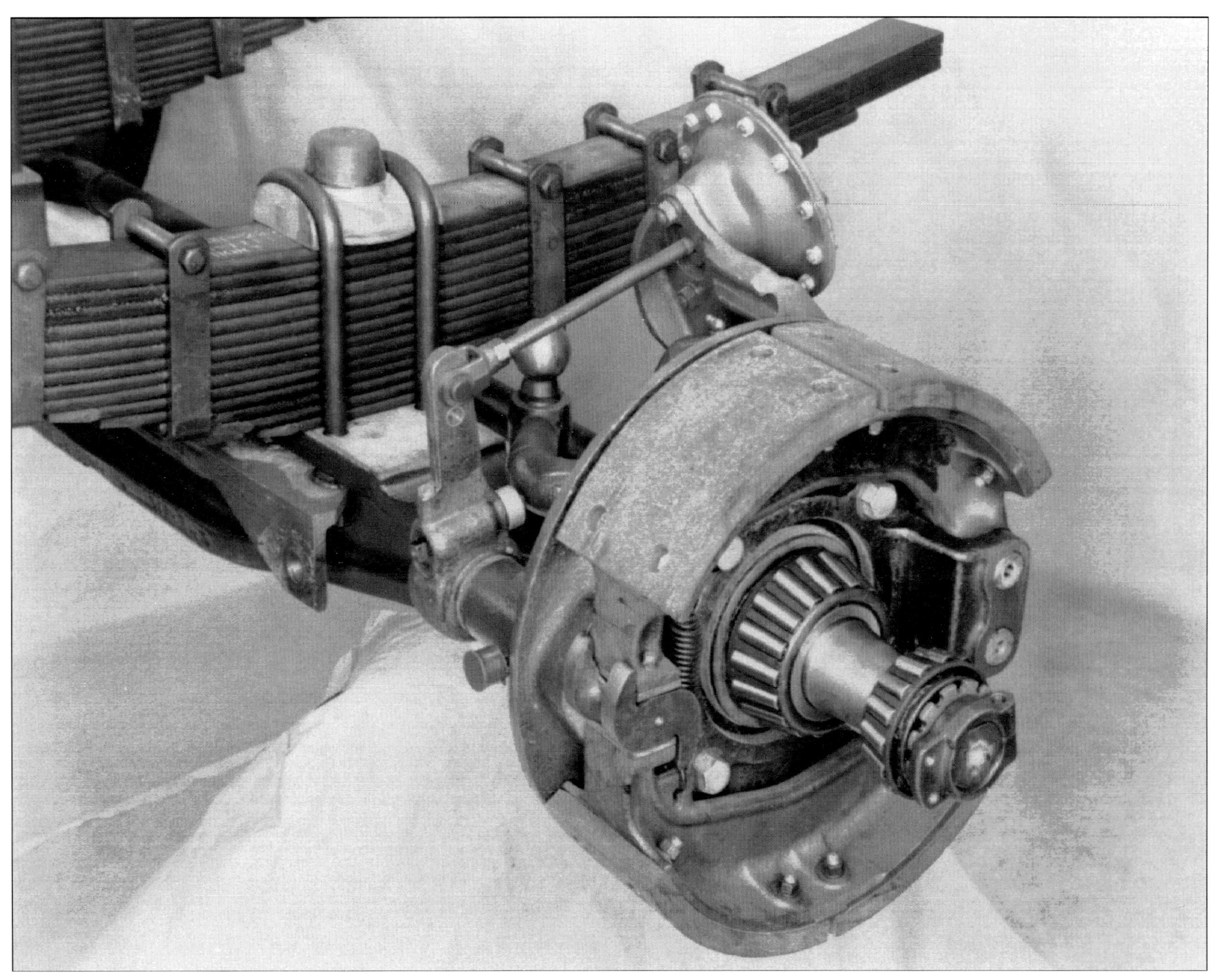

FCSW front wheel brake. (V6611)

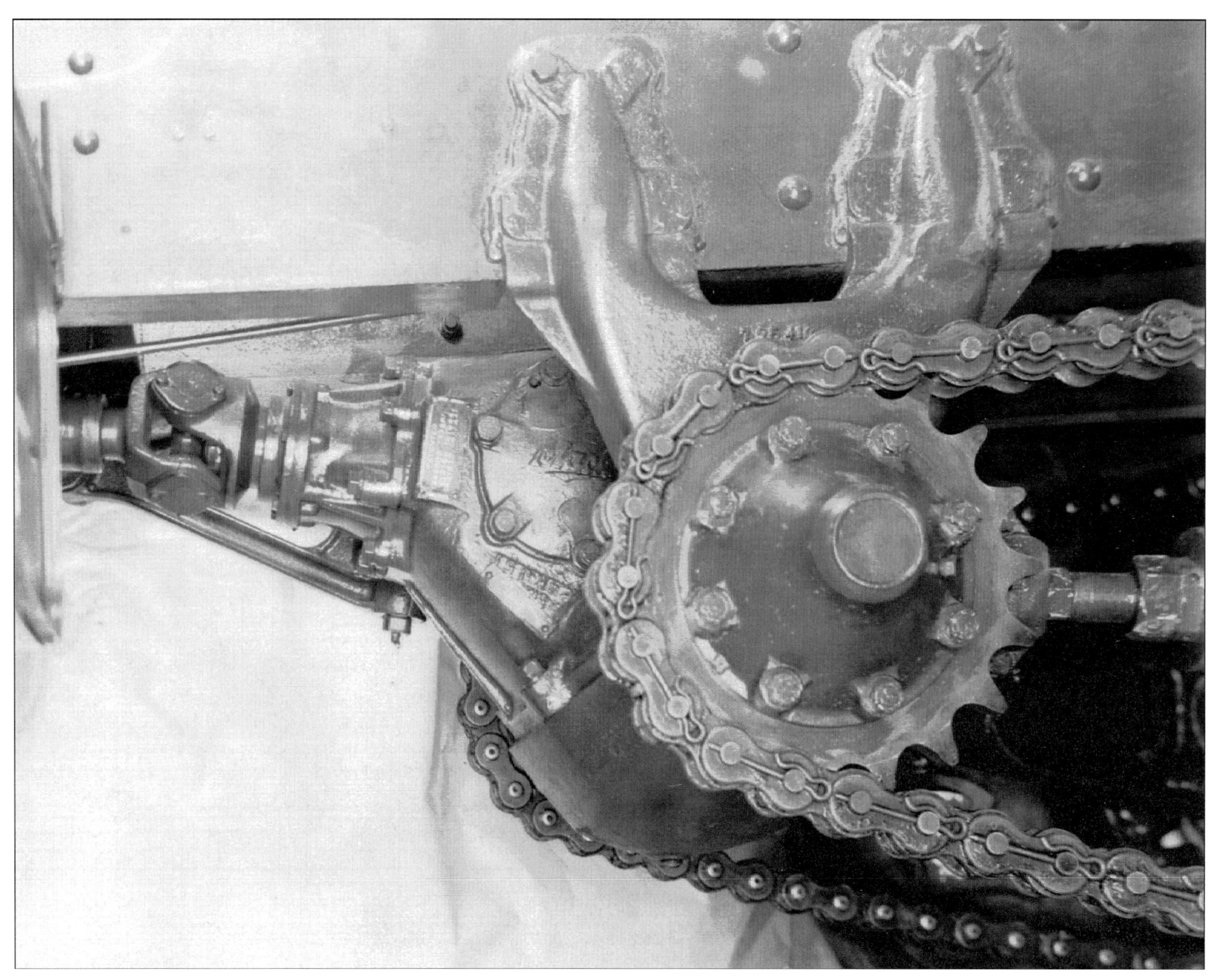

Jackshaft from one of the FCSW chassis built under General Sales Order #16 through #21. April 1943. (V6608)

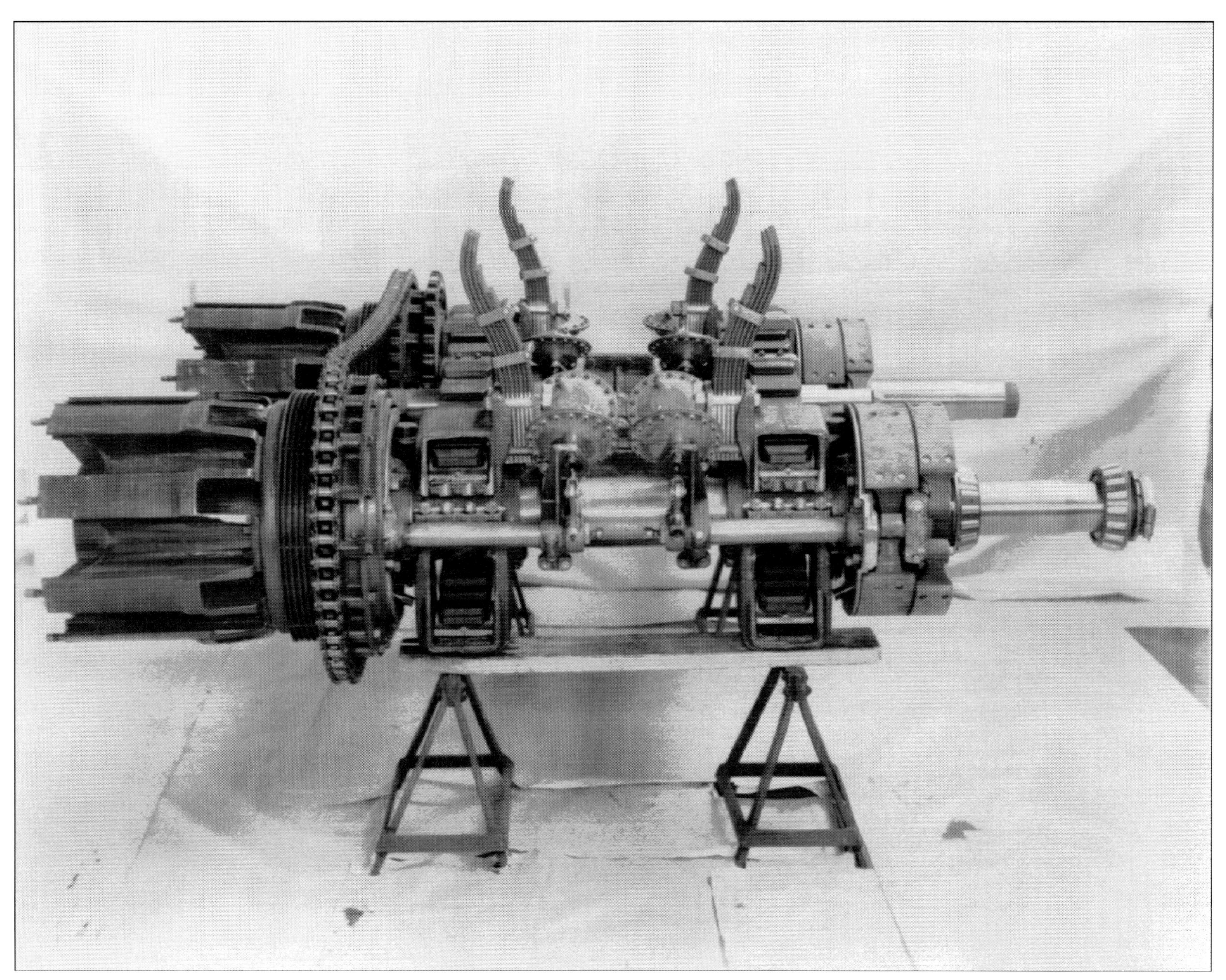

Bogie assembly from one of the FCSW chassis built under General Sales Order #16 through #21. April 1943. (V6615)

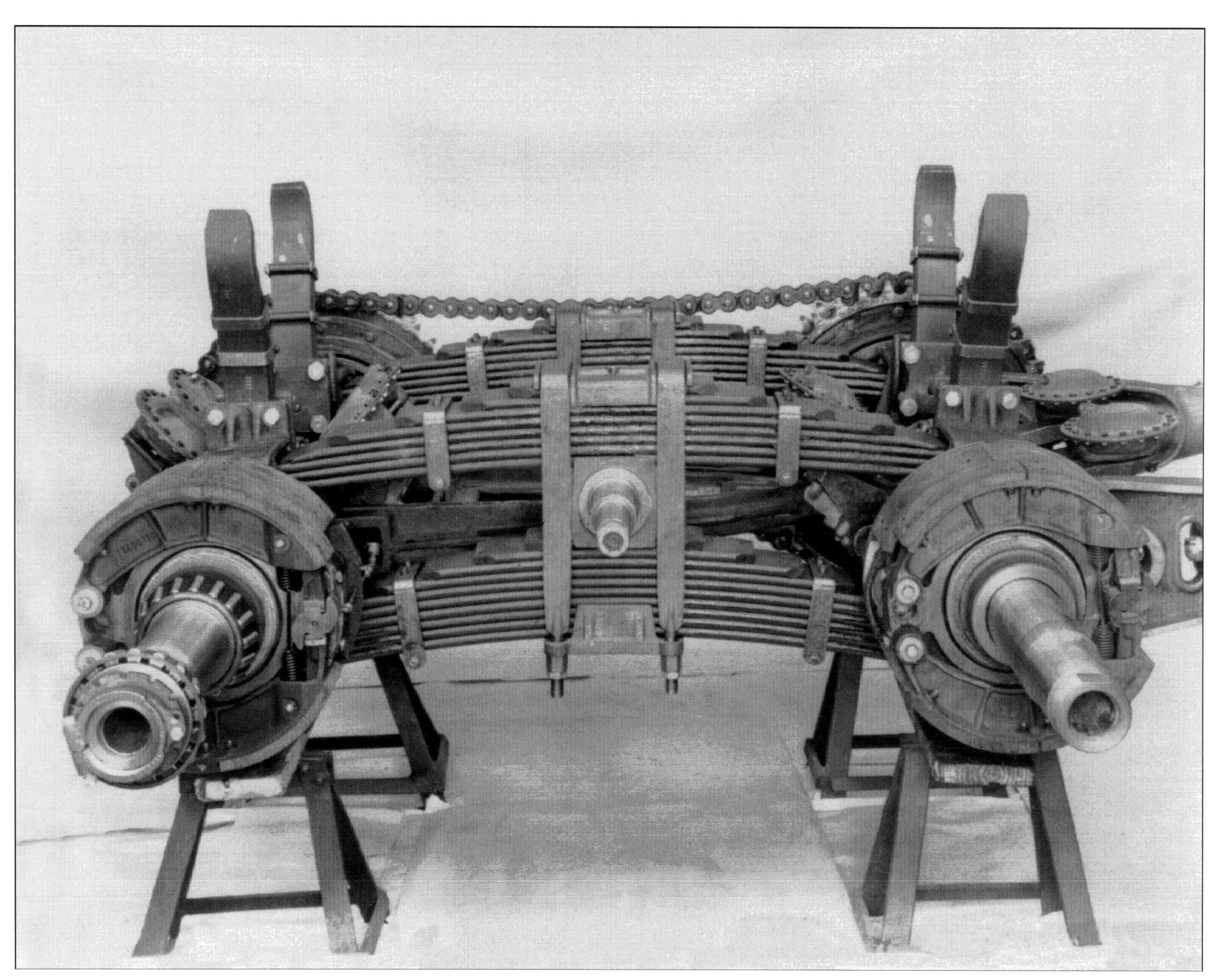

Two views of the bogie assembly from one of the FCSW chassis built under General Sales Order #16 through #21. April 1943. (V6616)

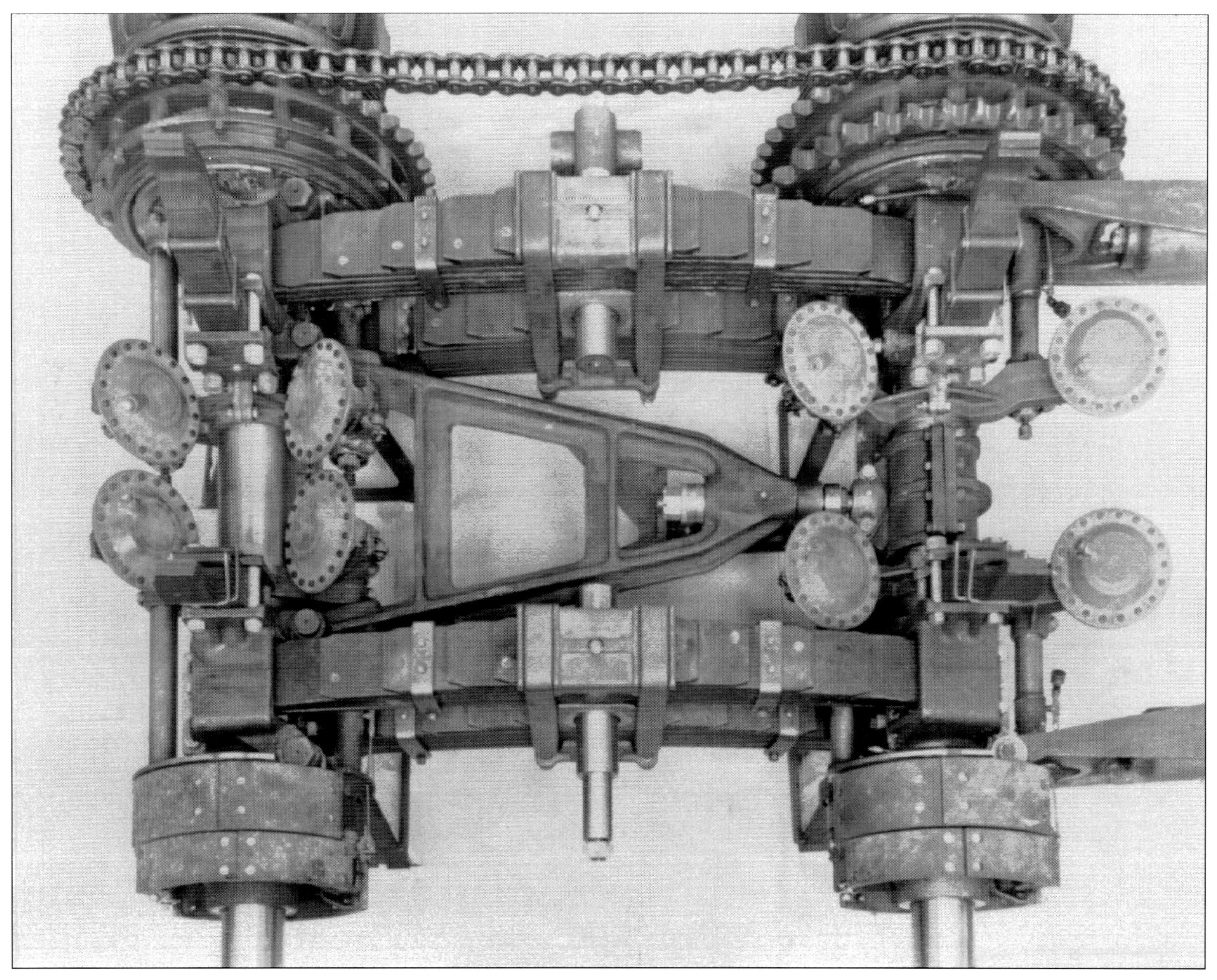

(V6618)

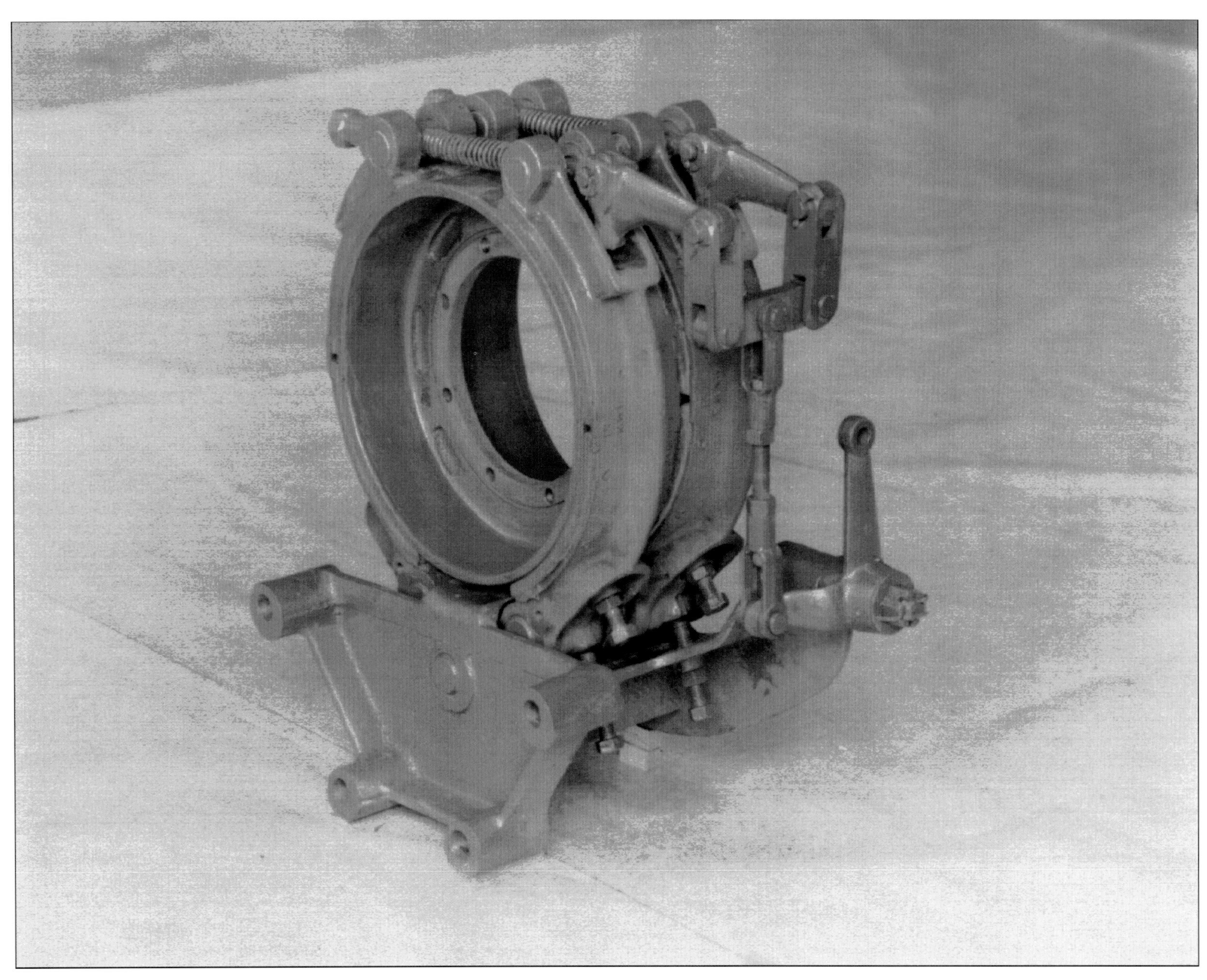

The parking brake from one of the FCSW chassis built under General Sales Order #16 through #21. April 1943. (V6586)

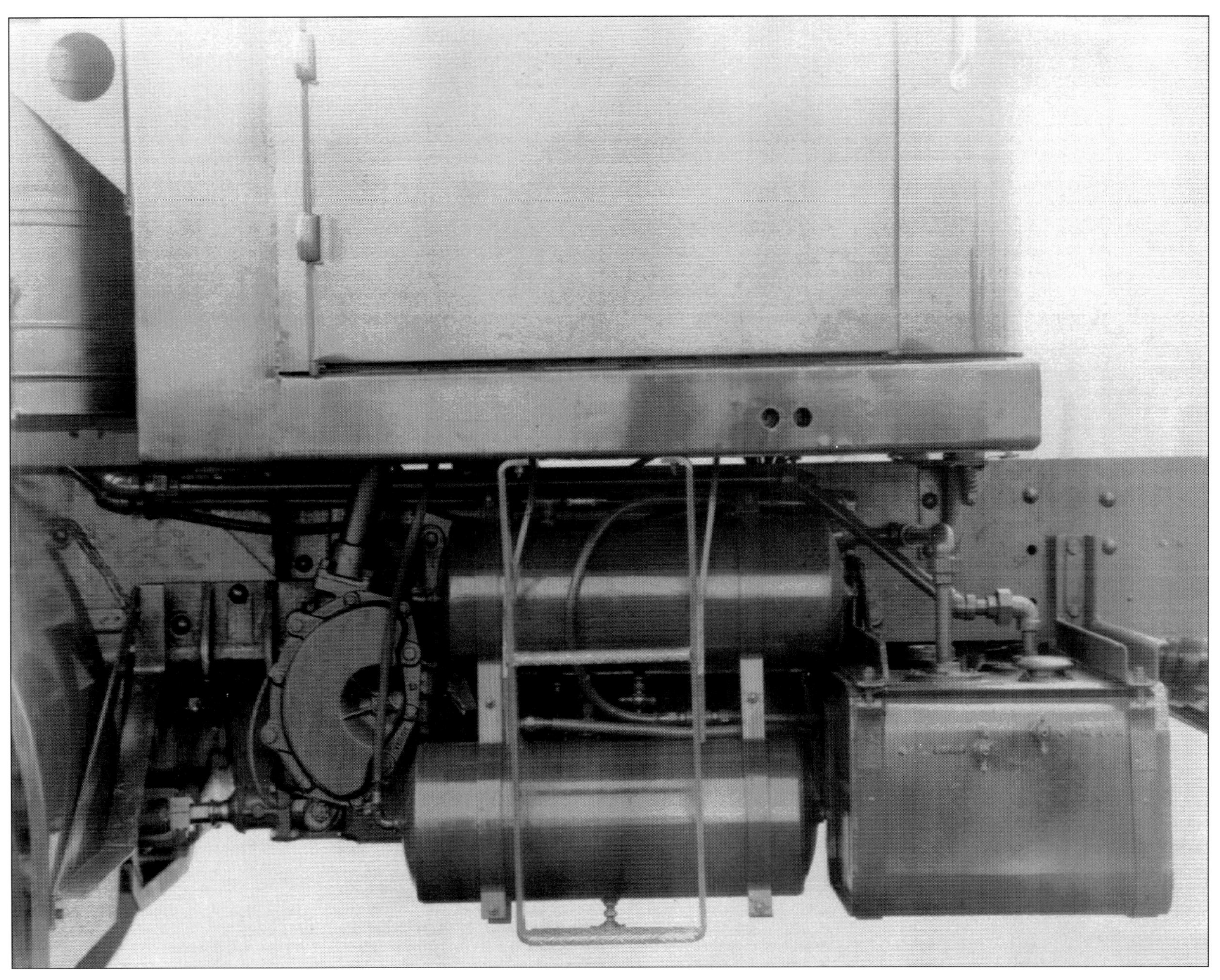

Chassis detail of one of the FCSW chassis built under General Sales Order #16 through #21. April 1943. (V6620)

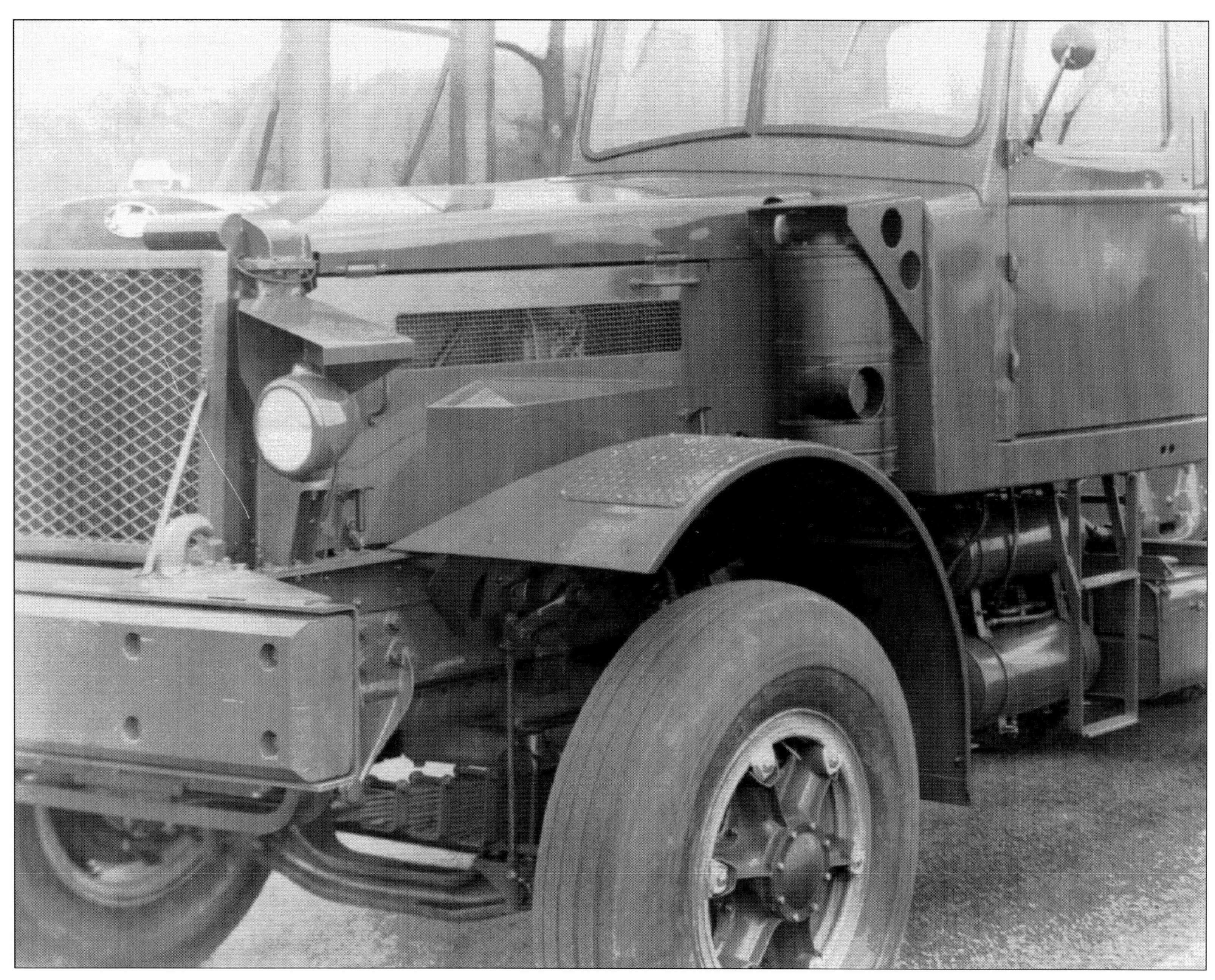

Two views of one of the six chassis with cab built under General Sales Order #16 through #21. April 1943. (V6621)

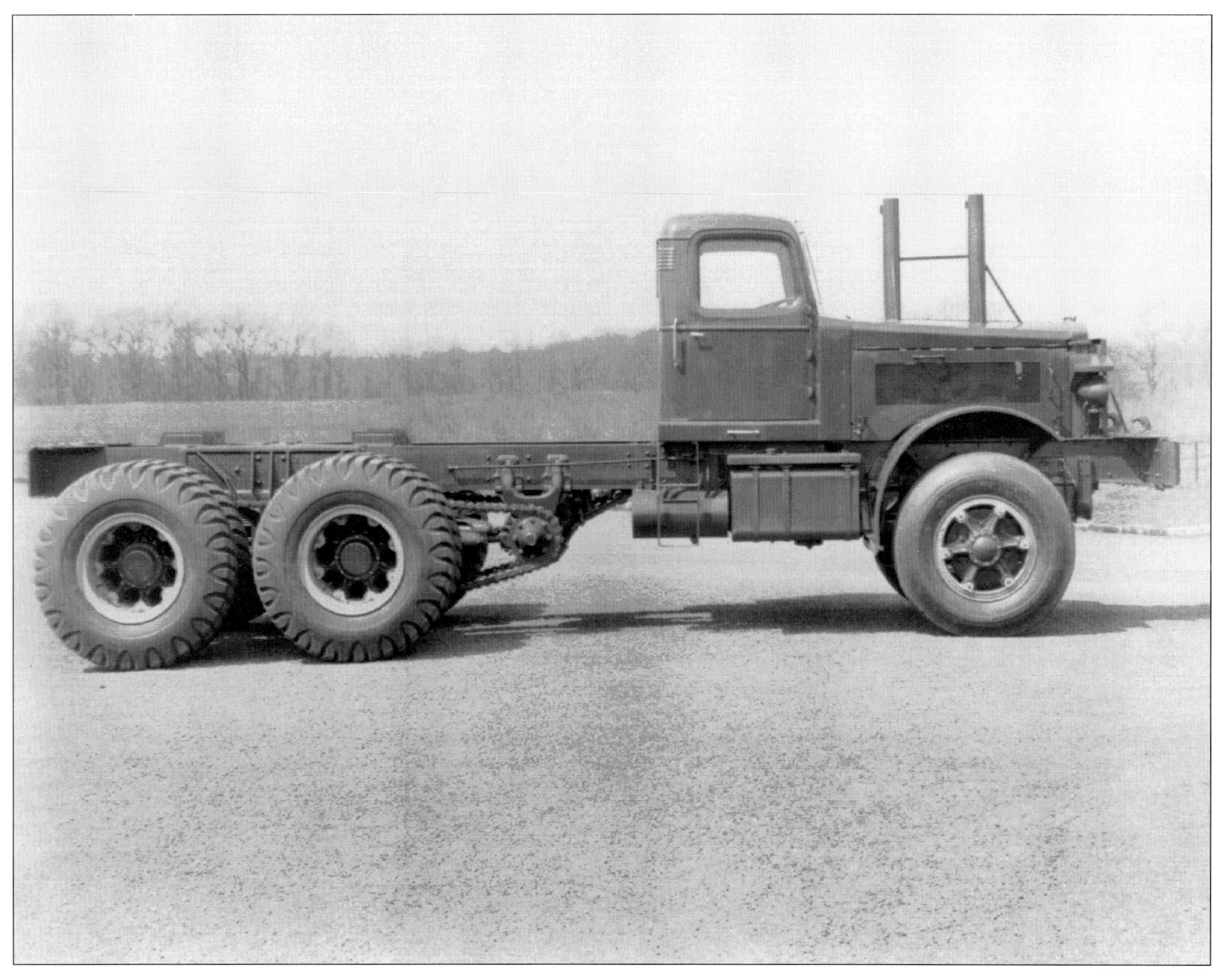

(V6624)

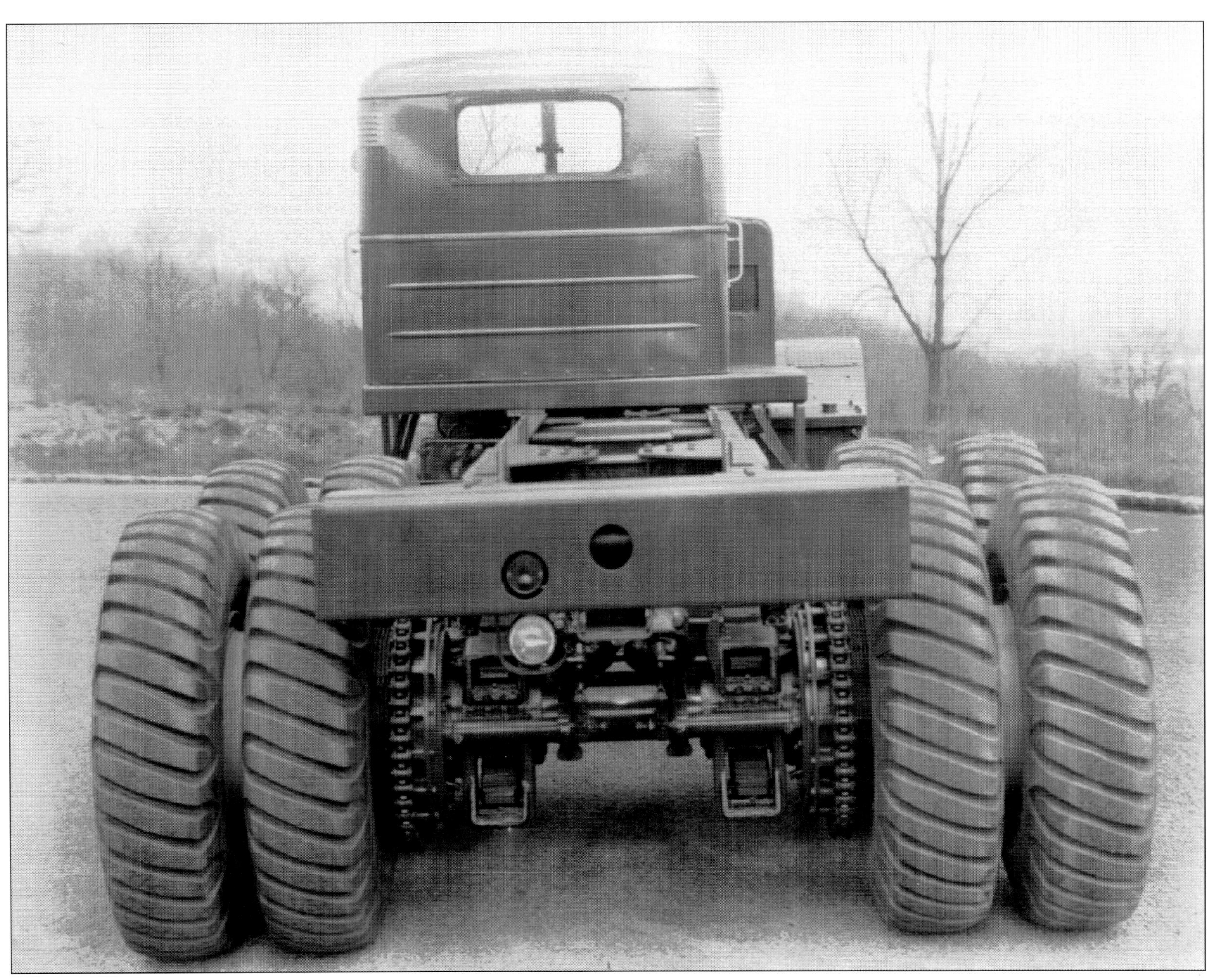

Rear views of one of the six chassis with cab built under General Sales Order #16 through #21. April 1943. (V6622)

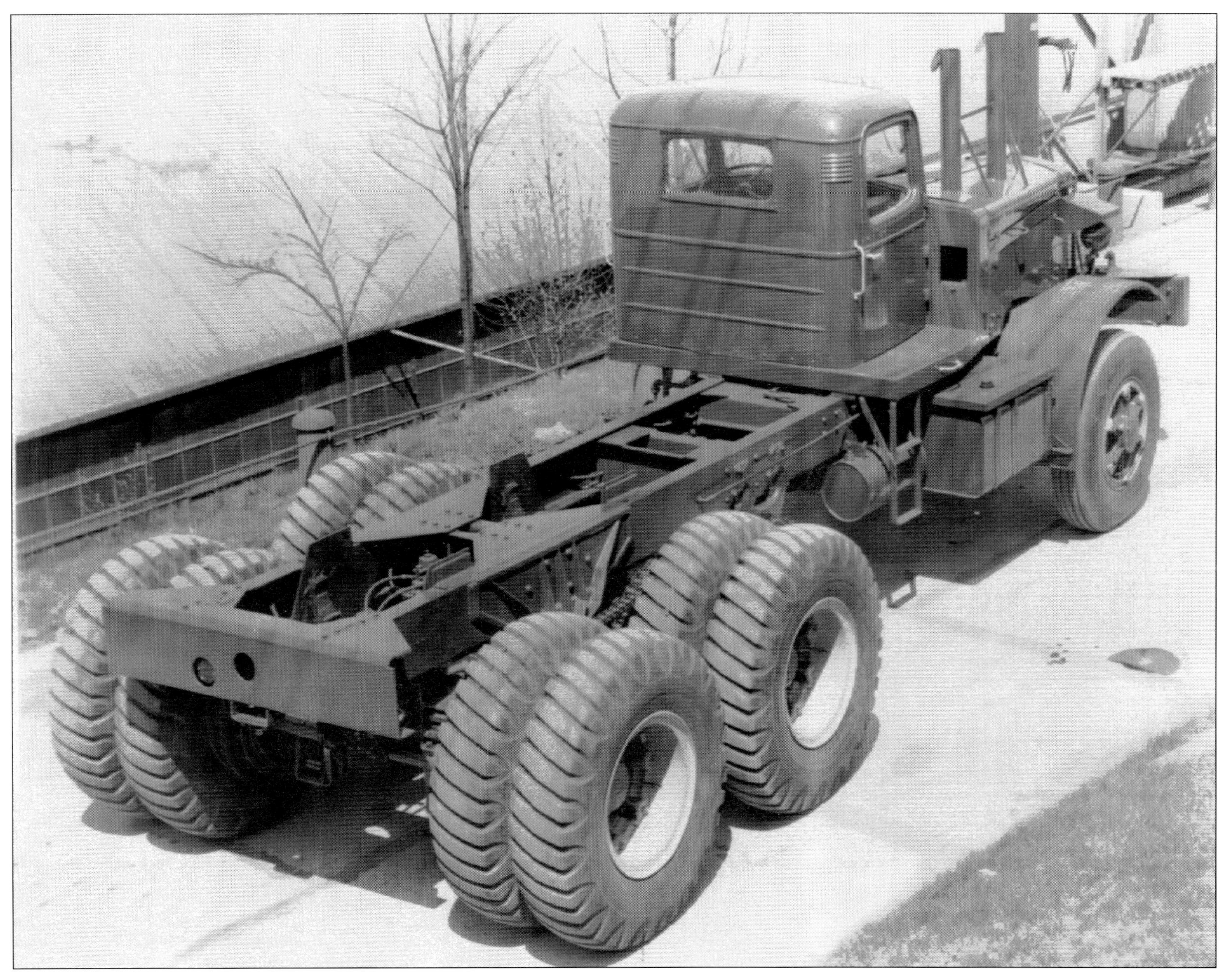

(V6628)

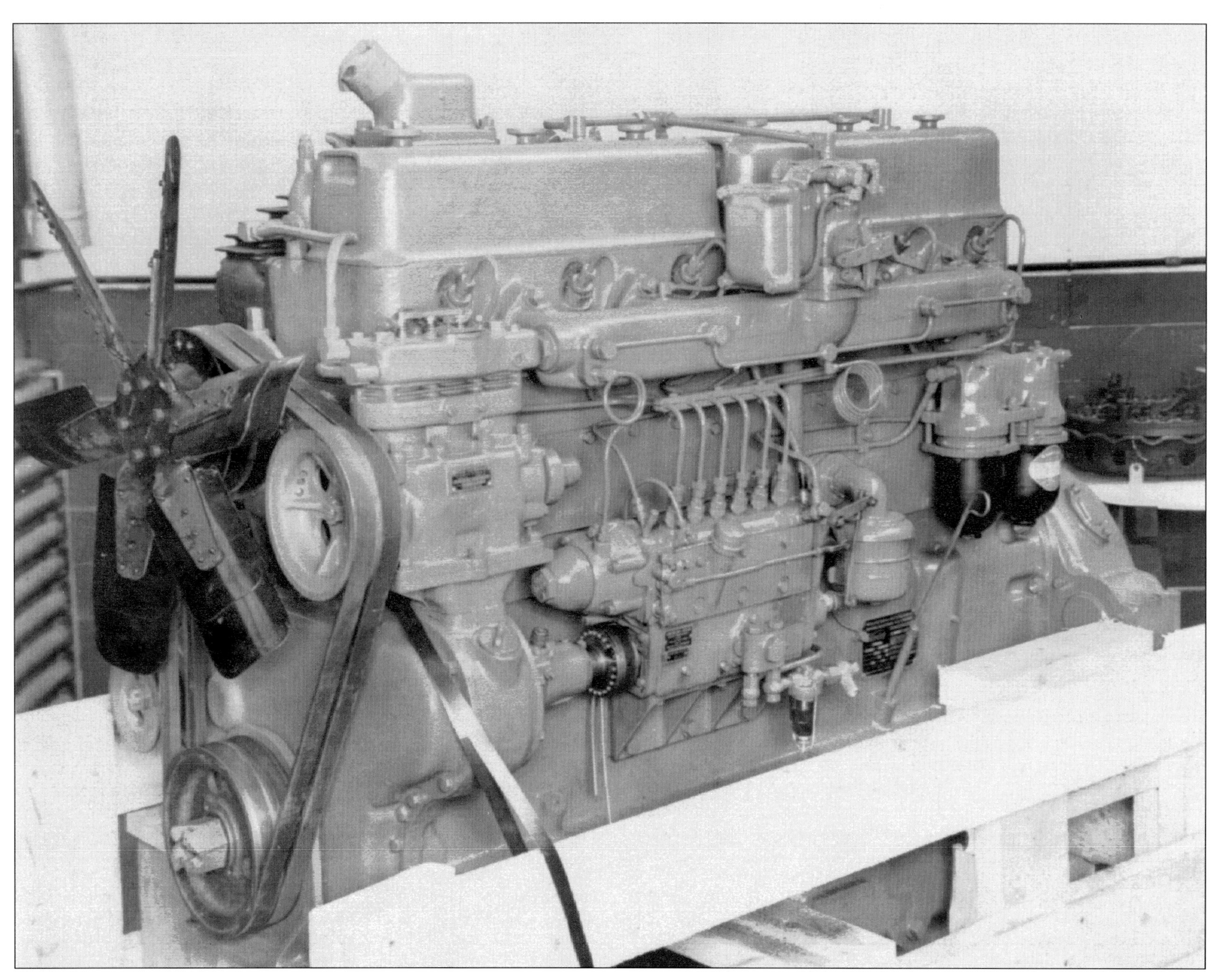

An example of the Waukesha Hesselman engine purchased for FCSW #16 through #21. (V6584)

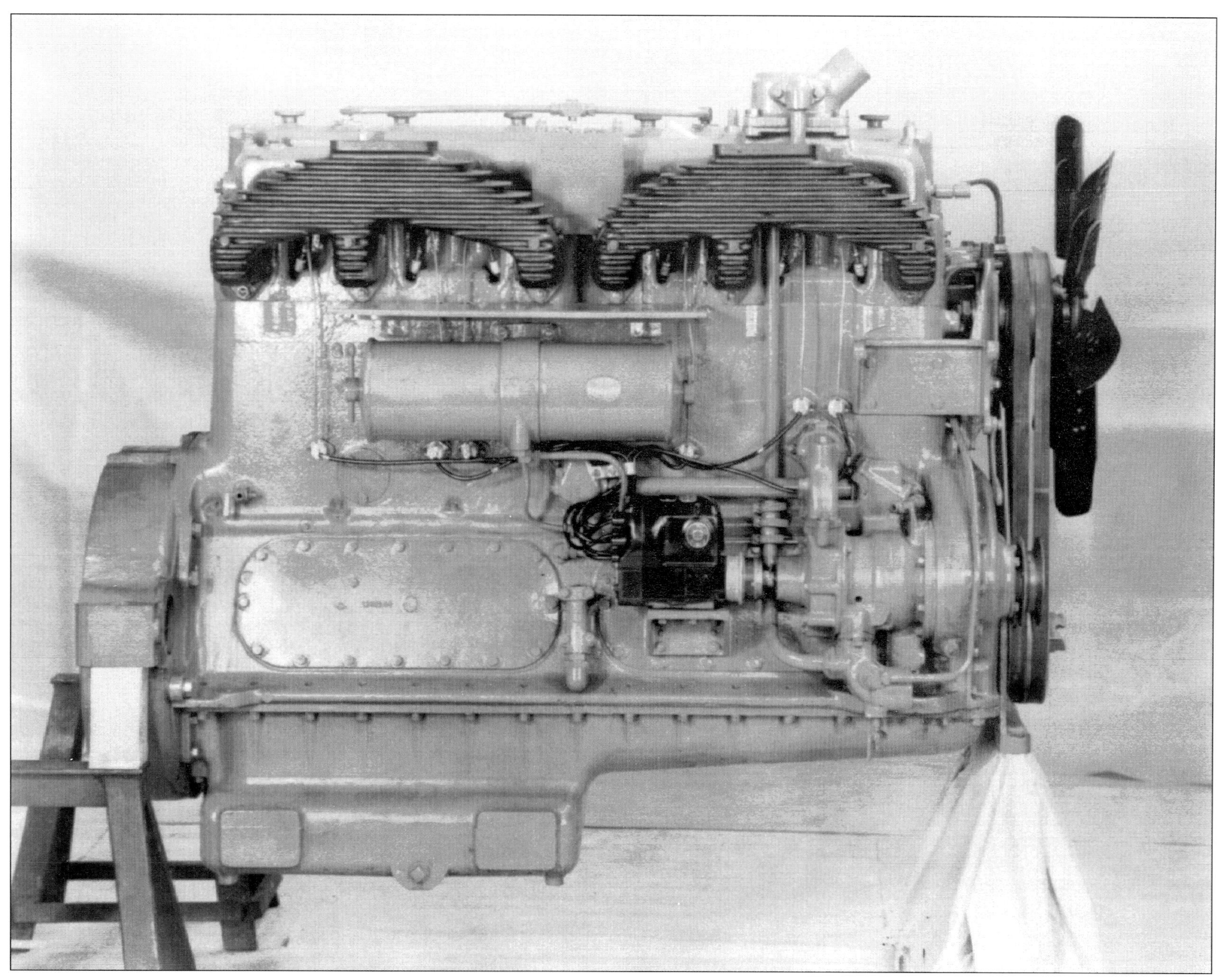

(V6634)

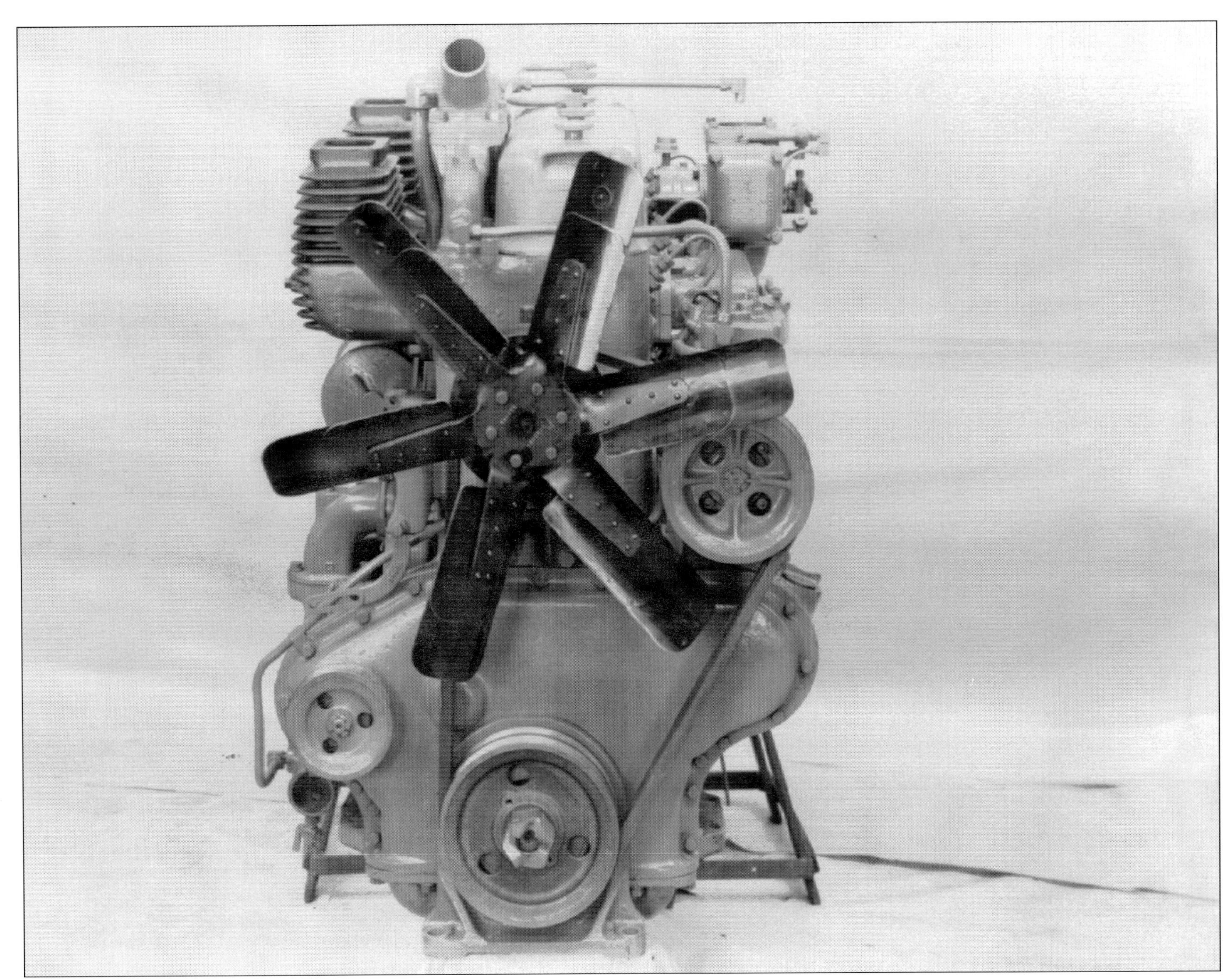

Front view of the Waukesha Hesselman engine. (V6632)

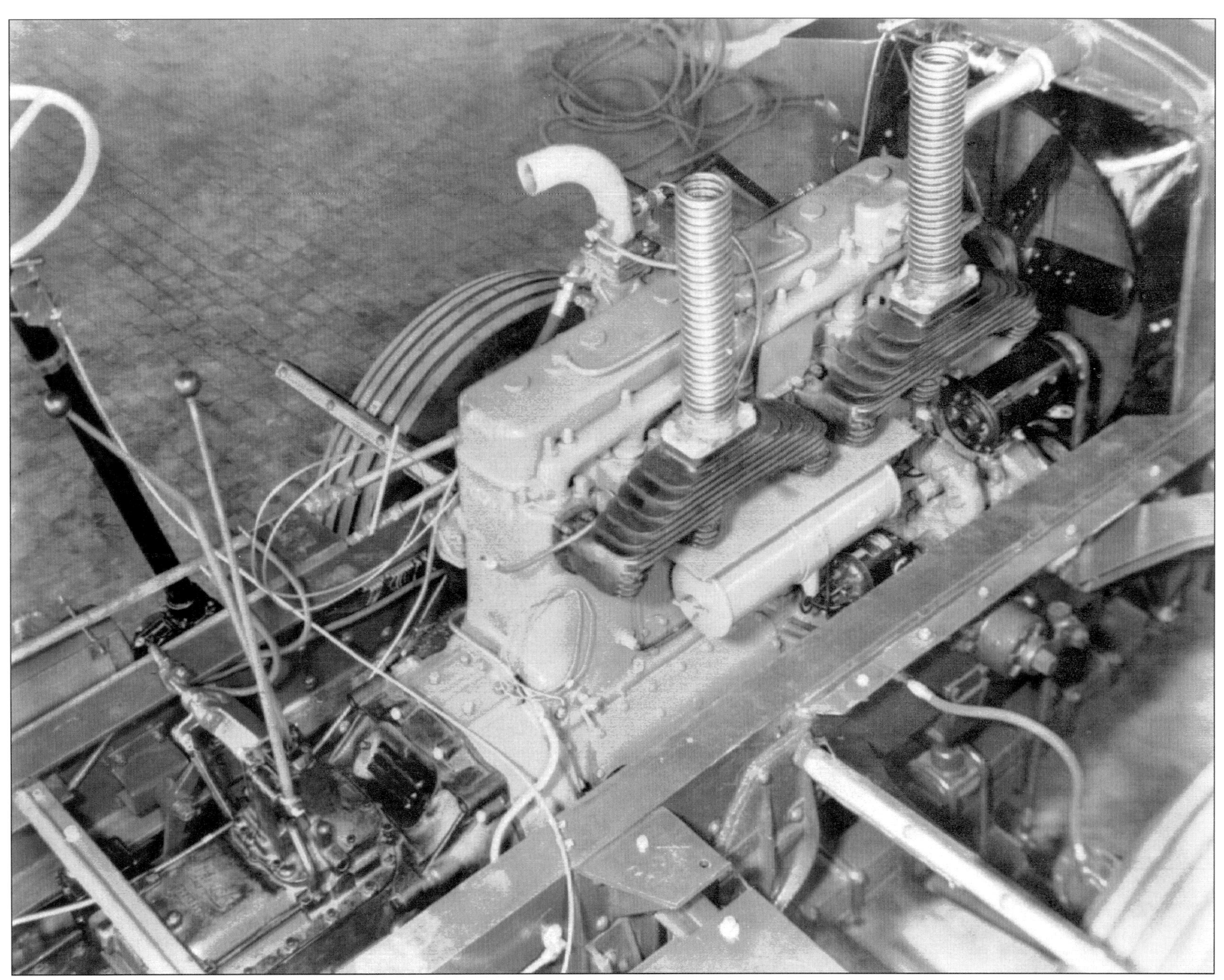

Waukesha Hesselman engine installed in a FCSW chassis. (V6646)

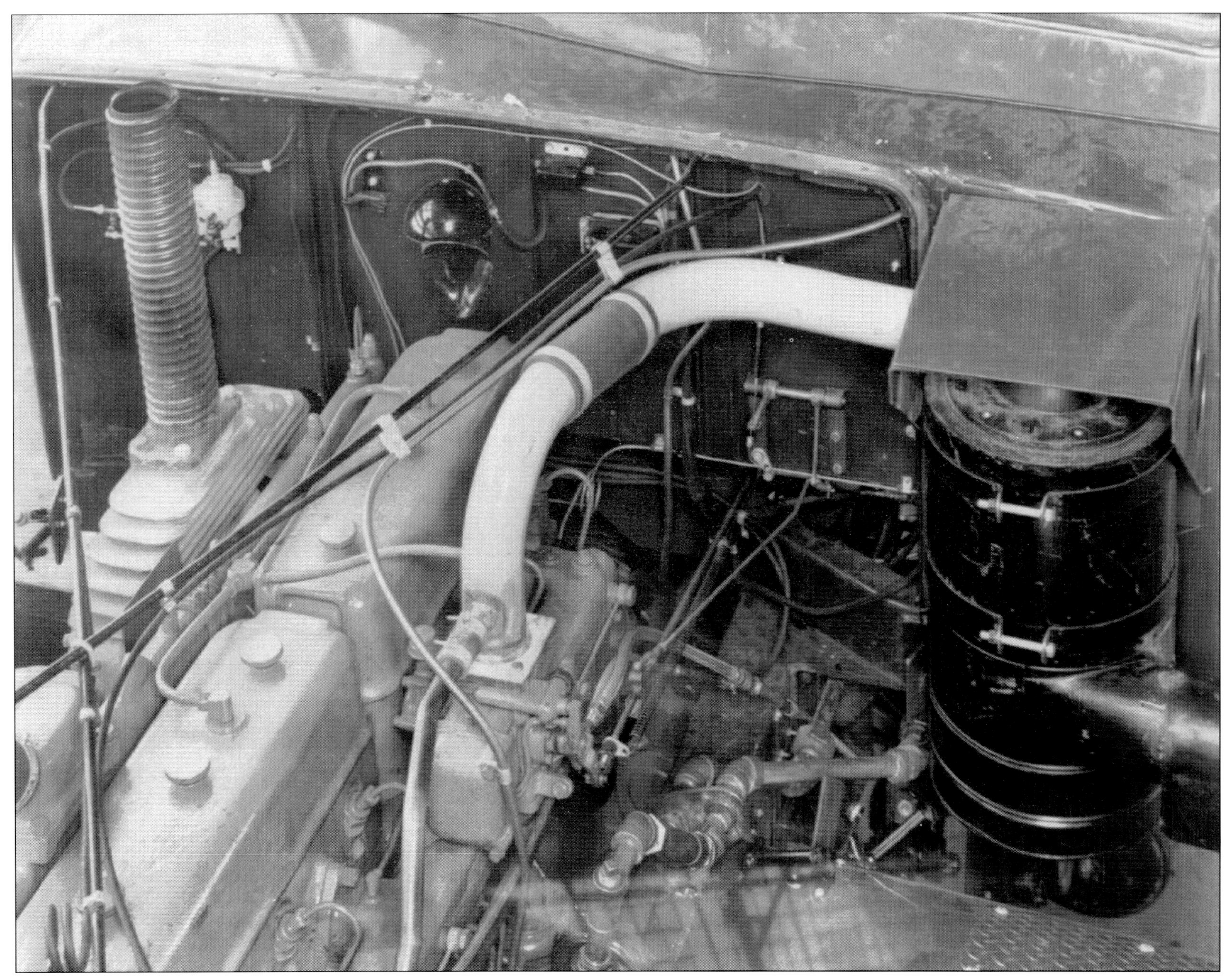

(V6722)

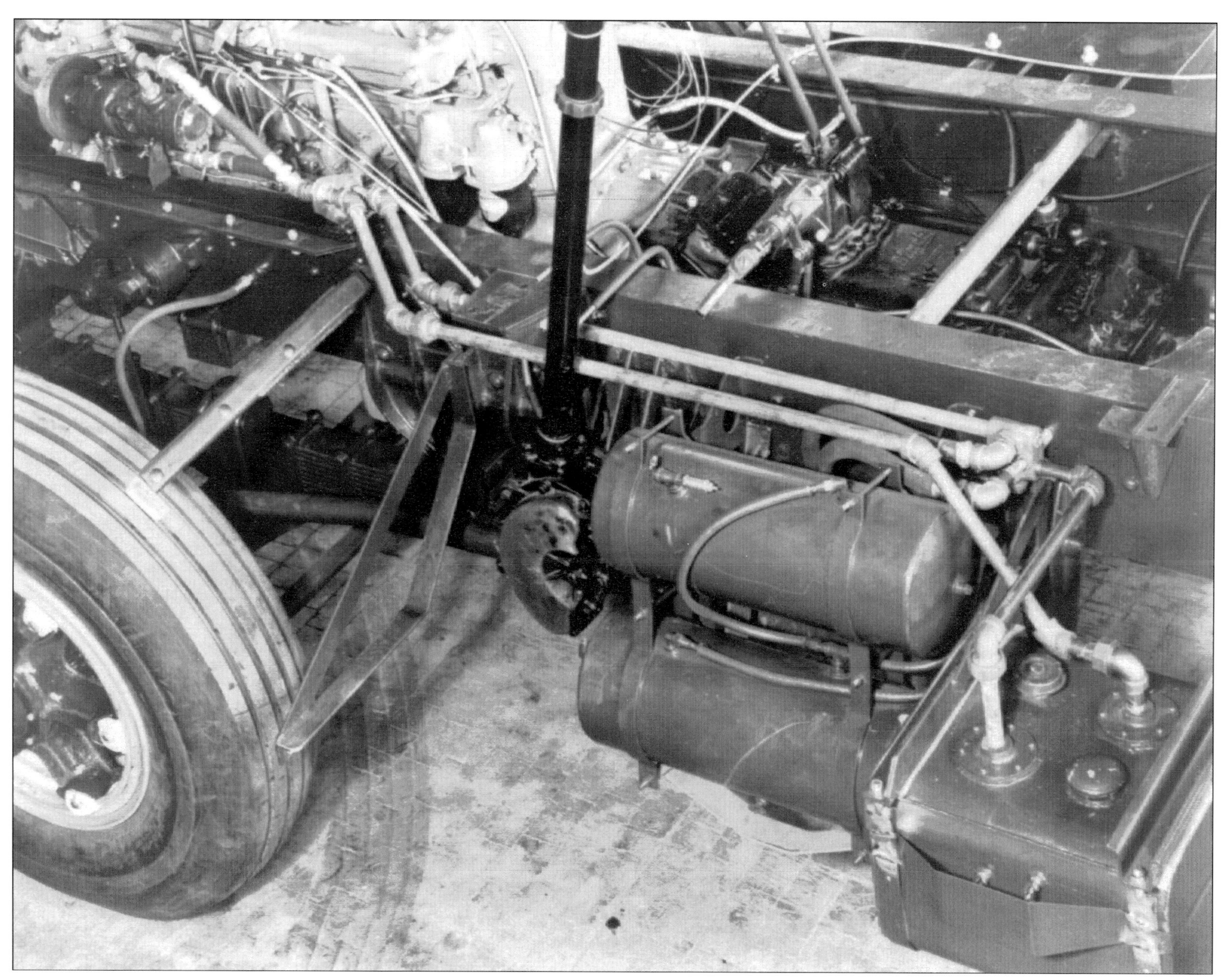

Power steering hydraulics fitted to one of the FCSW chassis built under General Sales Order #16 through #21.

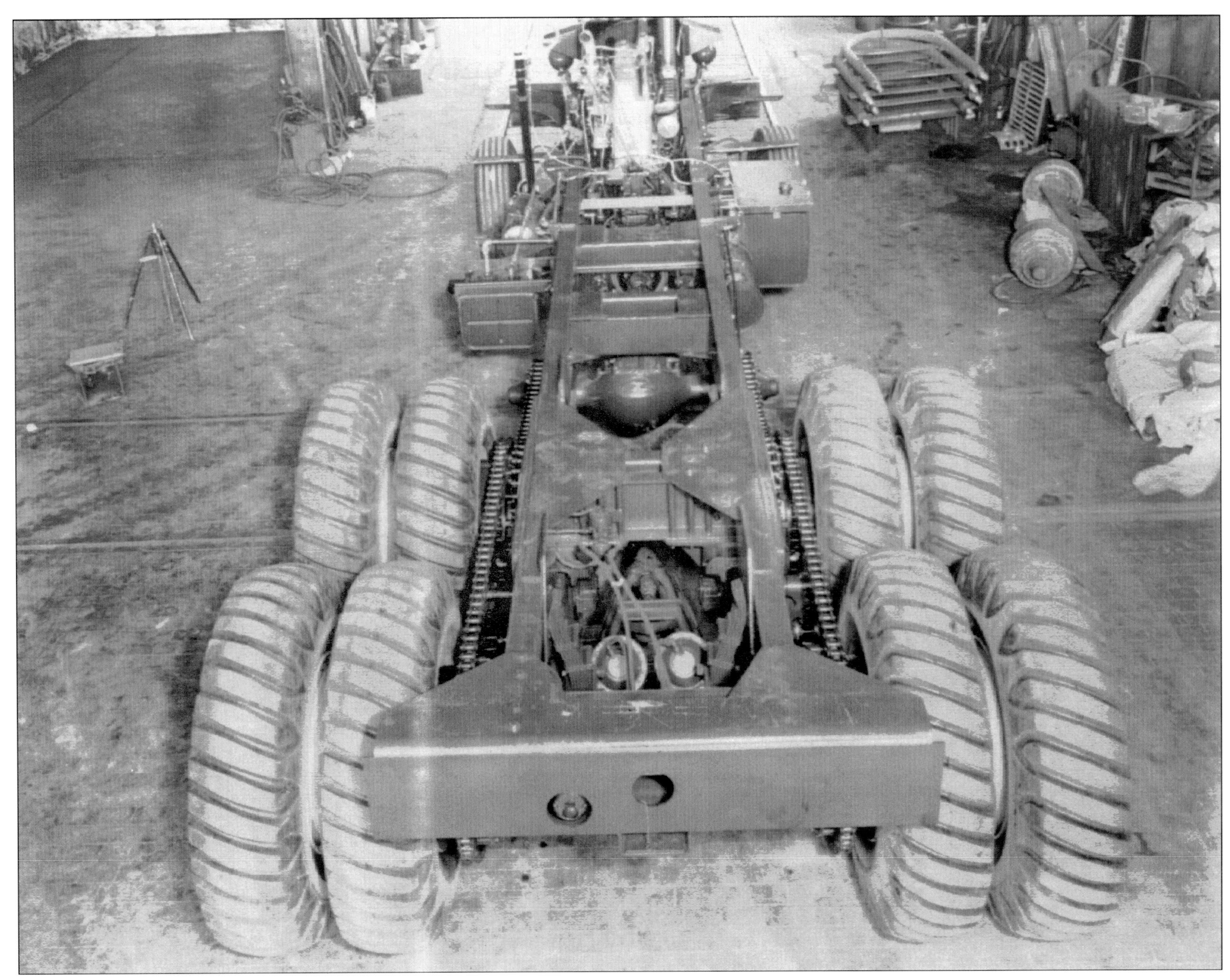

FCSW chassis details. (V6647)

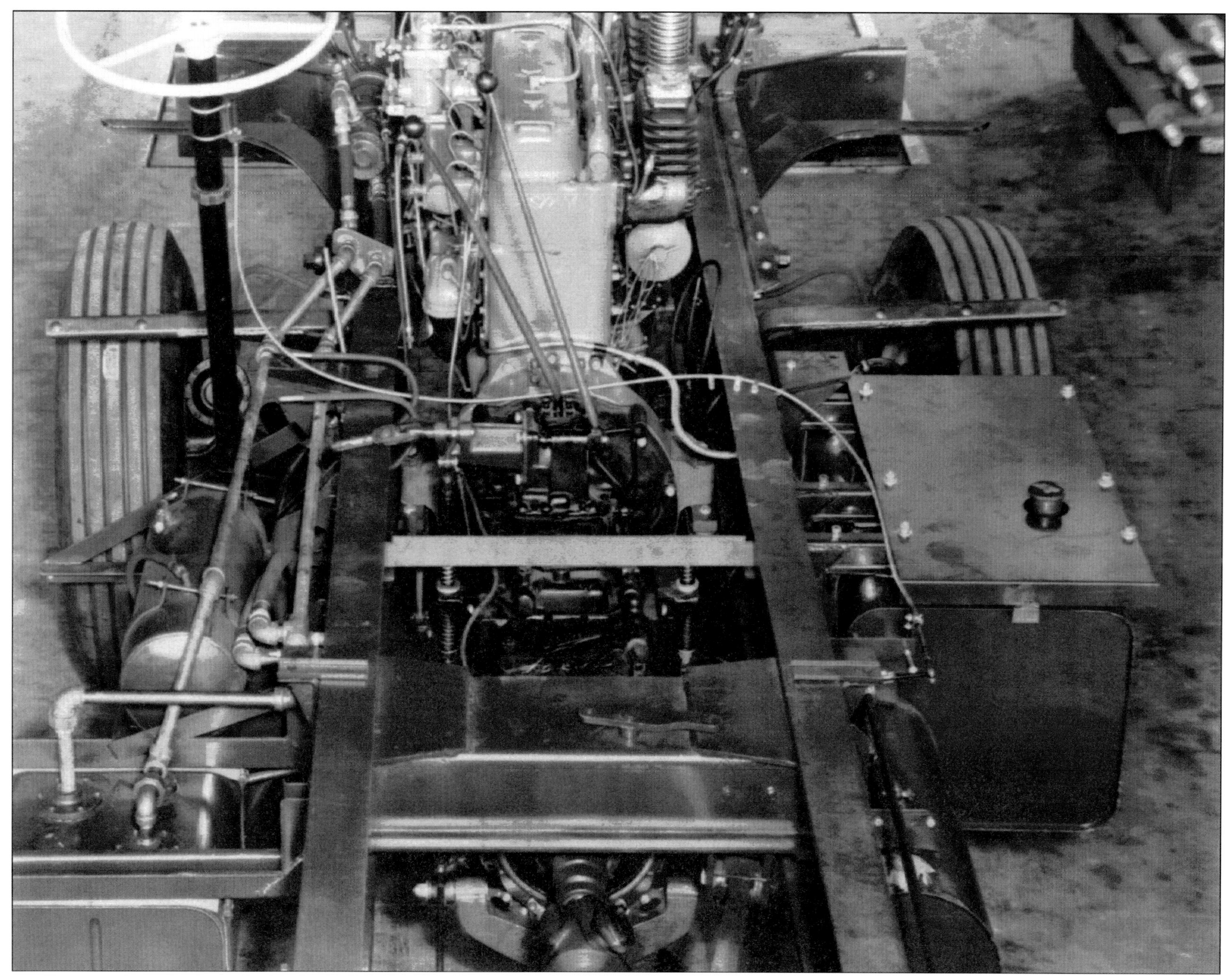

(V6641)

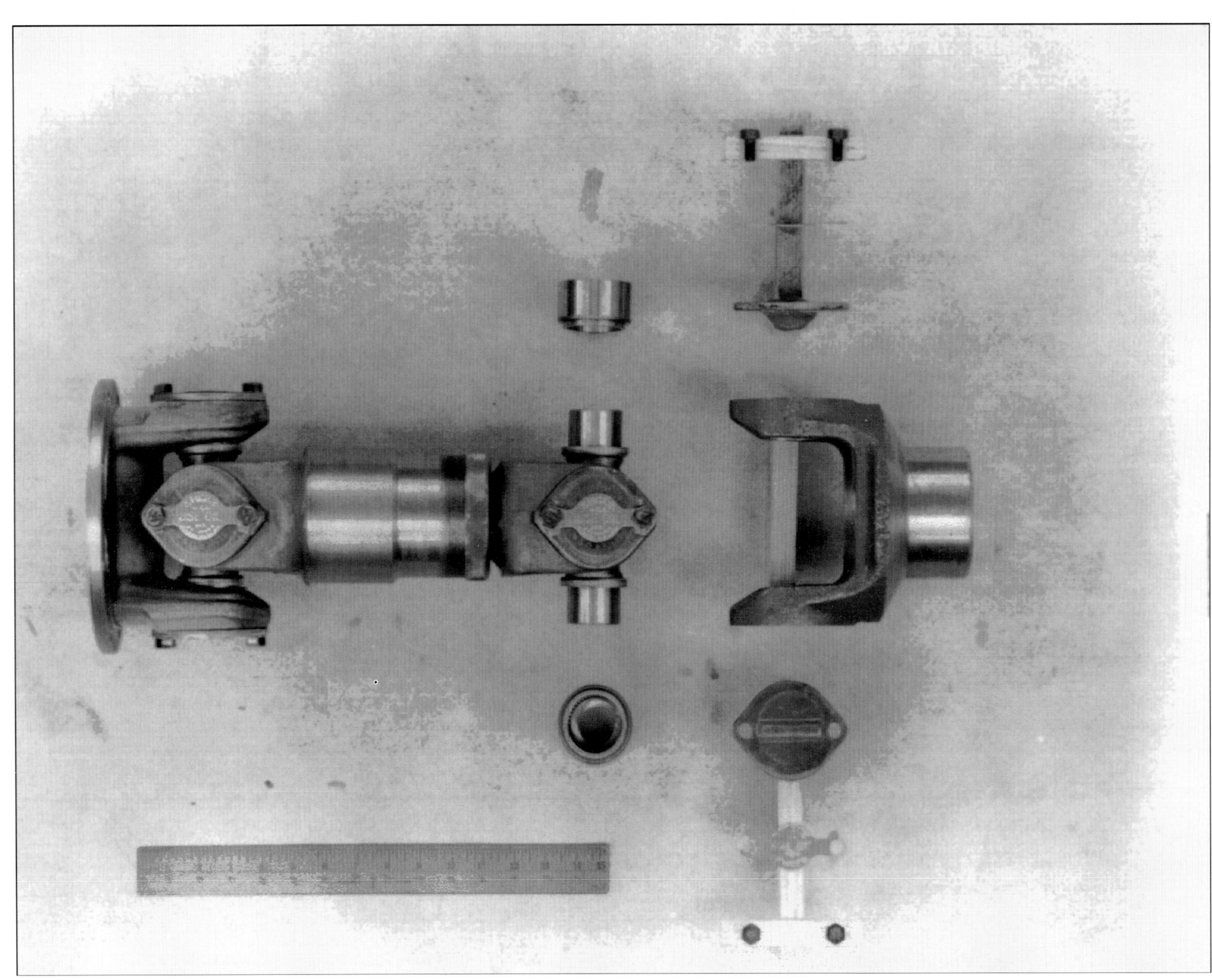

FCSW drive shaft with an exploded view of one universal joint. (V6775)

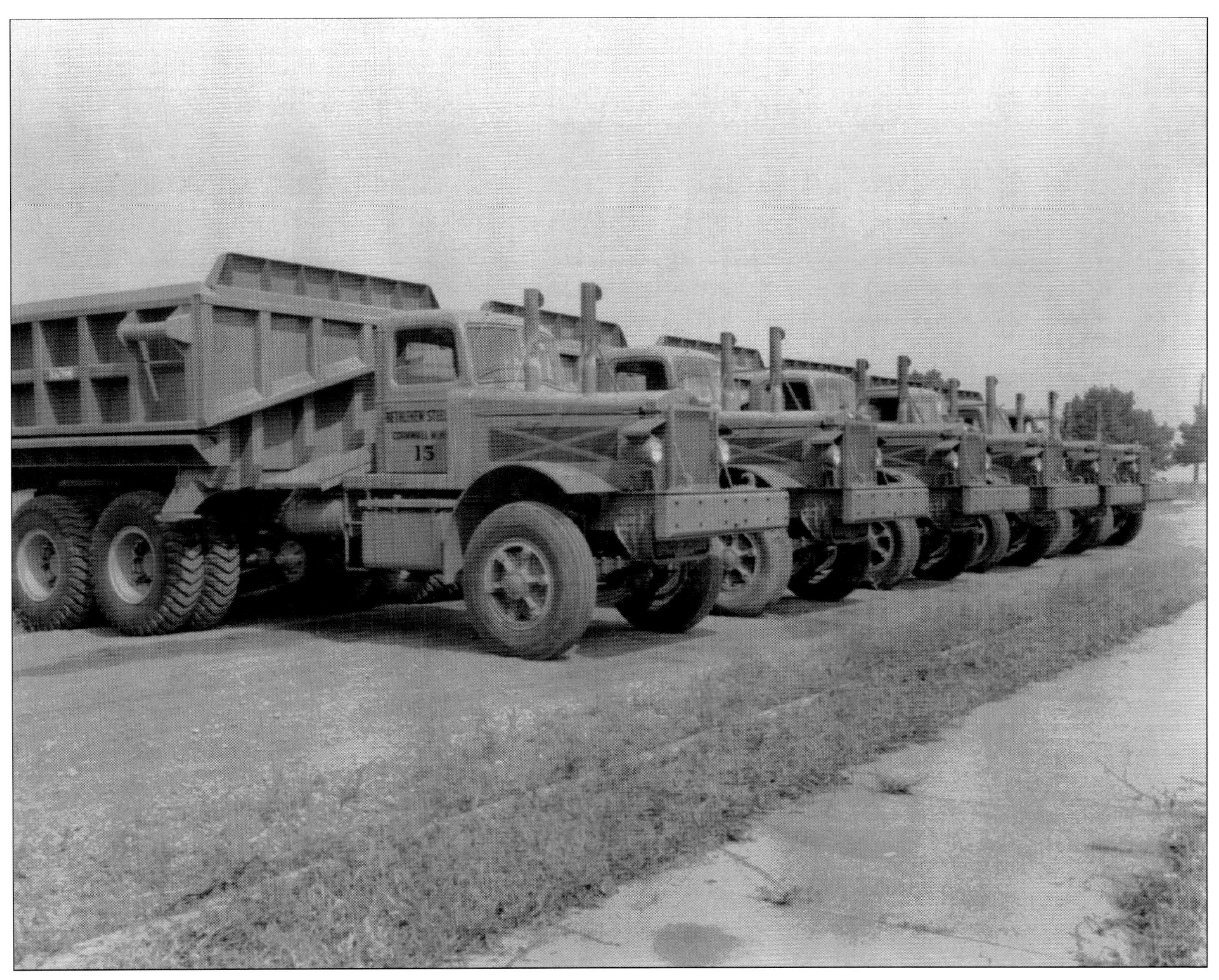

The FCSW chassis, #16 through #21, fitted with Easton side gate, side-dump, external hoist bodies, and sold to Bethlehem Steel Co., Cornwallis, Pennsylvania. July 1943. (V6972)

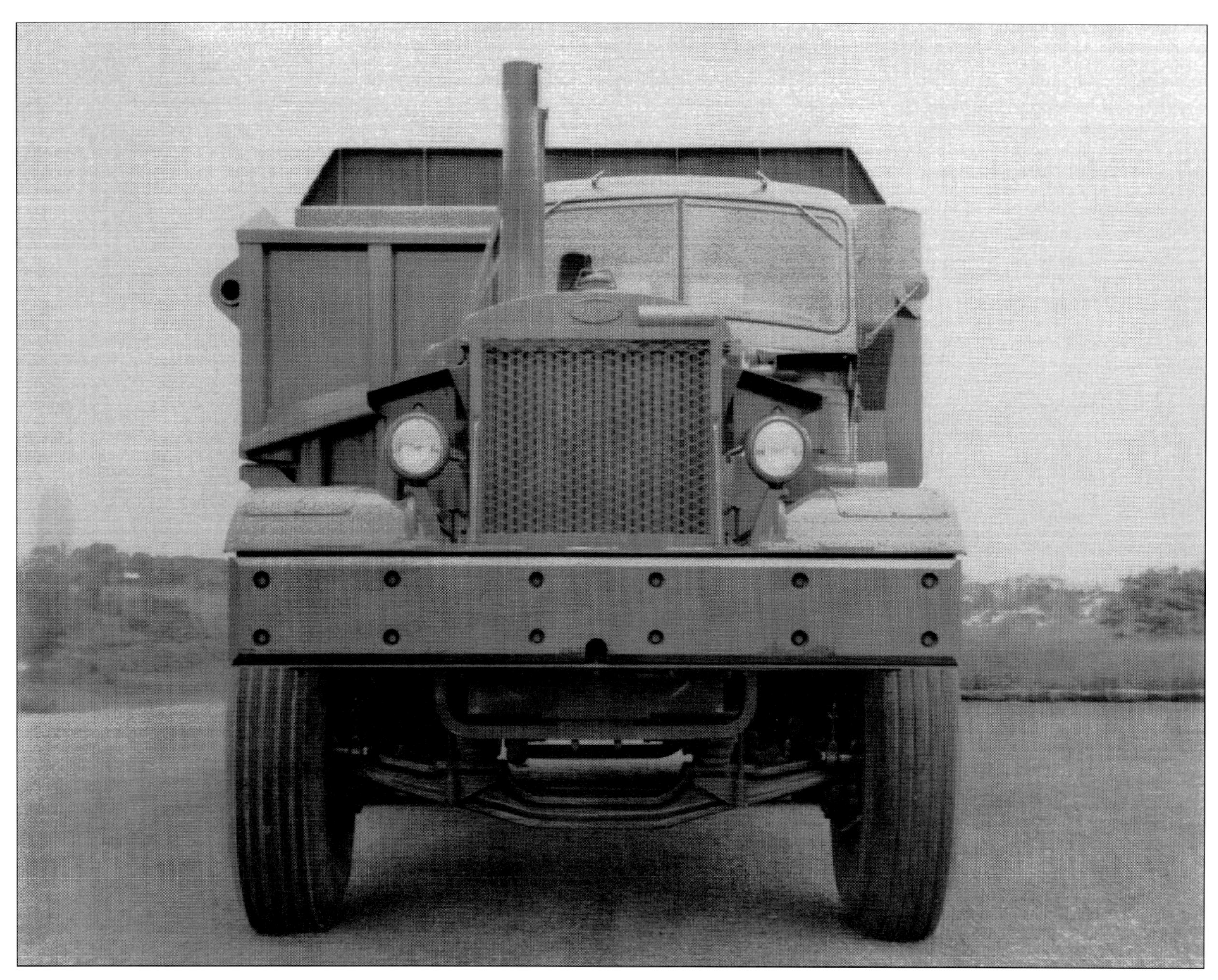

FC2C, chassis #1104D, mining truck with Easton side gate, side-dump, external hoist body, and sold to Bethlehem Steel Co. Steeleton, Pennsylvania. November 1943. (V6779)

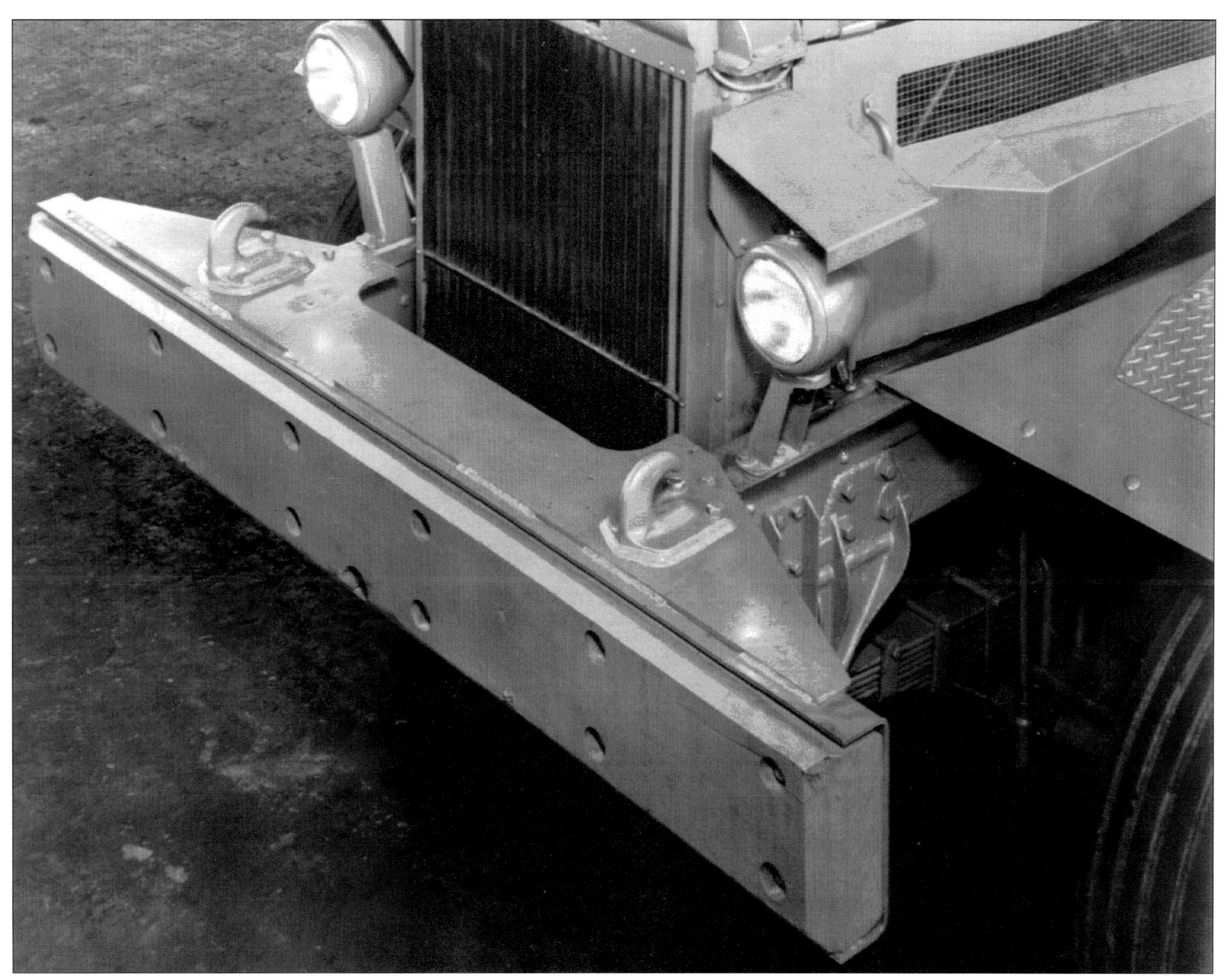

Tow hooks welded to the front bumper of FC2C #1104D. (V7249)

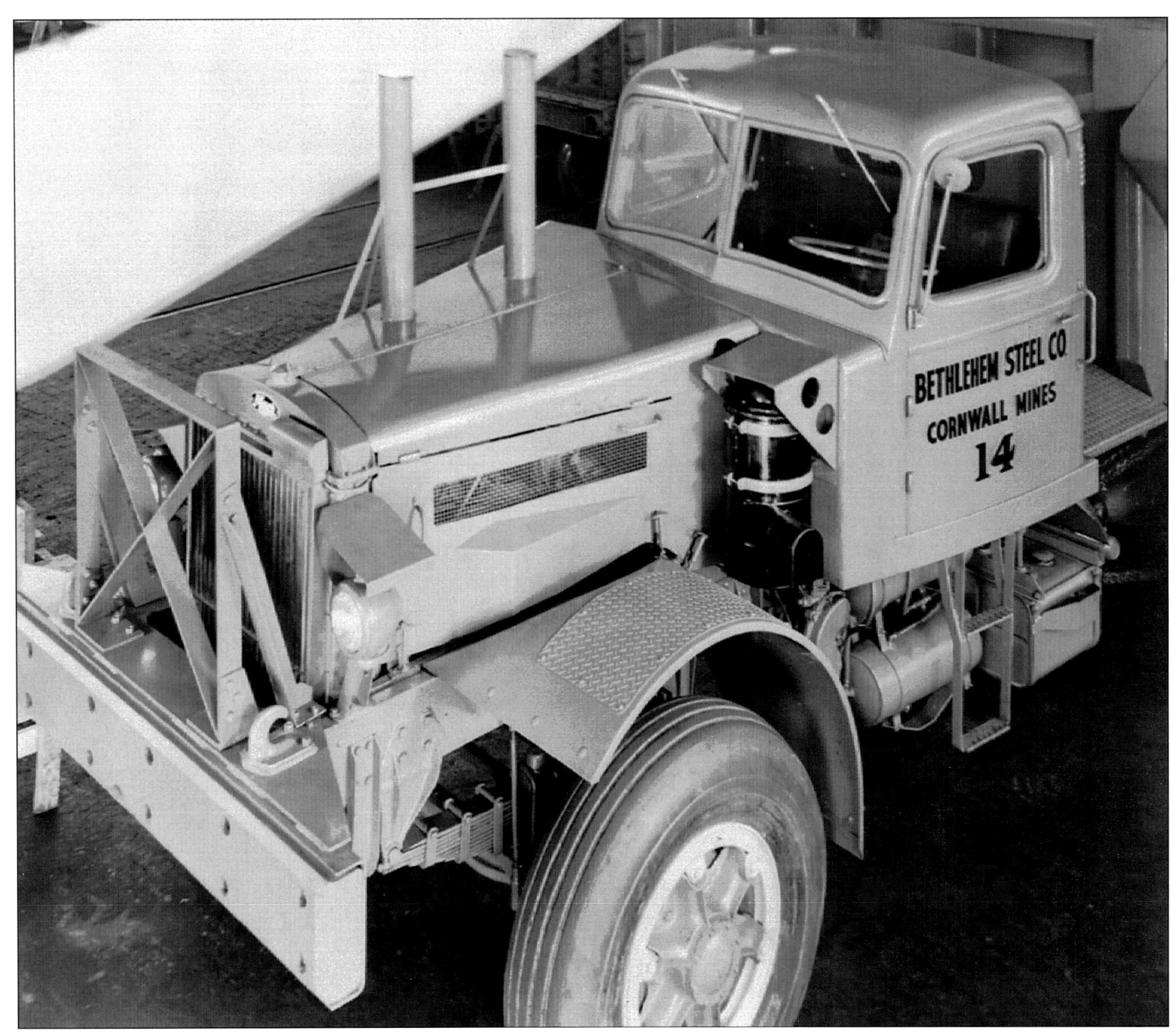

External and internal views of the cab fitted to FC2C #1104D. (V7253)

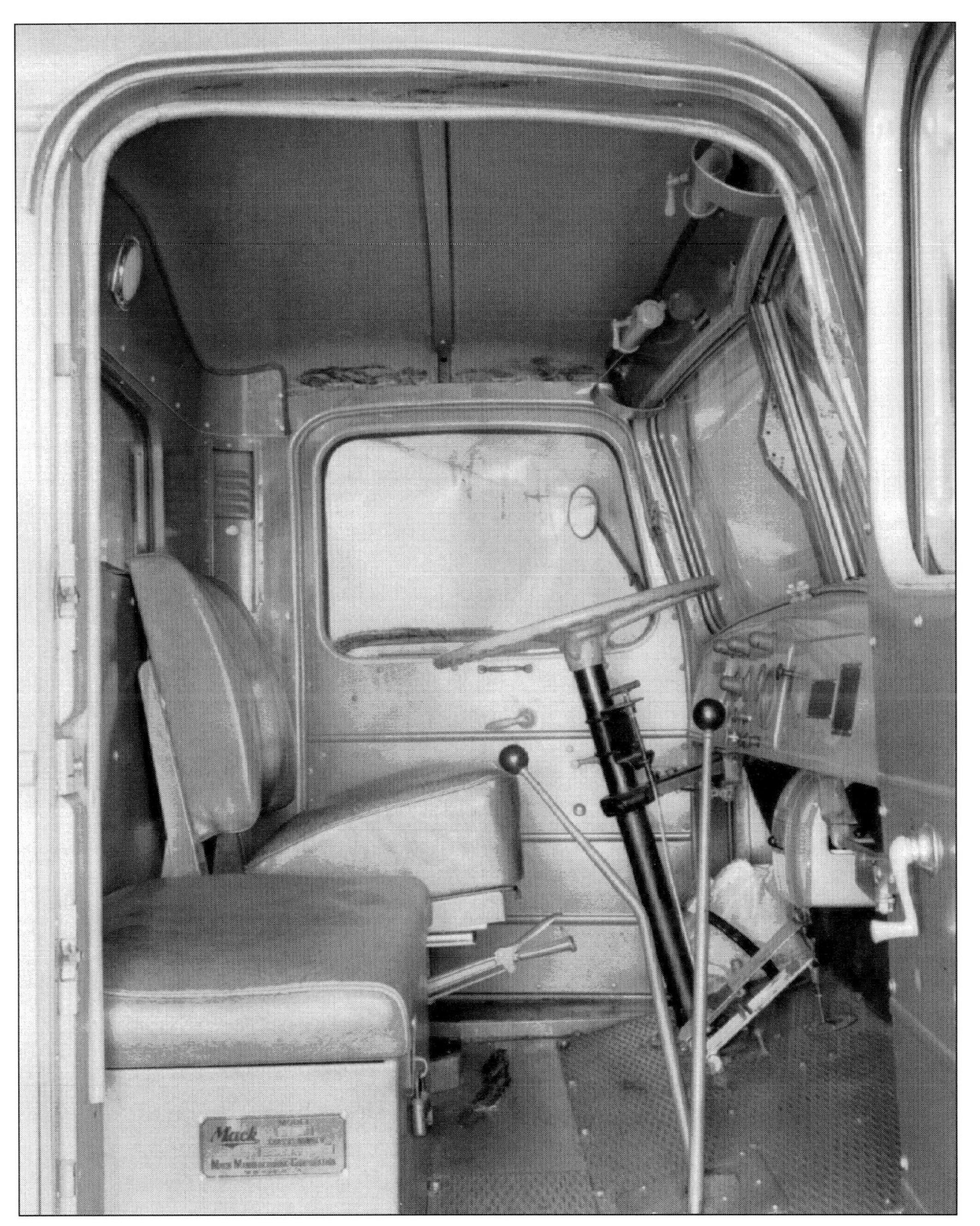

(V7285)

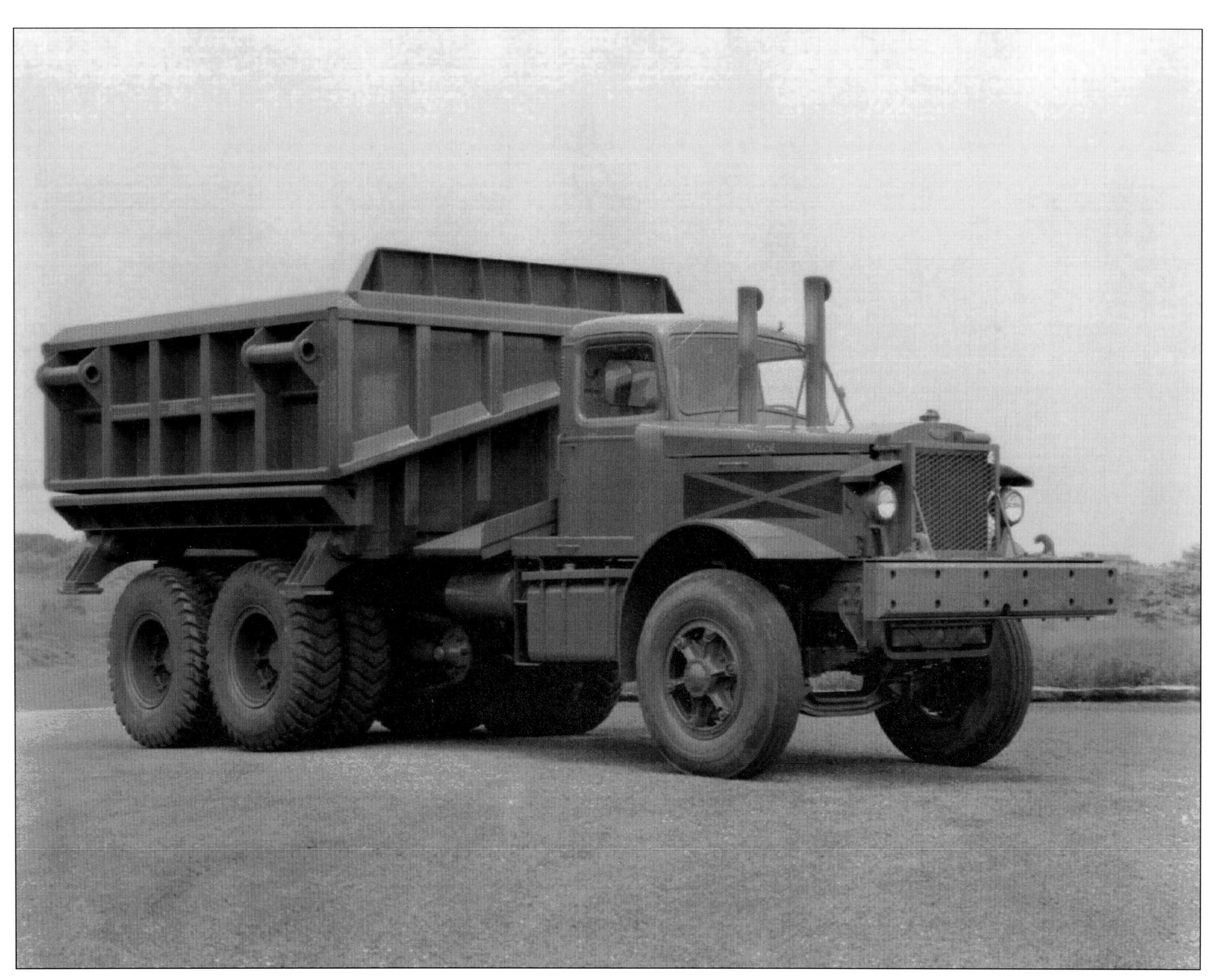

Two views of the Easton side gate, side-dump, external hoist body, as fitted to FC2C #1104D. (V6785)

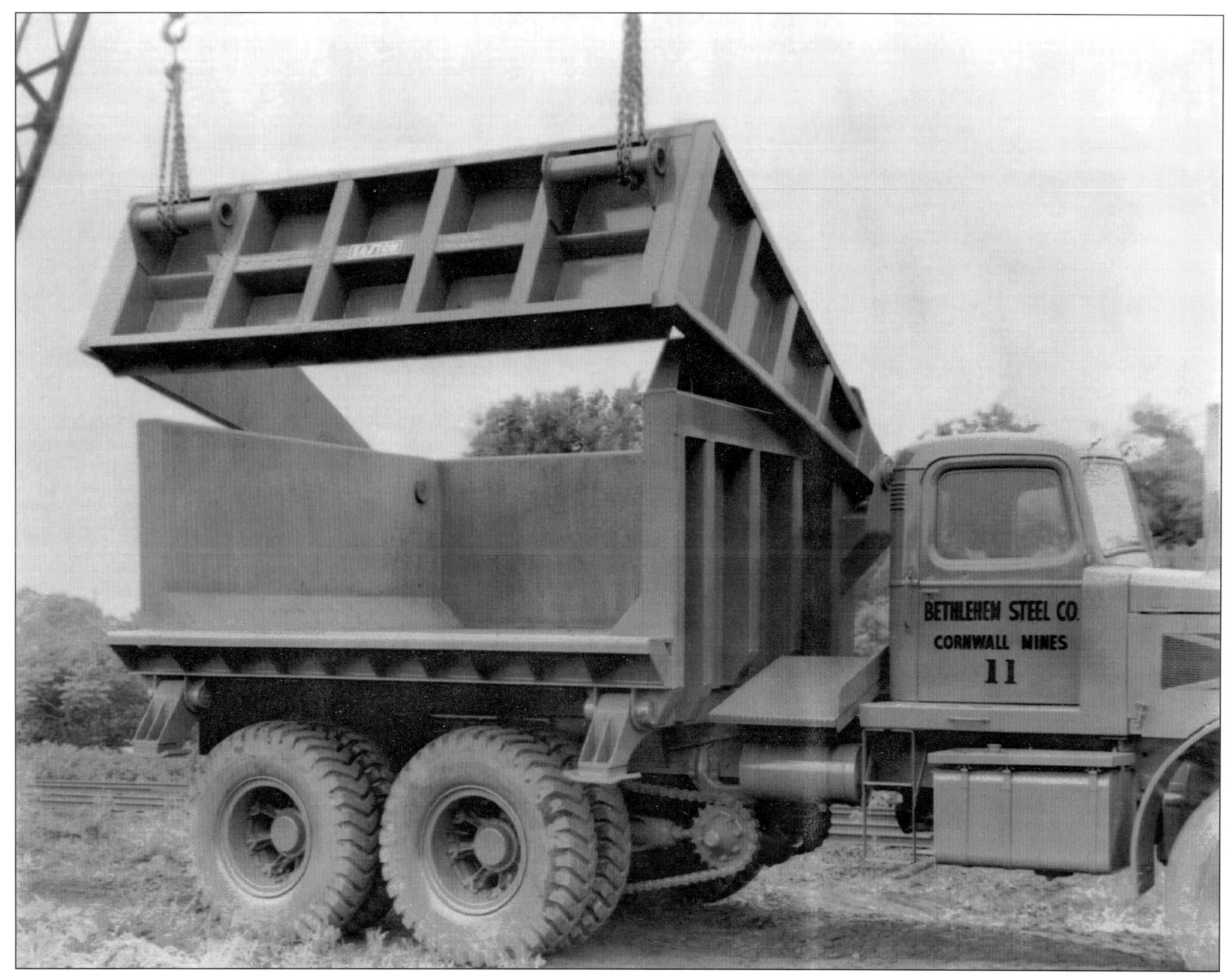

(V6809)

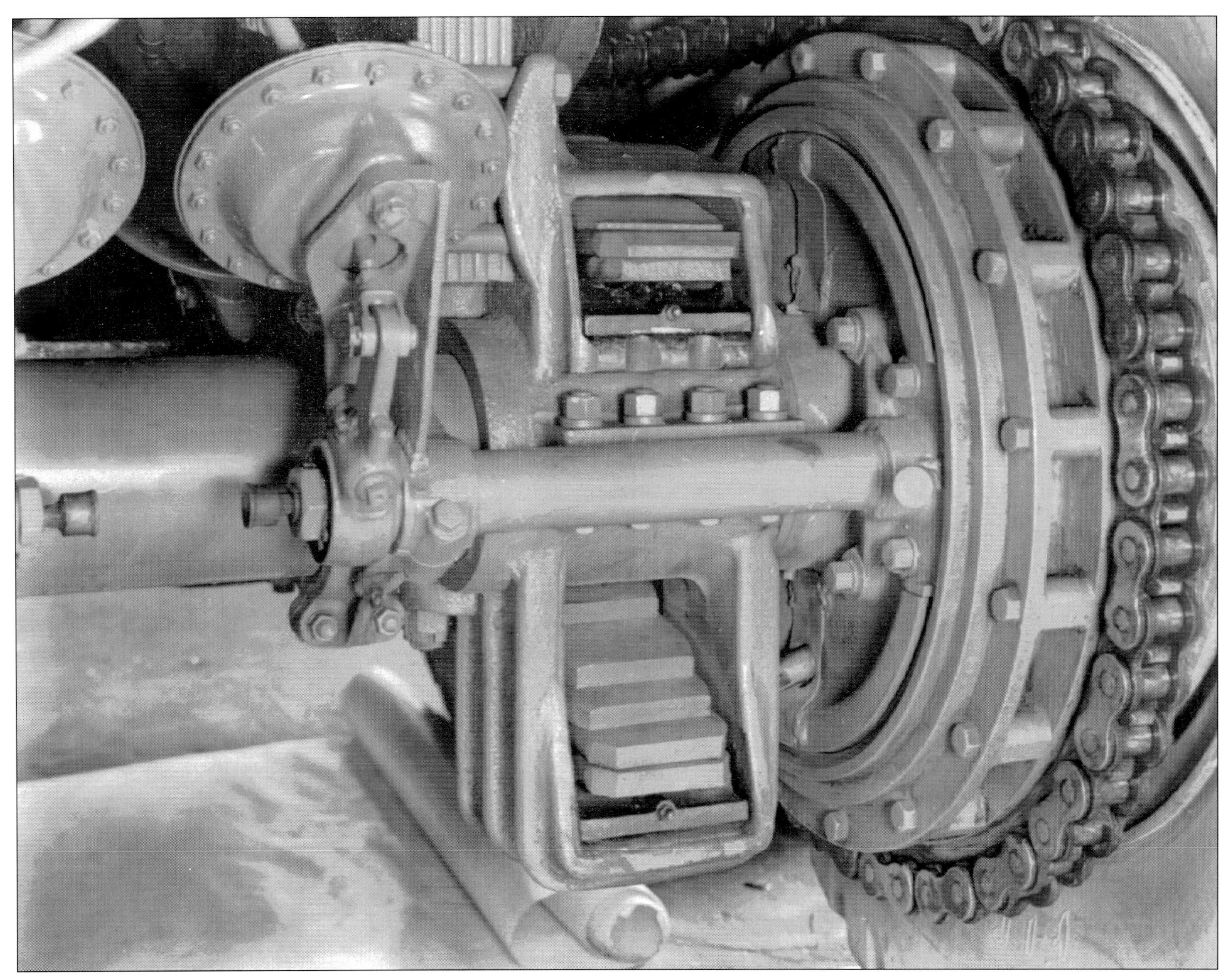

Views of the drive chain and axle fitted to FC2C #1104D. (V7284)

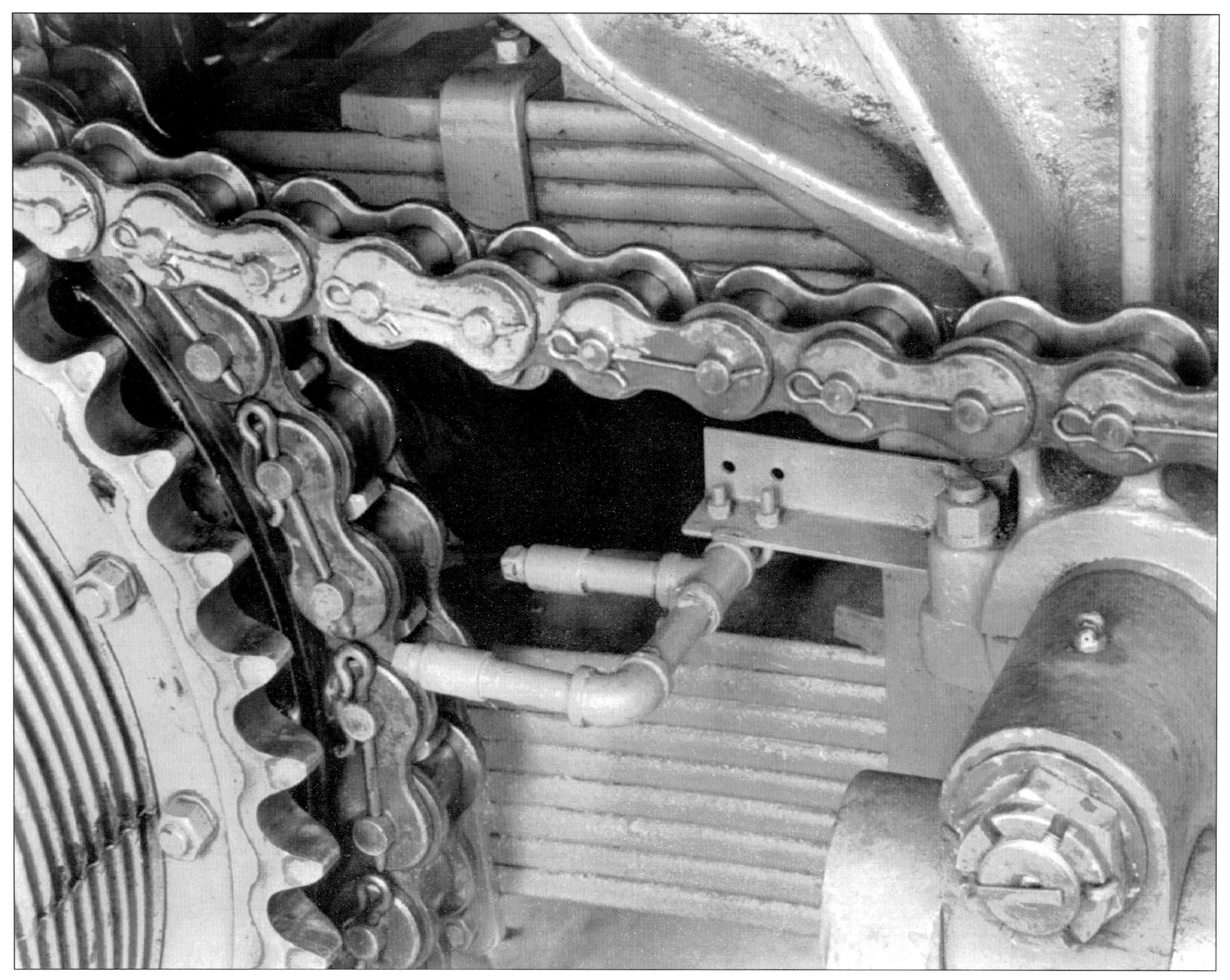

(V7245)

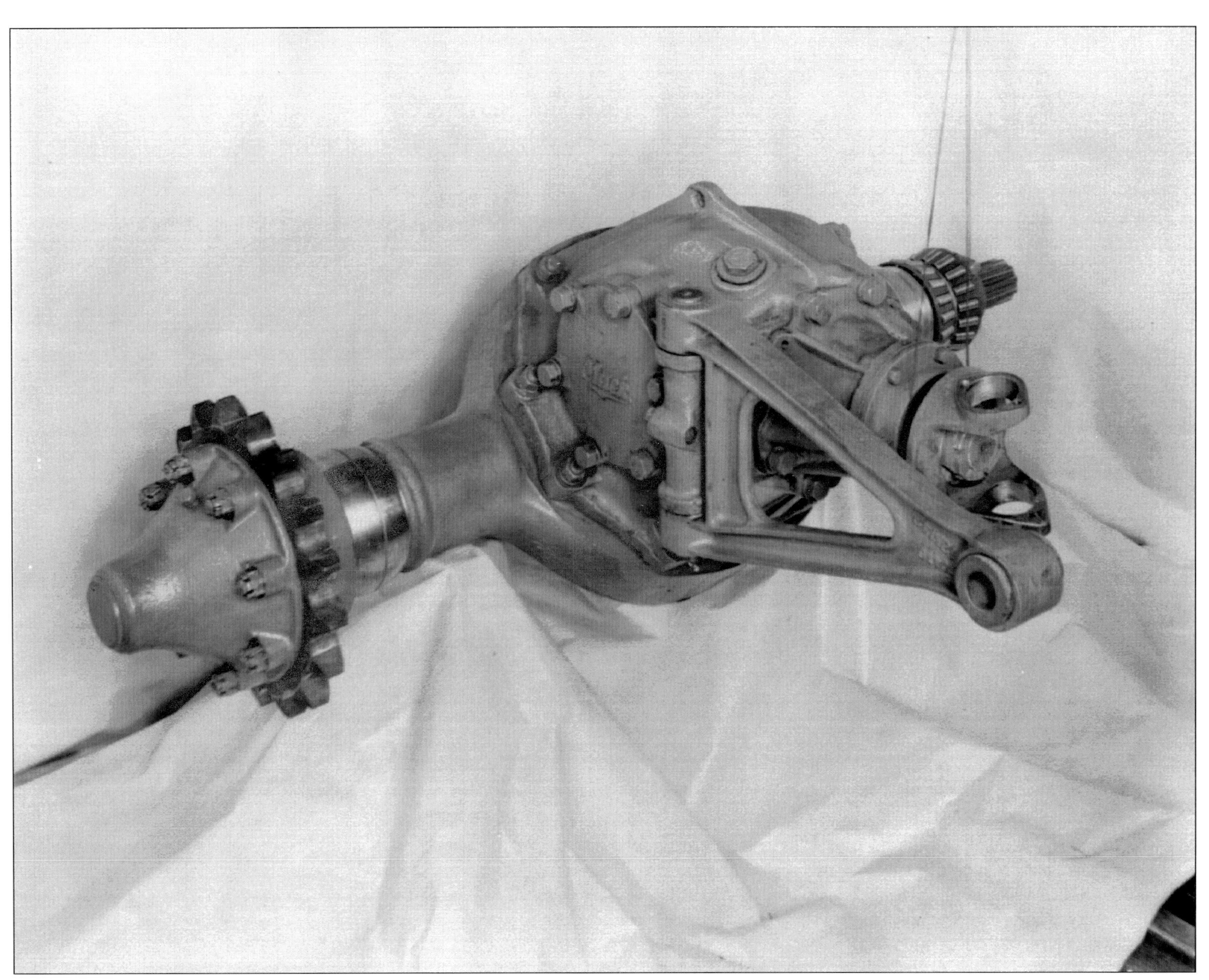

Jackshaft fitted to FC2C #1104D.

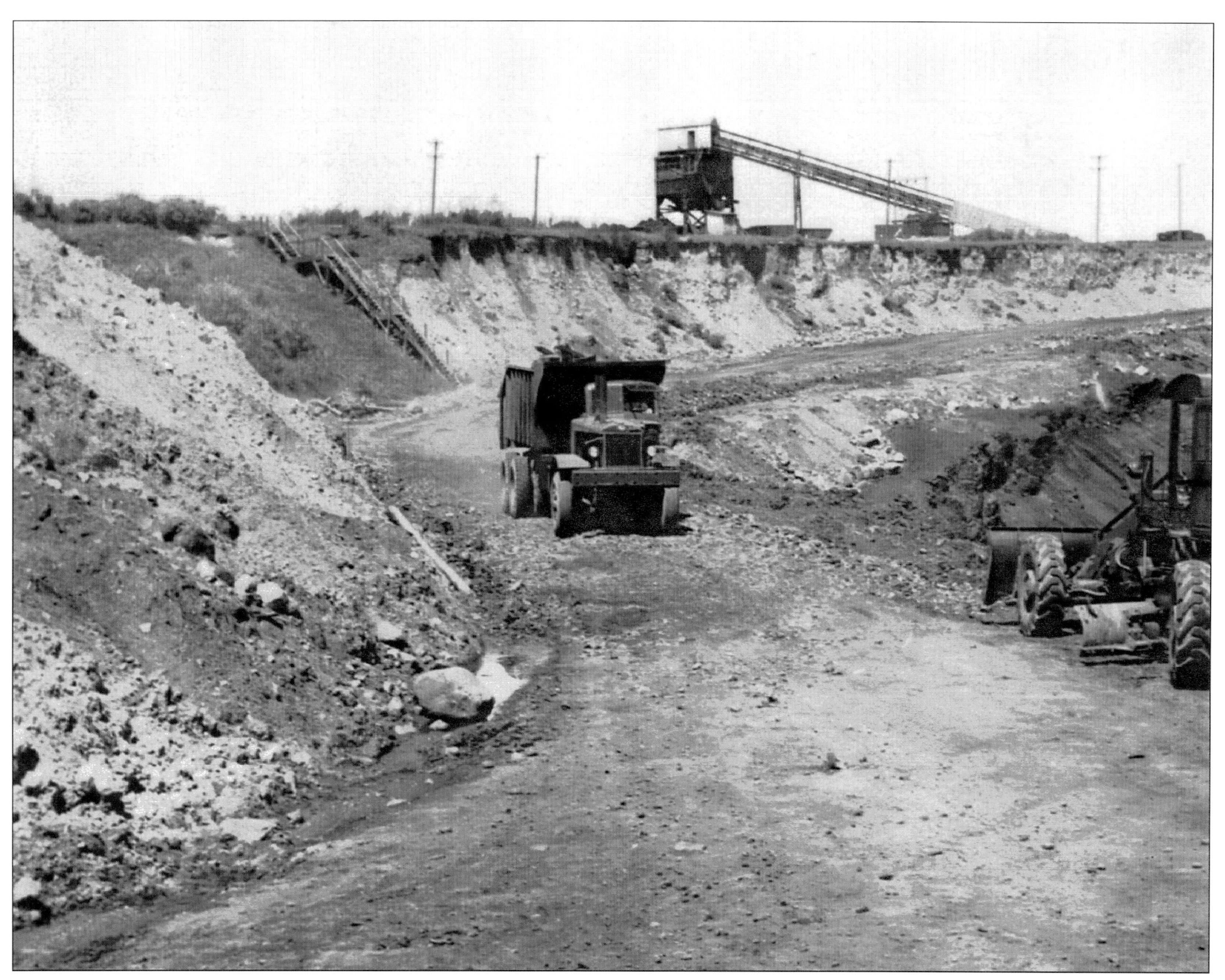

FCSW mining truck operated by Inter-State Iron Co., Virginia, Minnesota. July 1943. (M7355)

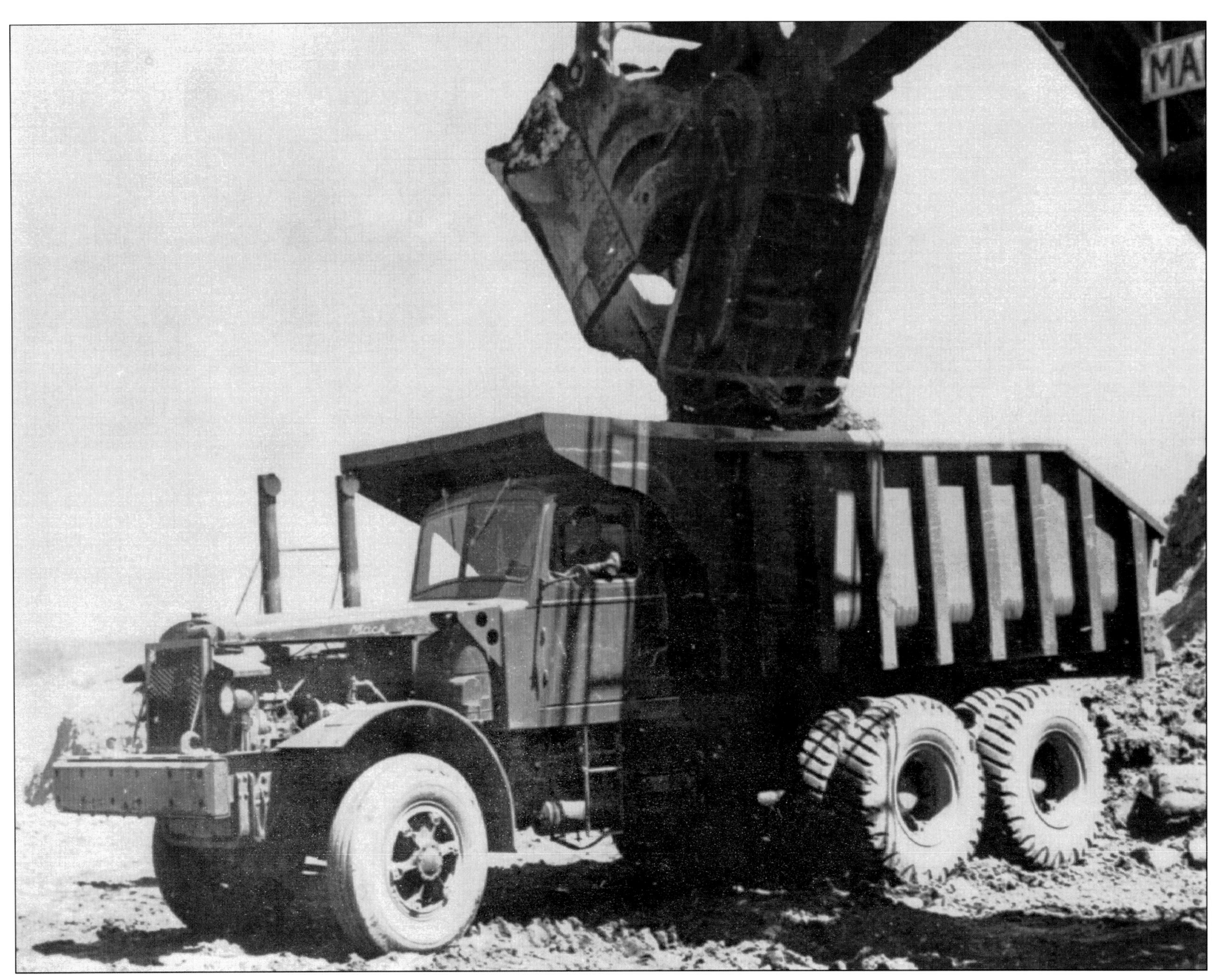

FCSW mining truck operated by Inter-State Iron Co., Virginia, Minnesota. July 1943. (M7349)

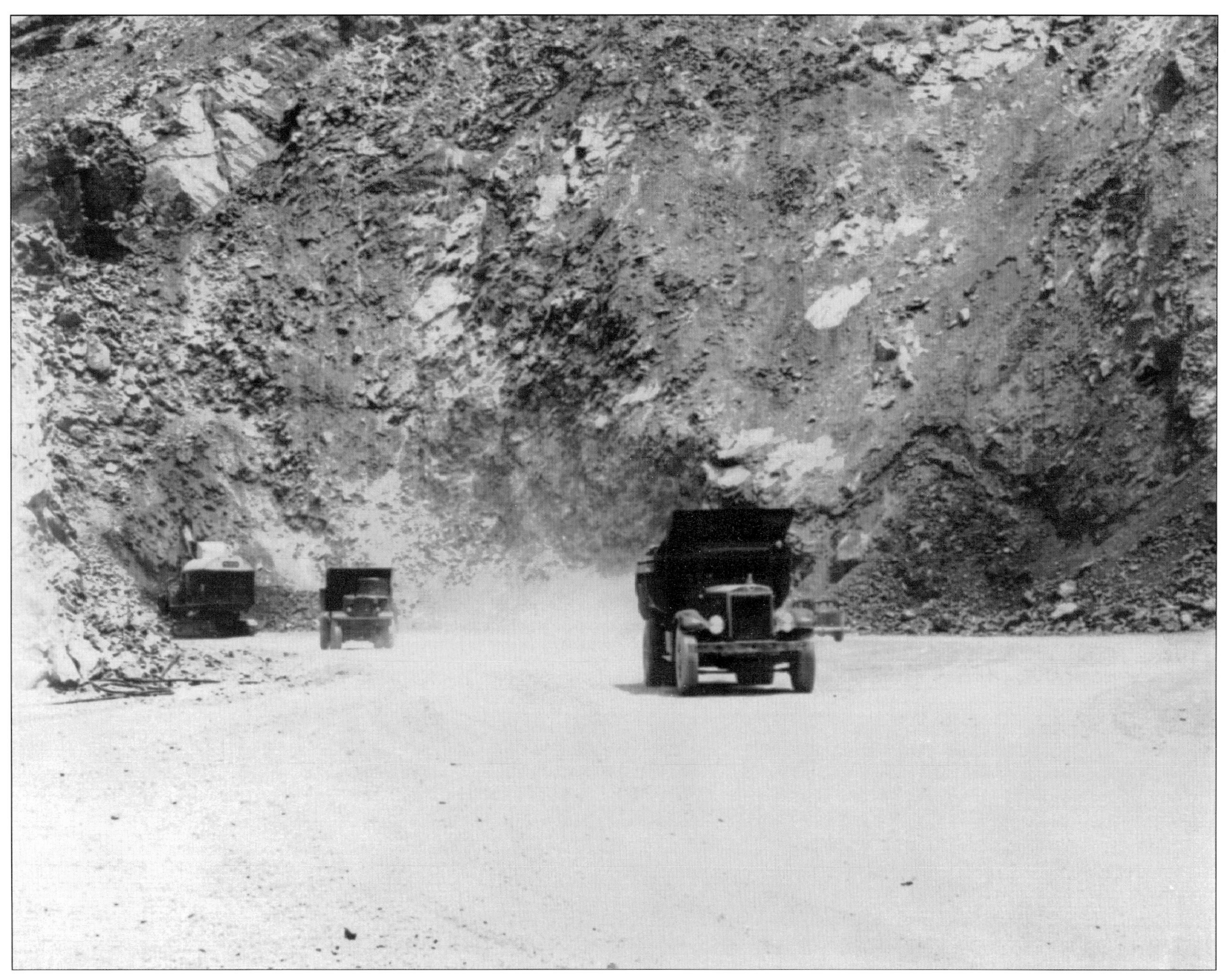

FCSW mining trucks operated by Colorado Fuel and Iron Co., Monarch, Colorado. July 1943. (M7360)

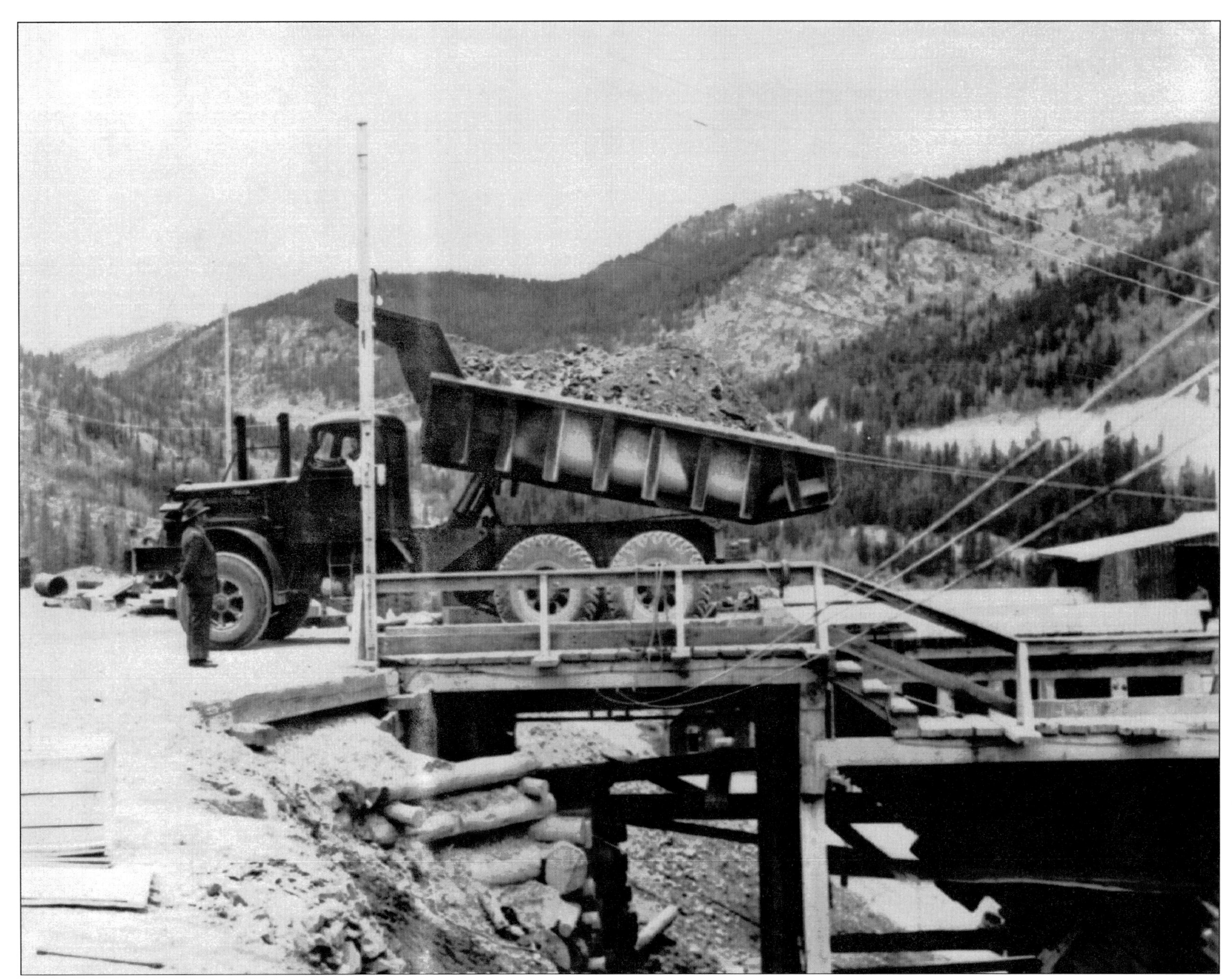

FCSW mining truck operated by Colorado Fuel and Iron Co., Monarch, Colorado. July 1943. (M7363)

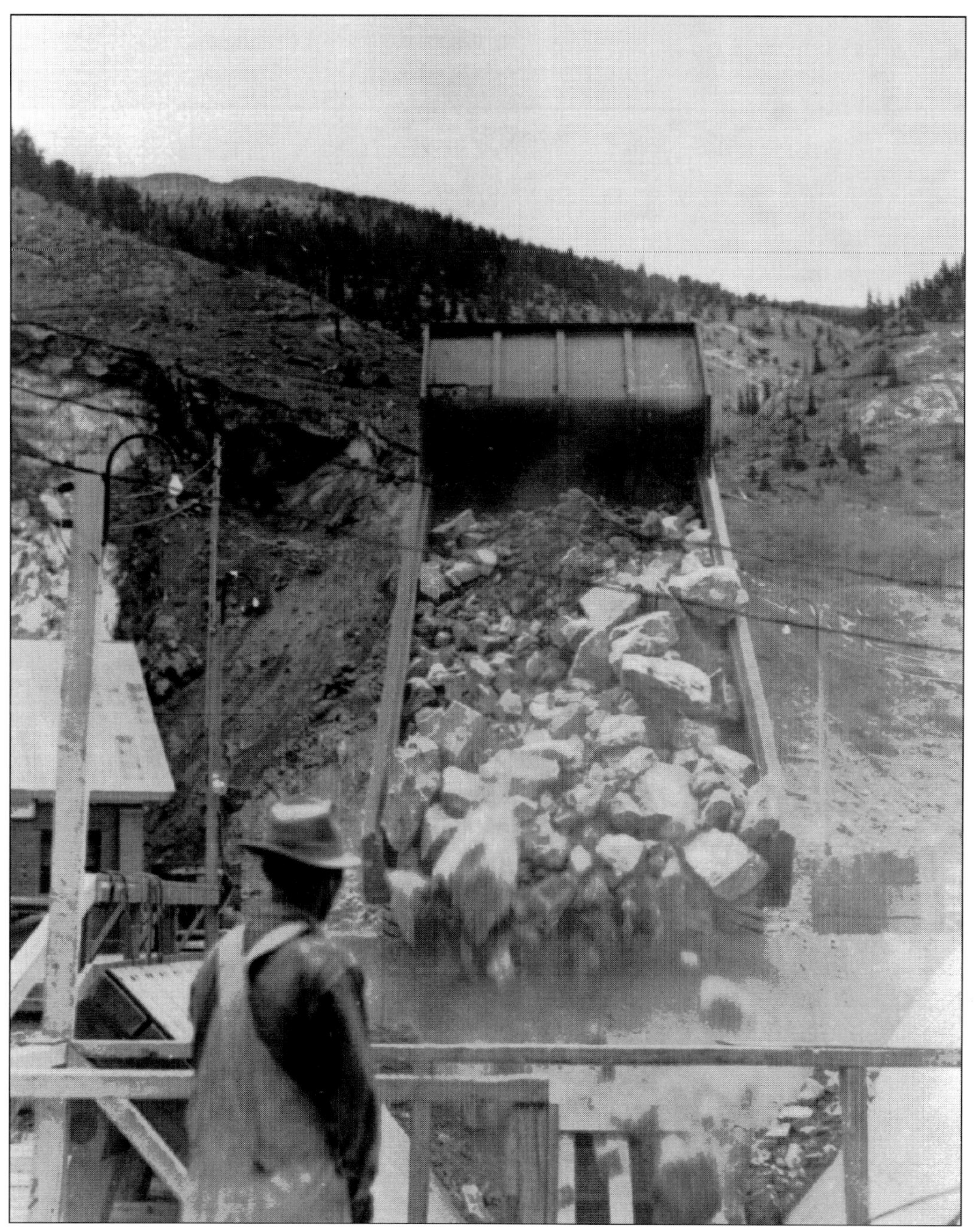

(M7366)

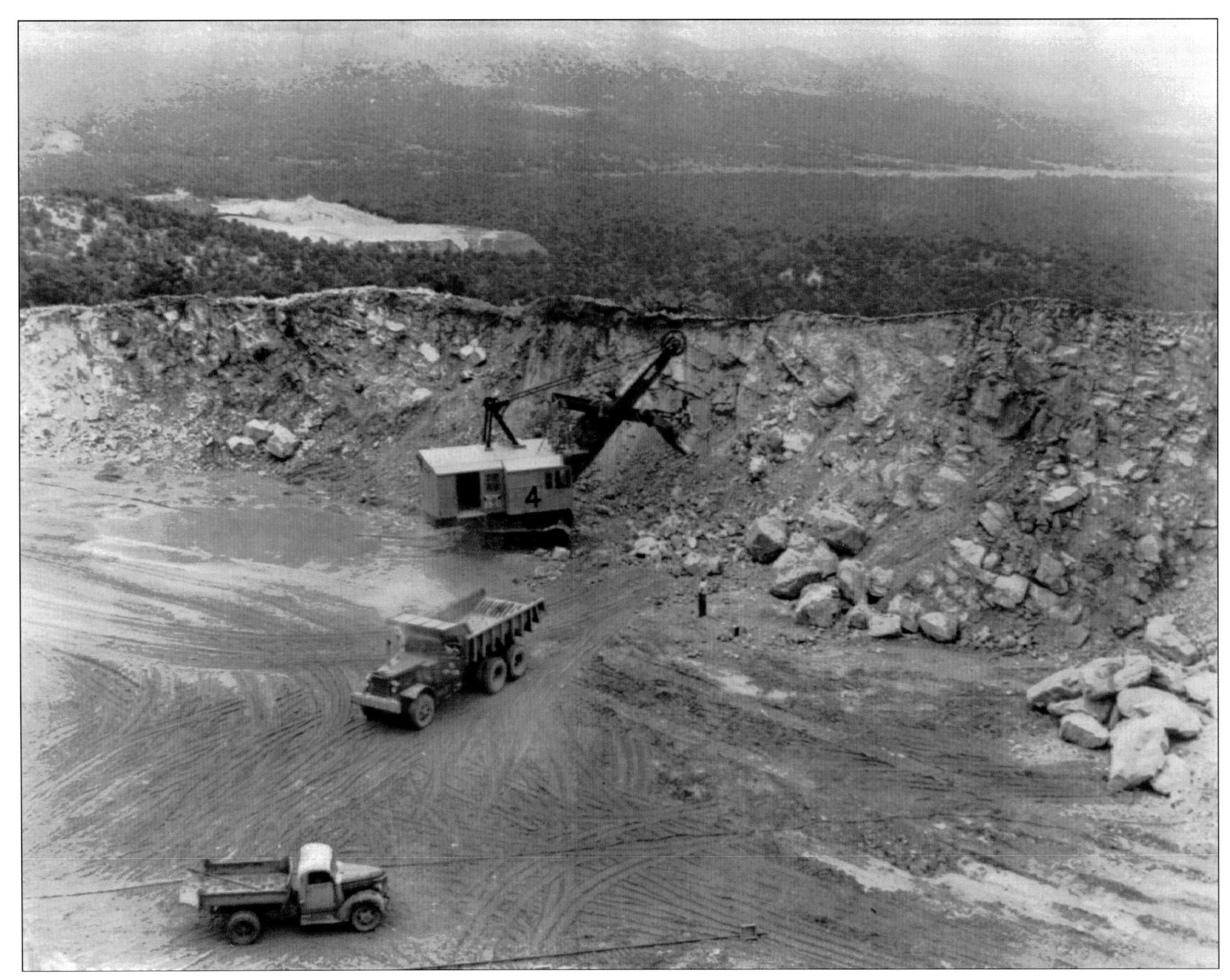

FCSW mining truck operated by Columbia Iron Mining Co., Cedar City, Utah. October 1943. (M7476)

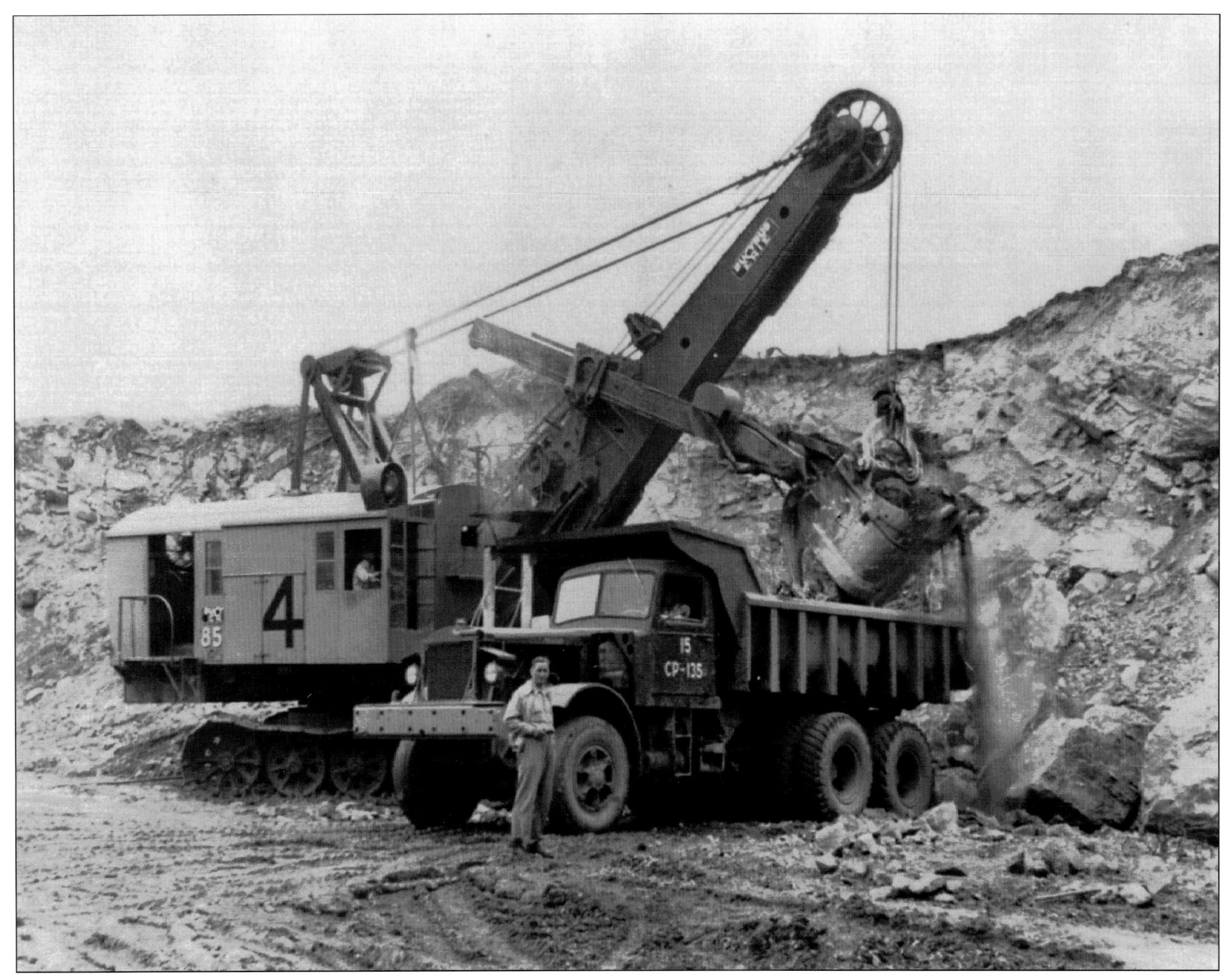

(M7477)

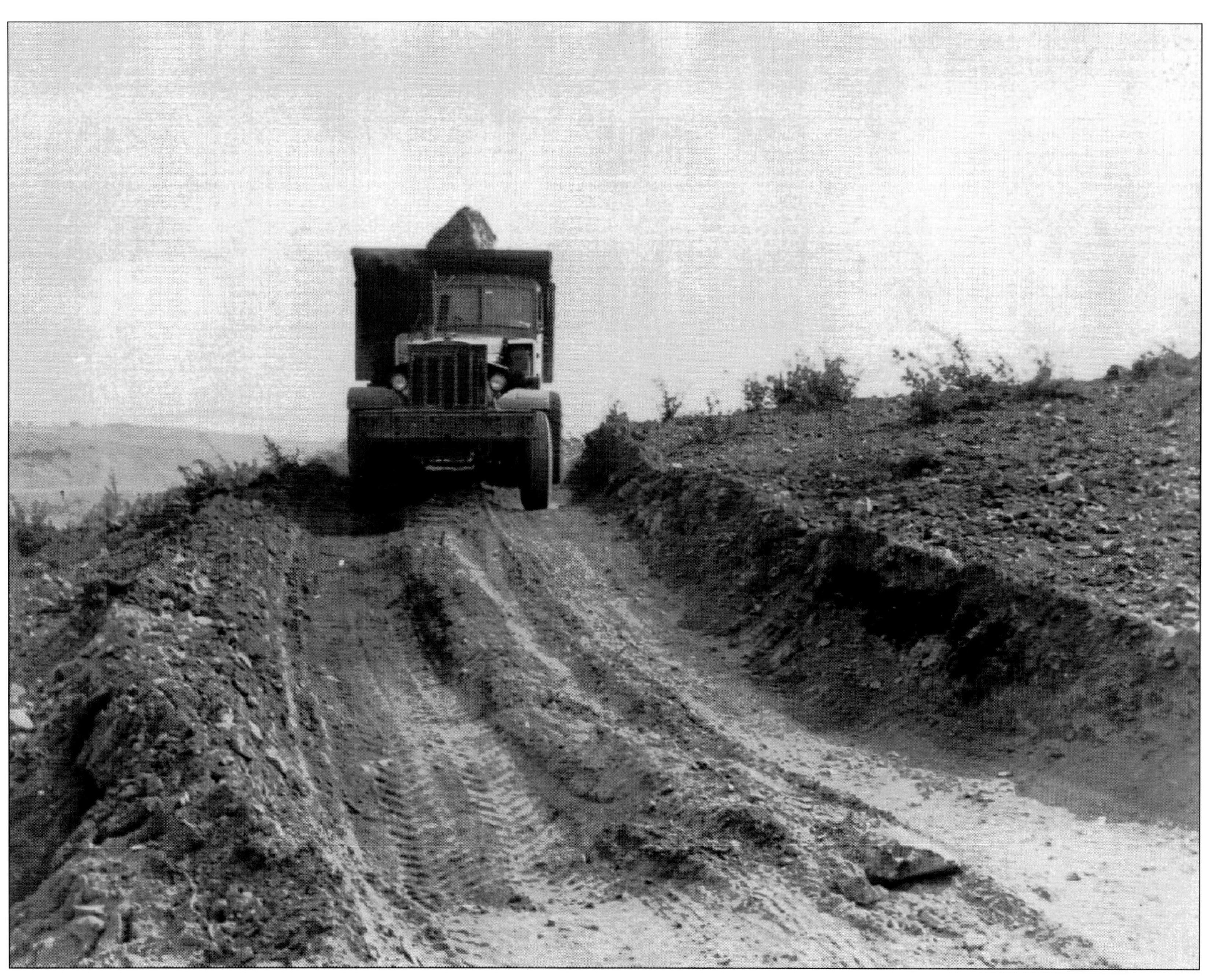

FCSW mining truck operated by Greene Cananea Copper Co., Cananea, Mexico. October 1943. (M7490)

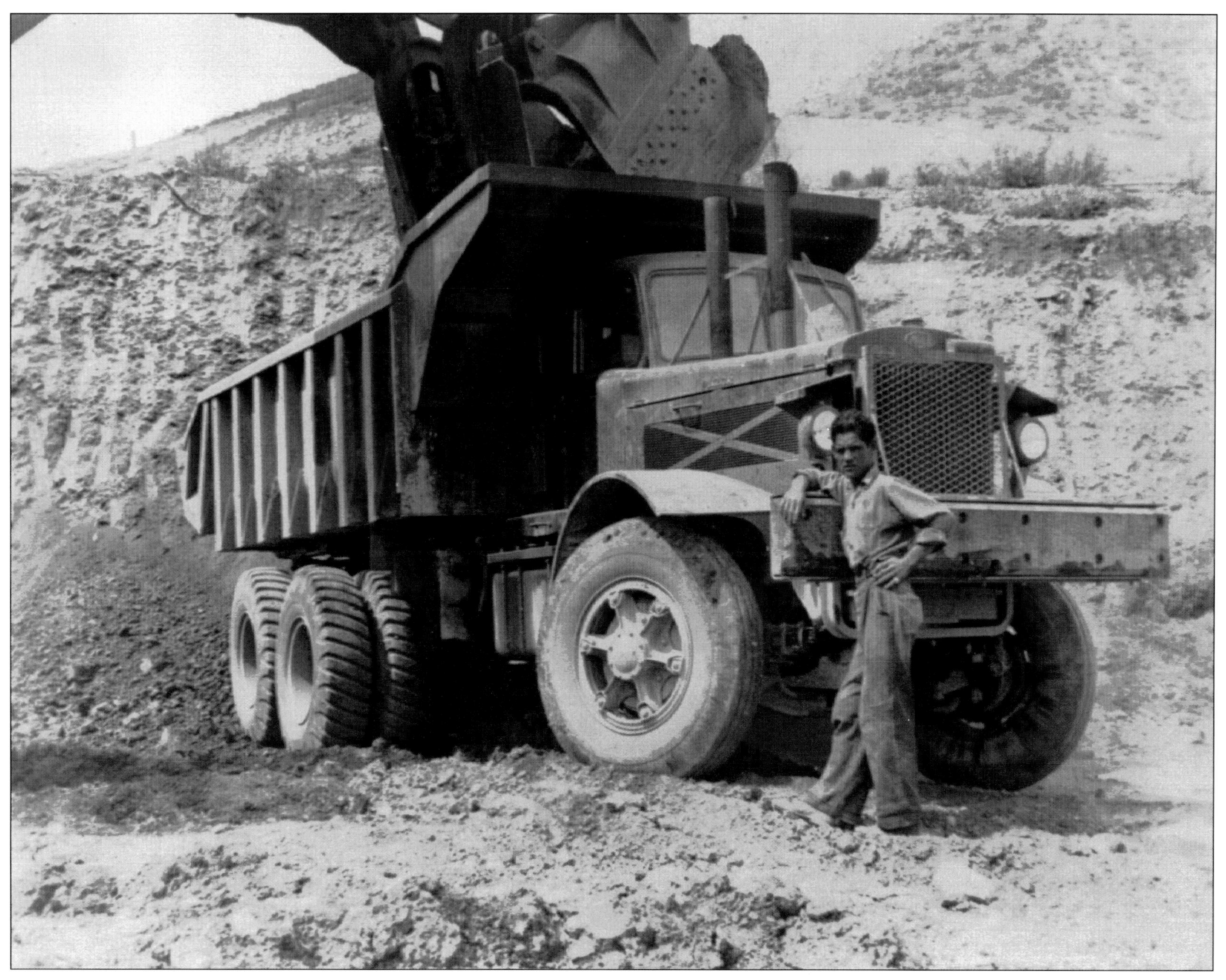

(M7489)

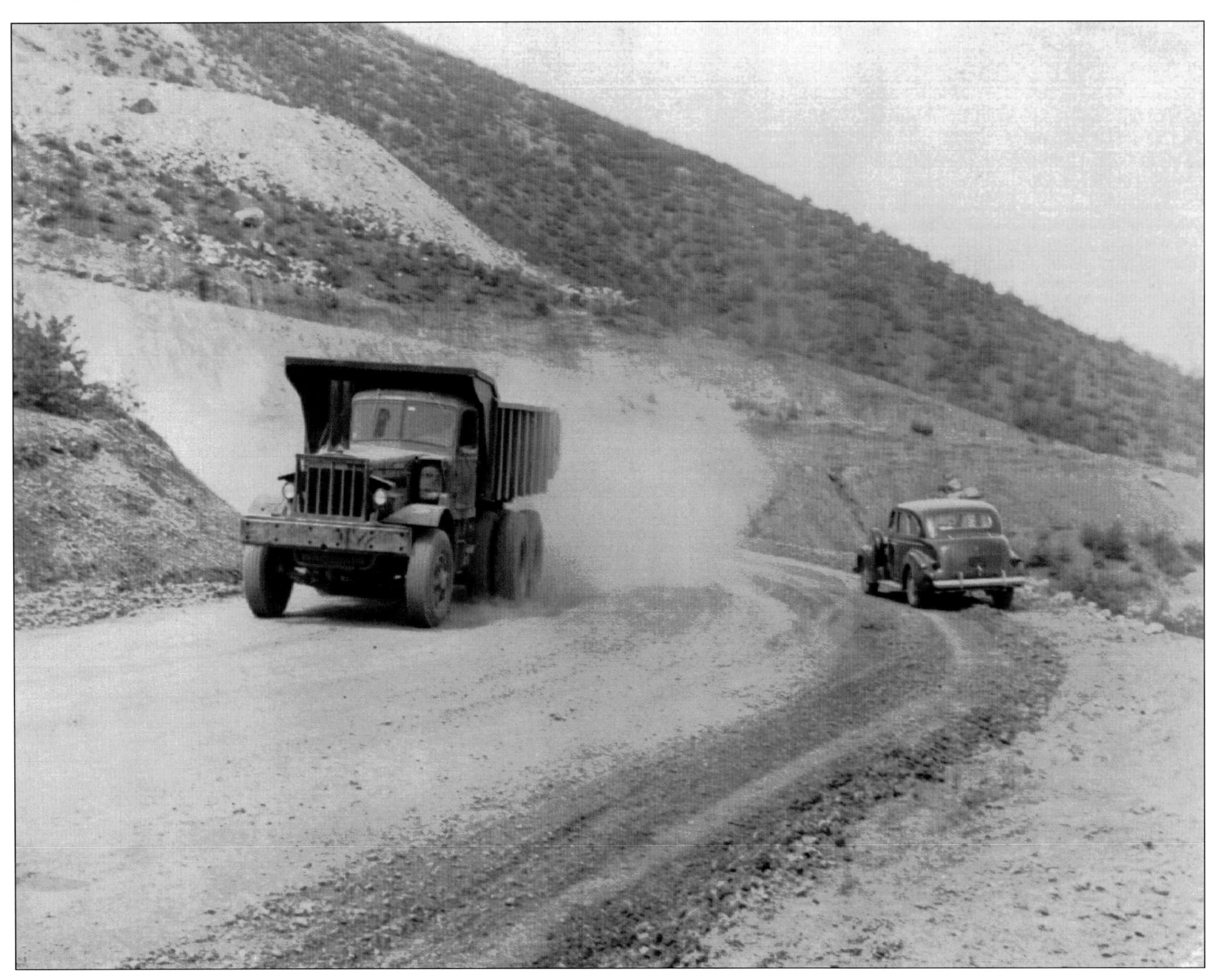

FCSW mining truck operated by Greene Cananea Copper Co., Cananea, Mexico. October 1943. (M7485)

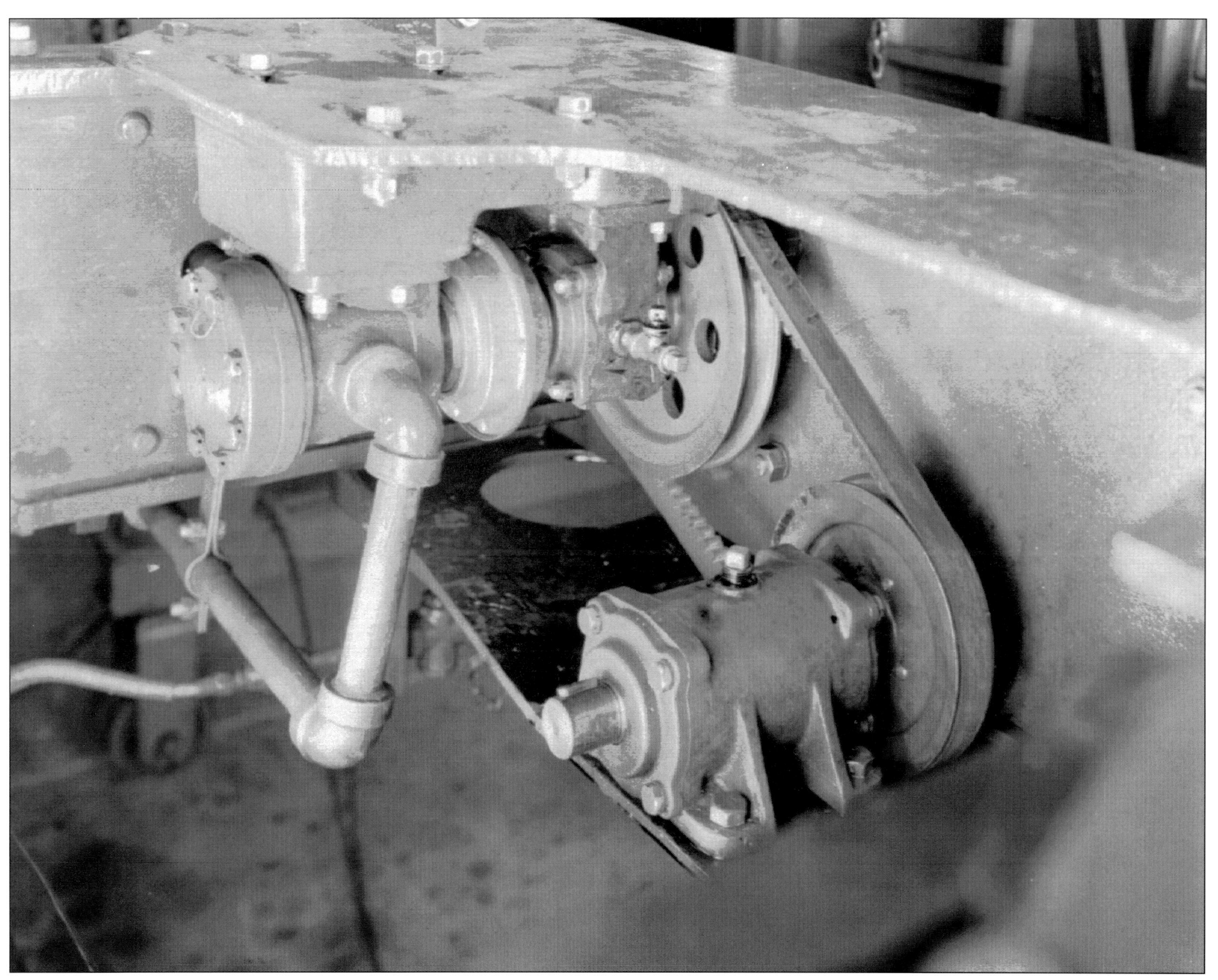

Hydraulic pump drive fitted to FCSW chassis built under General Works Order #24. June 1944. (V7597)

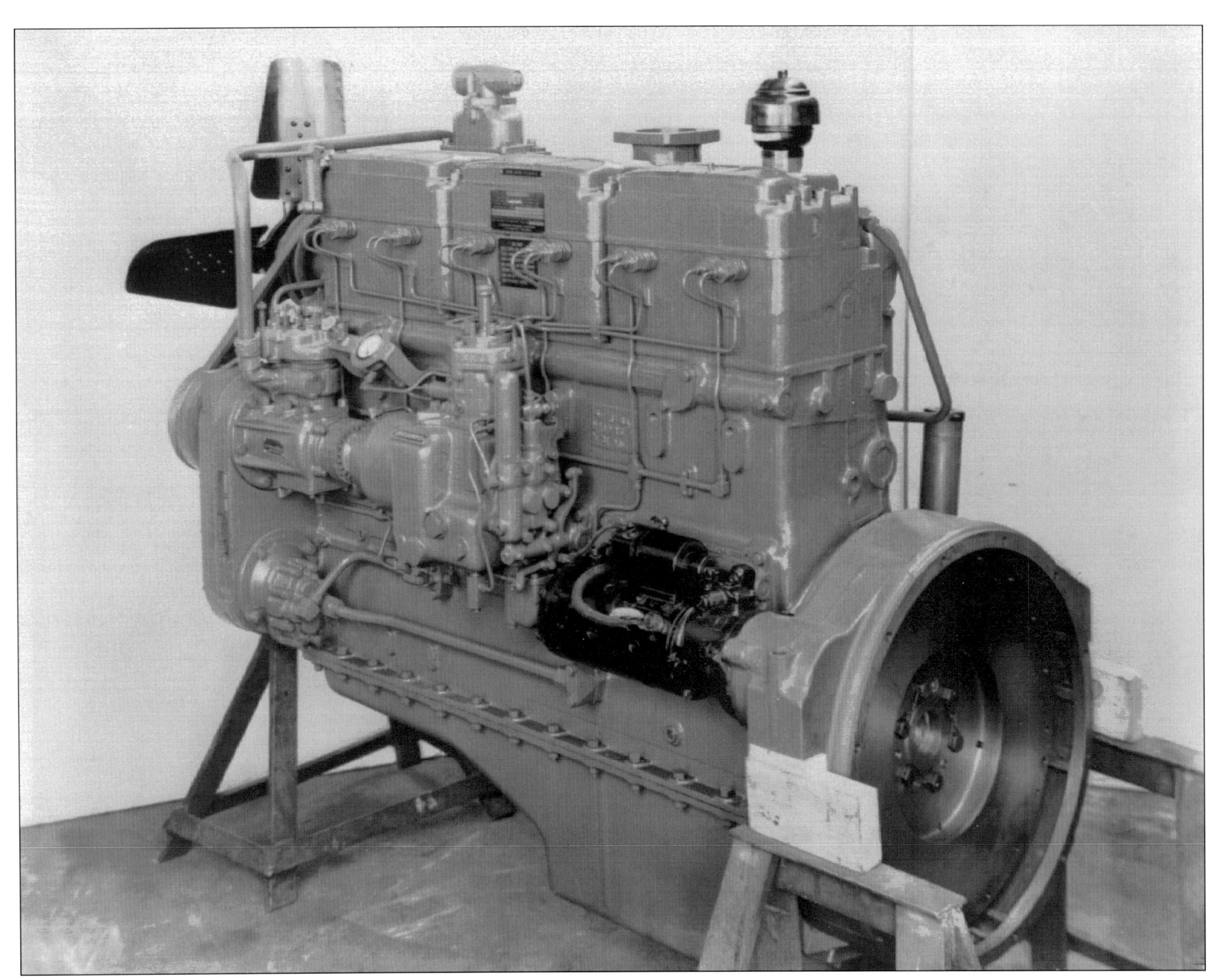

Cummins diesel engine fitted to FCSW chassis built under General Works Order #24. (7590)

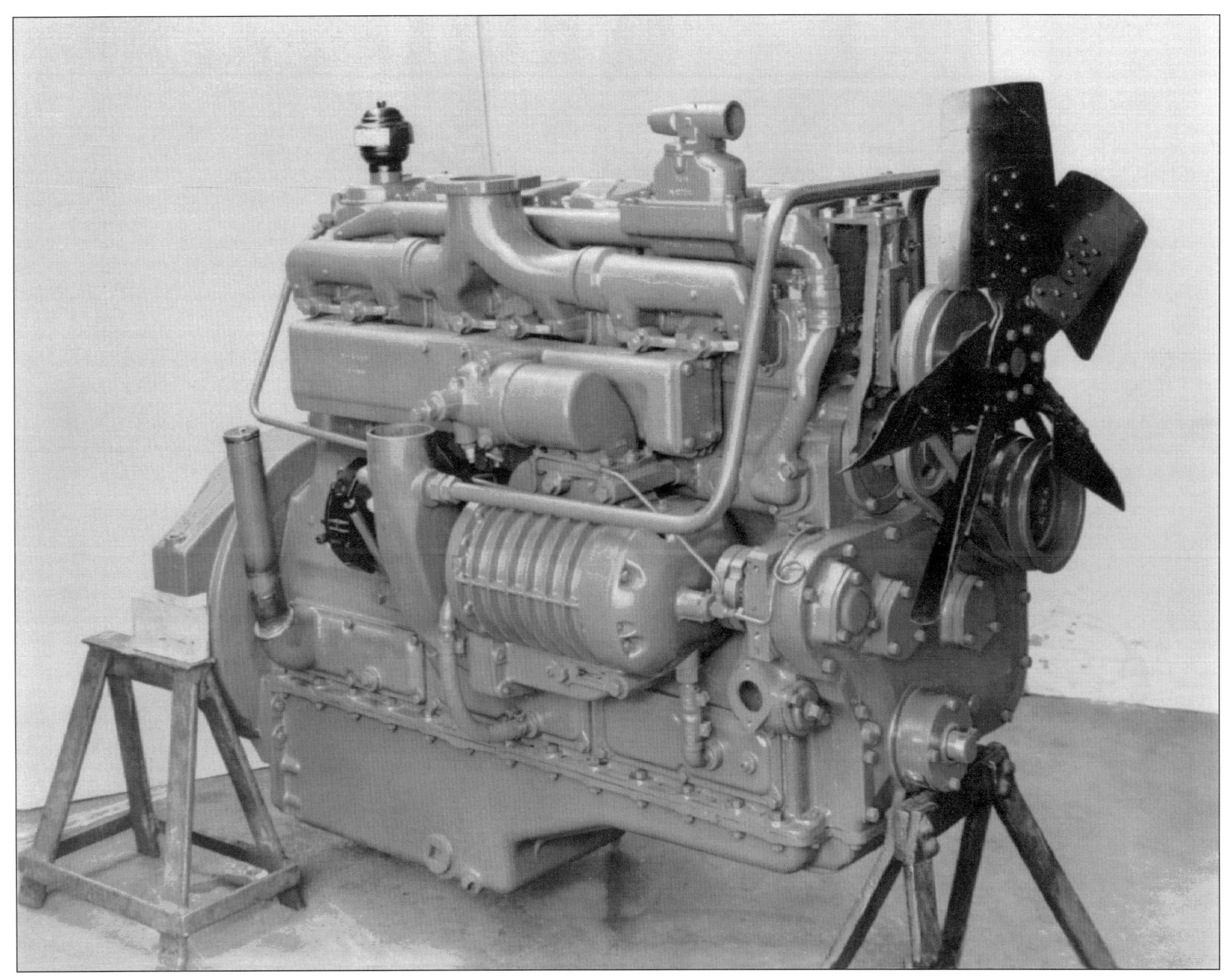

(V7589)

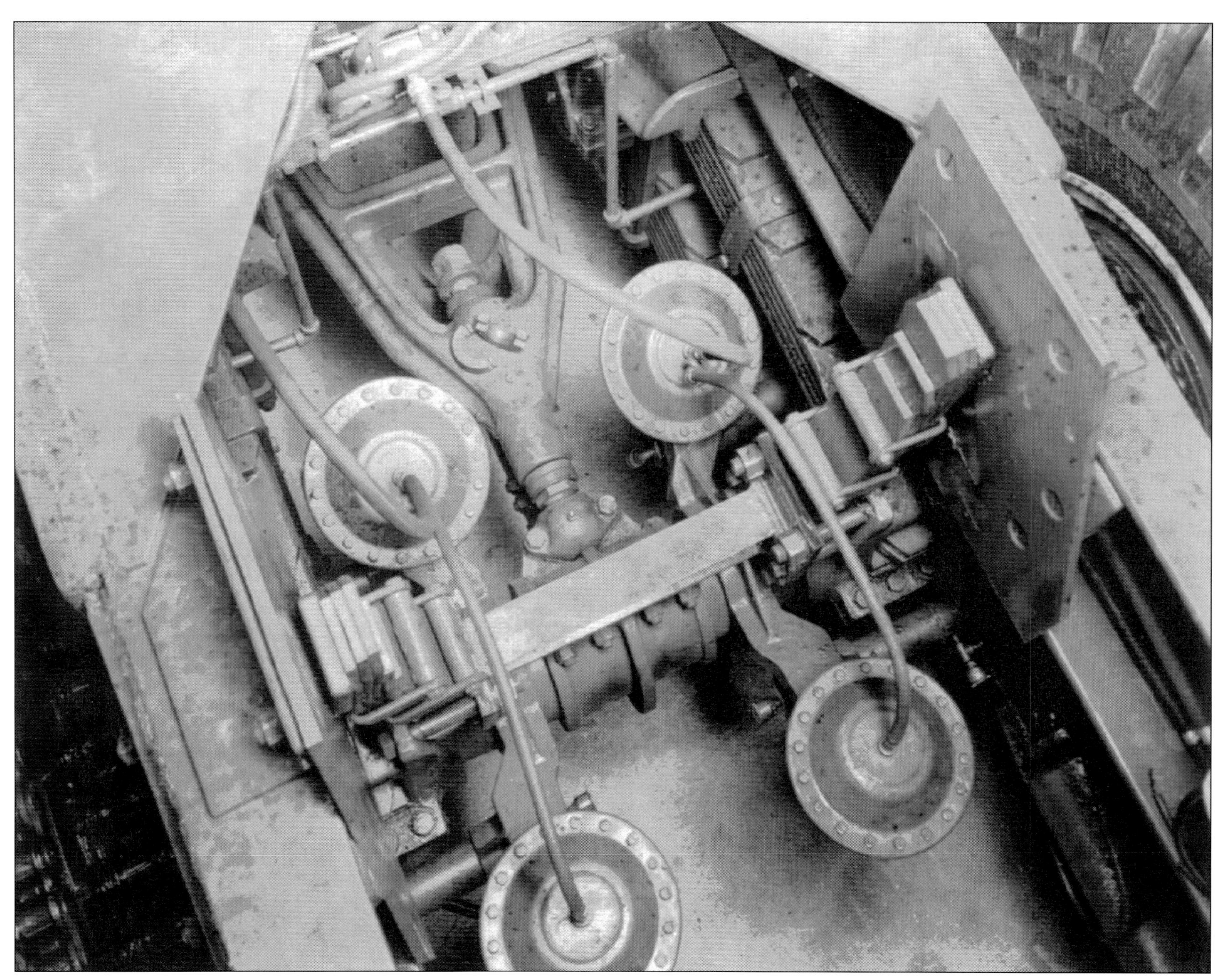

Bogie mounted to the chassis of FCSW built under General Works Order #24. (V7599)

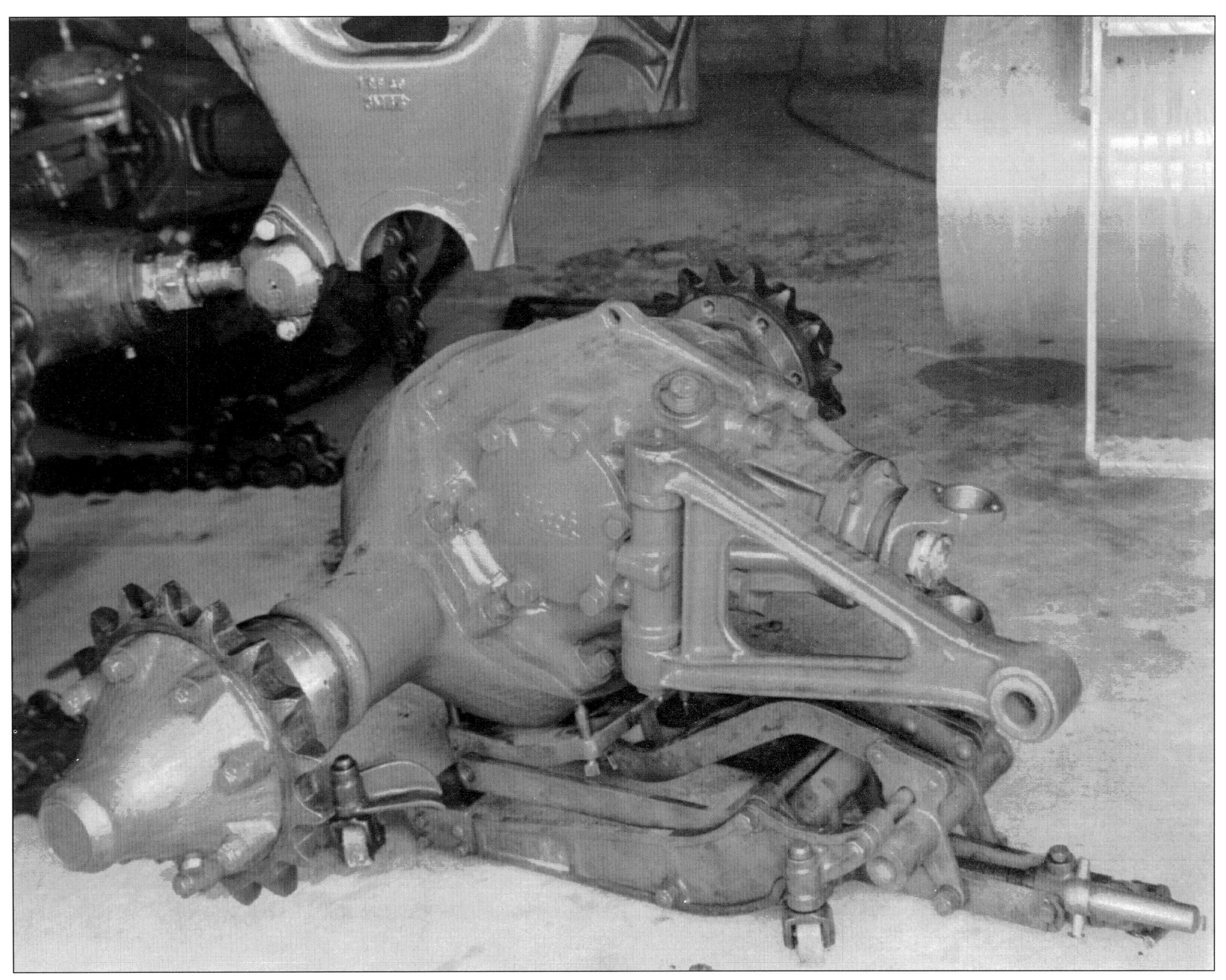

Jackshaft fitted to the chassis of FCSW built under General Works Order #24. (V7599)

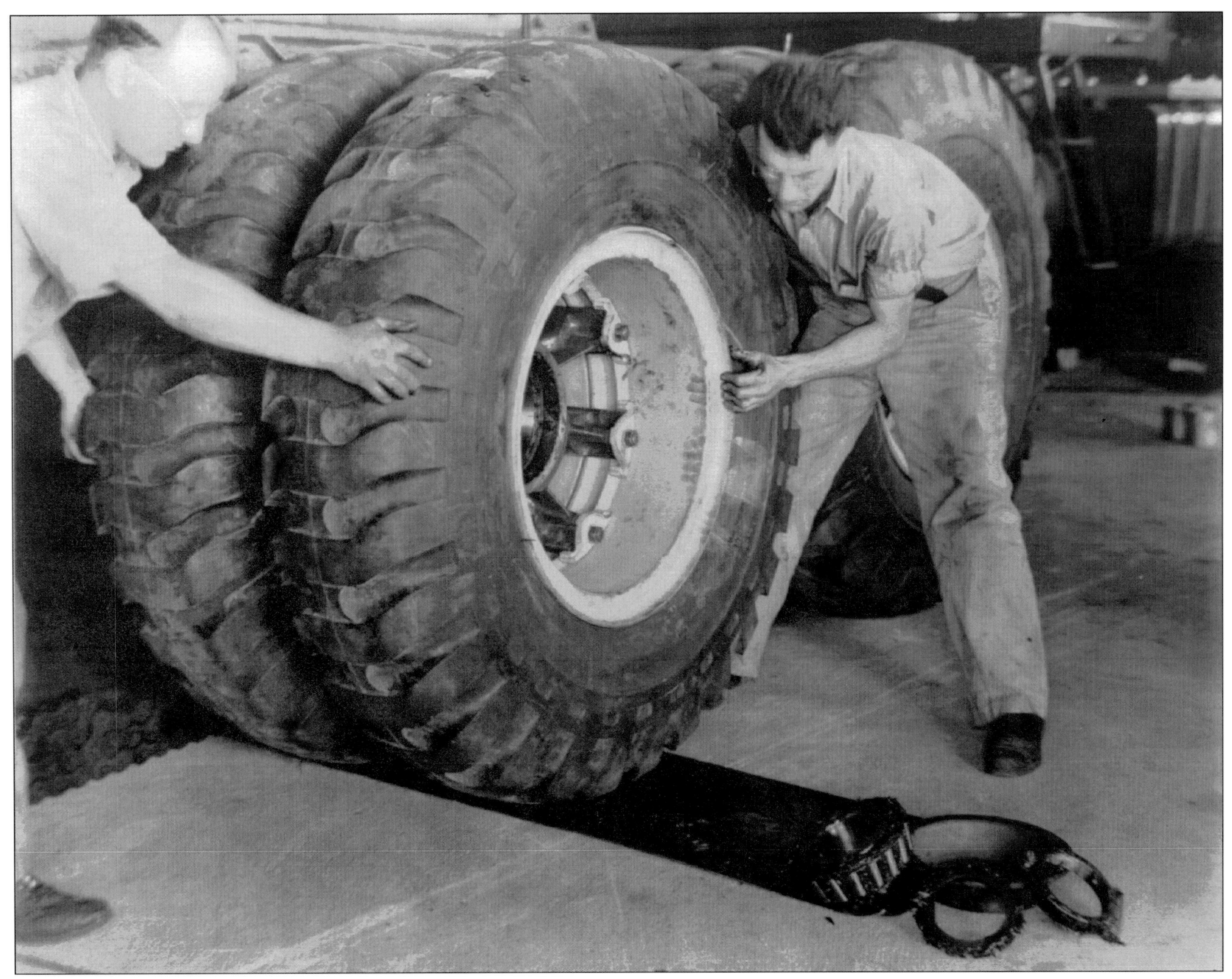

(V7616)

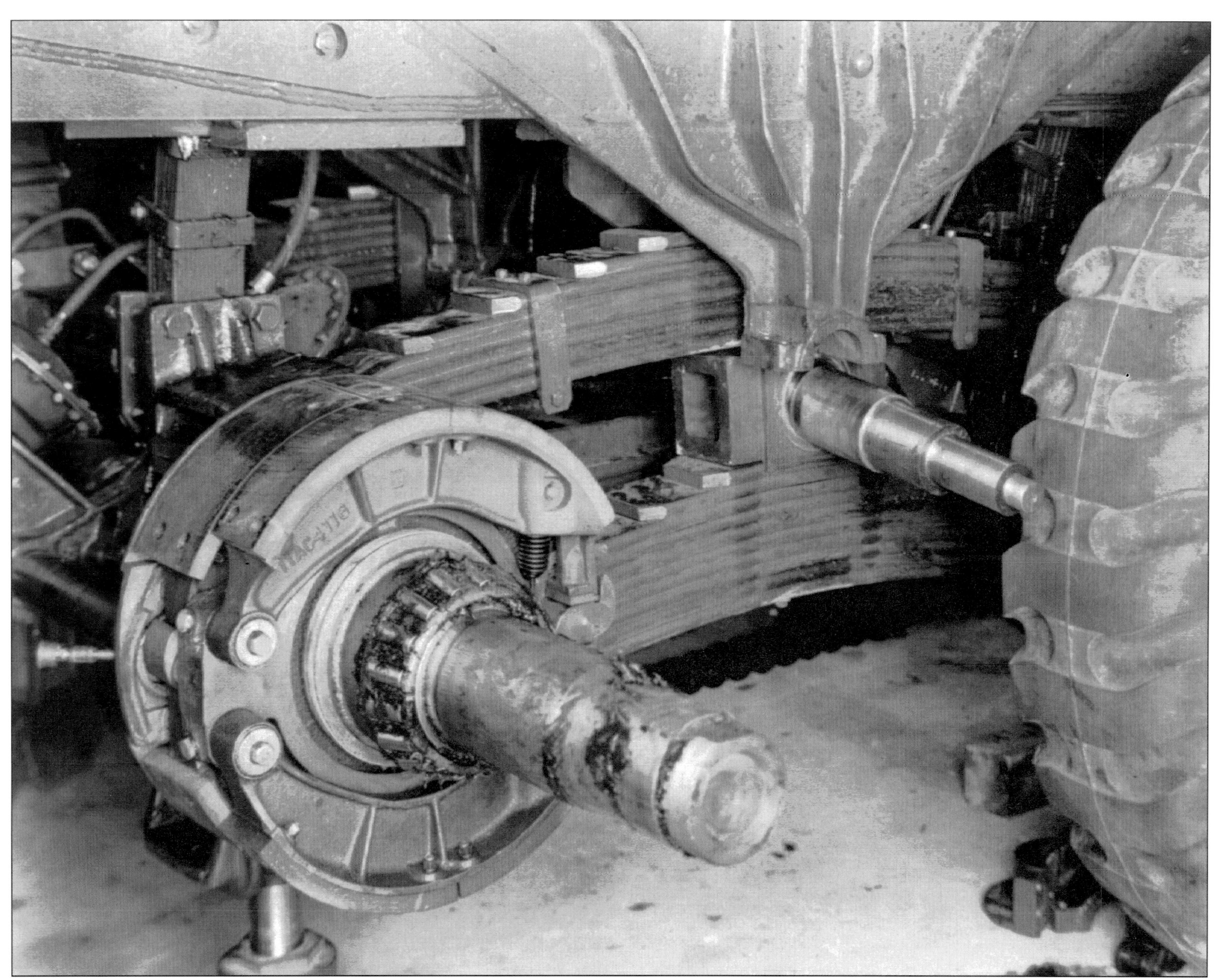

Axle detail on the FCSW chassis built under General Works Order #24. (V7618)

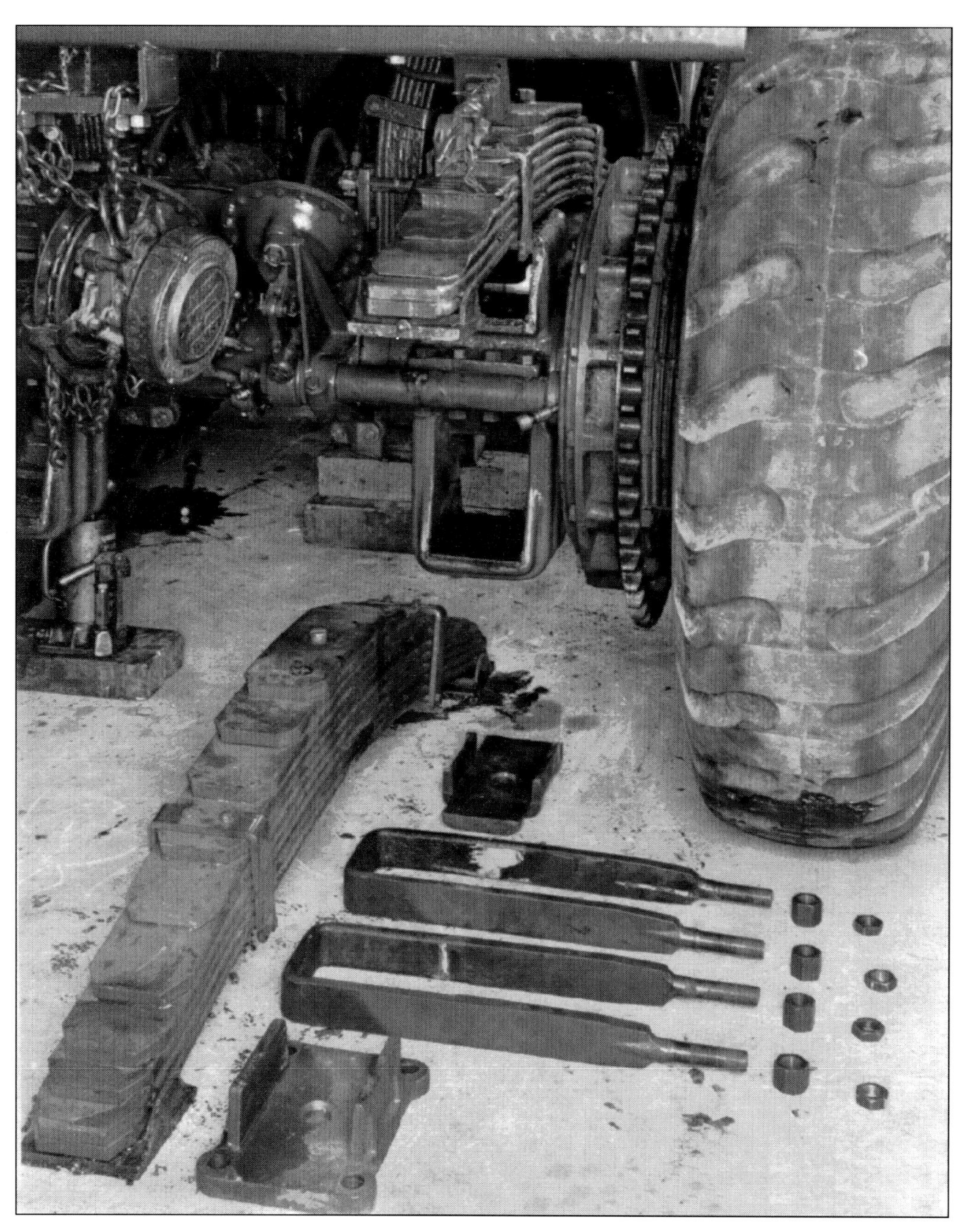

Bogie and spring on the FCSW chassis built under General Works Order #24. (V7619)

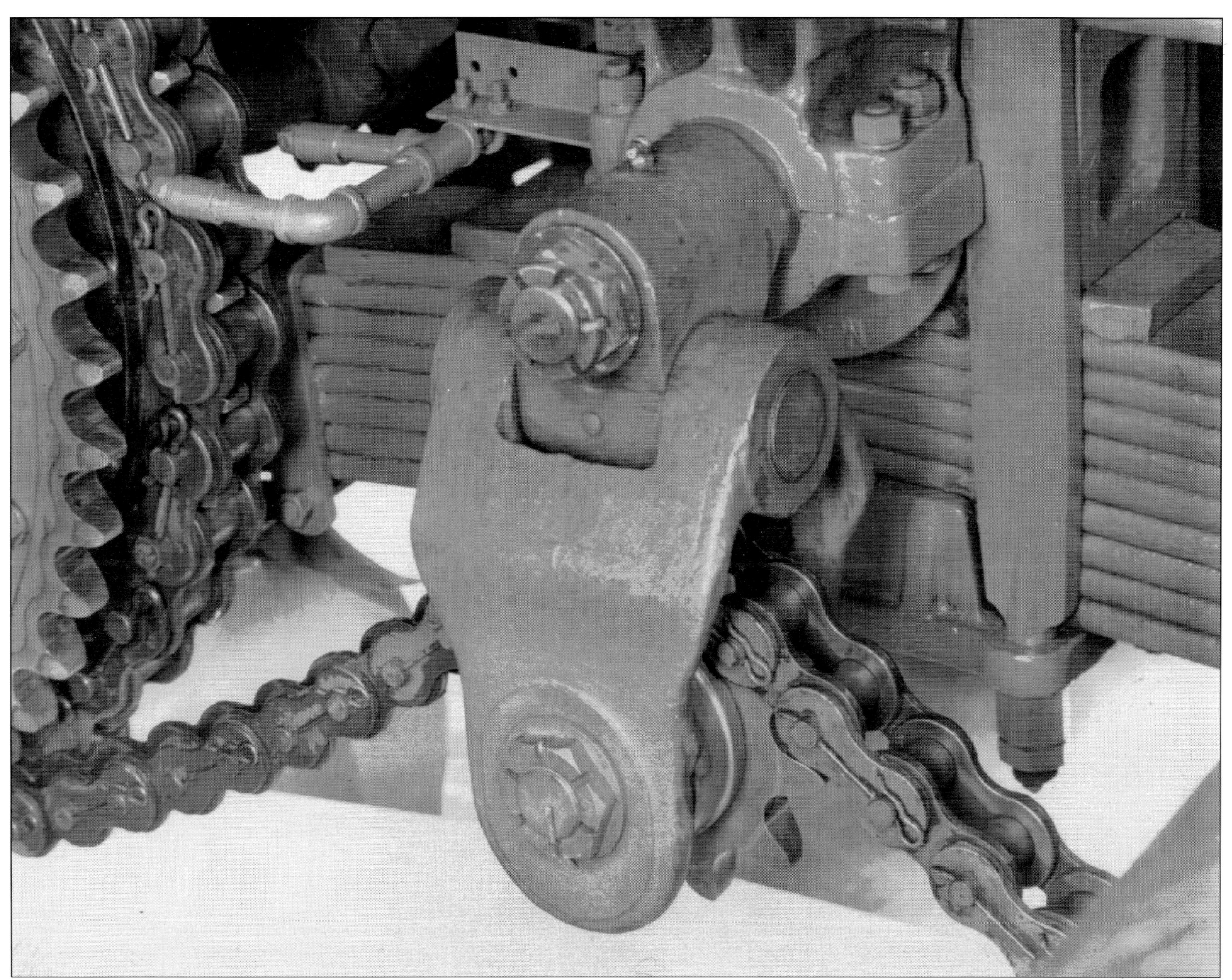

Drive chain guide and idler sprocket on the FCSW.

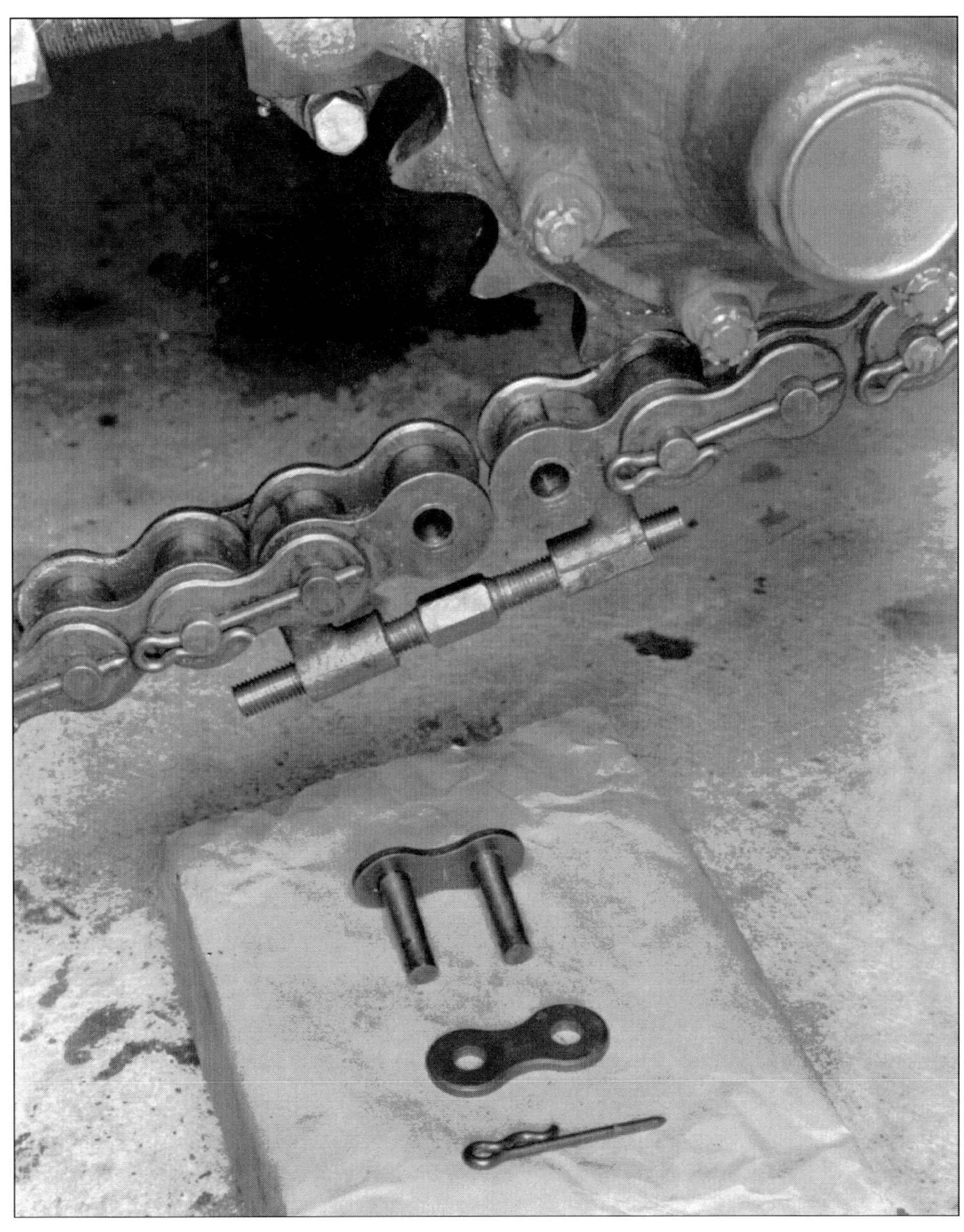

Detail of chain link repair to the FCSW drive chain. (V7620)

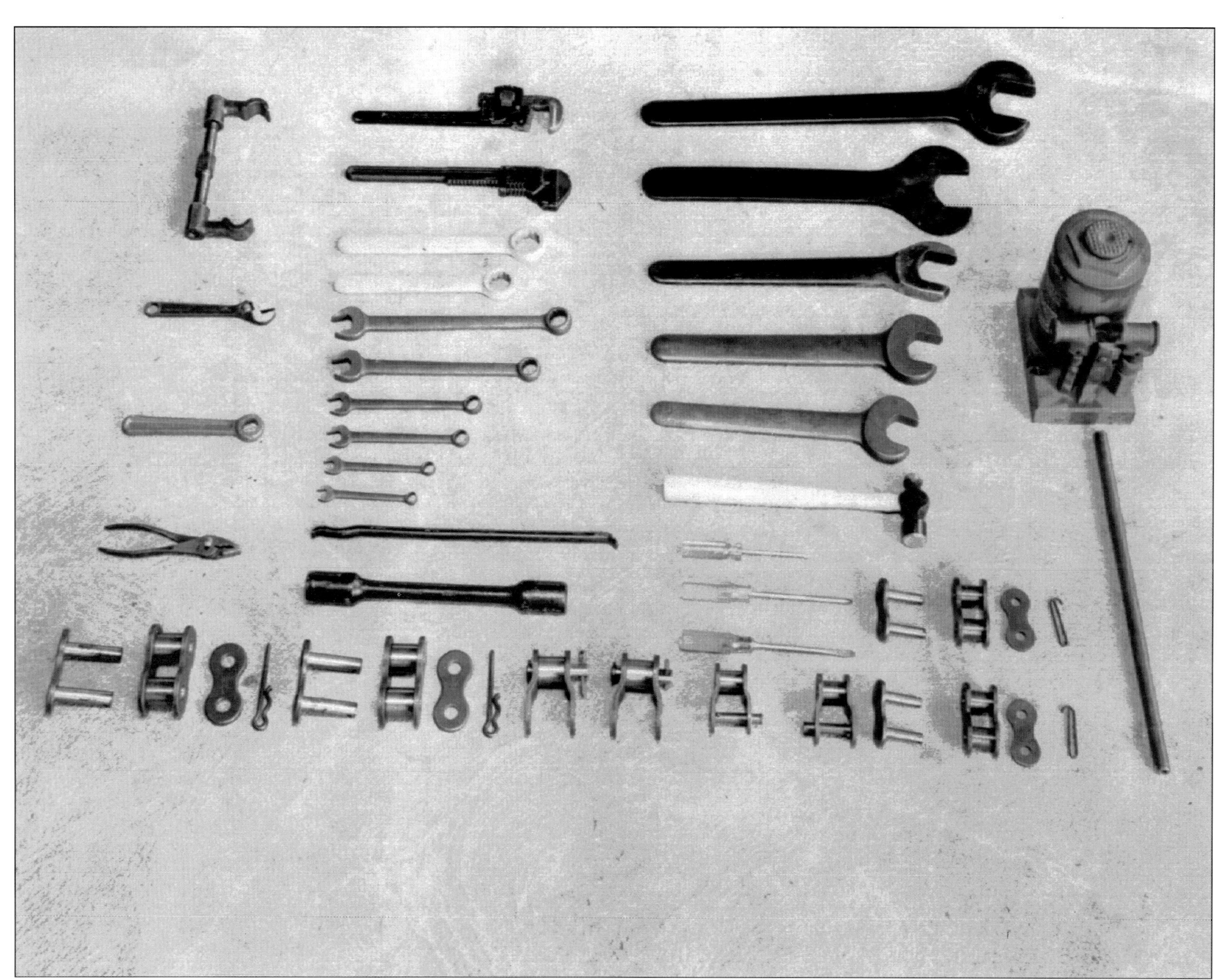

Chain repair tools for the FCSW. (V7631)

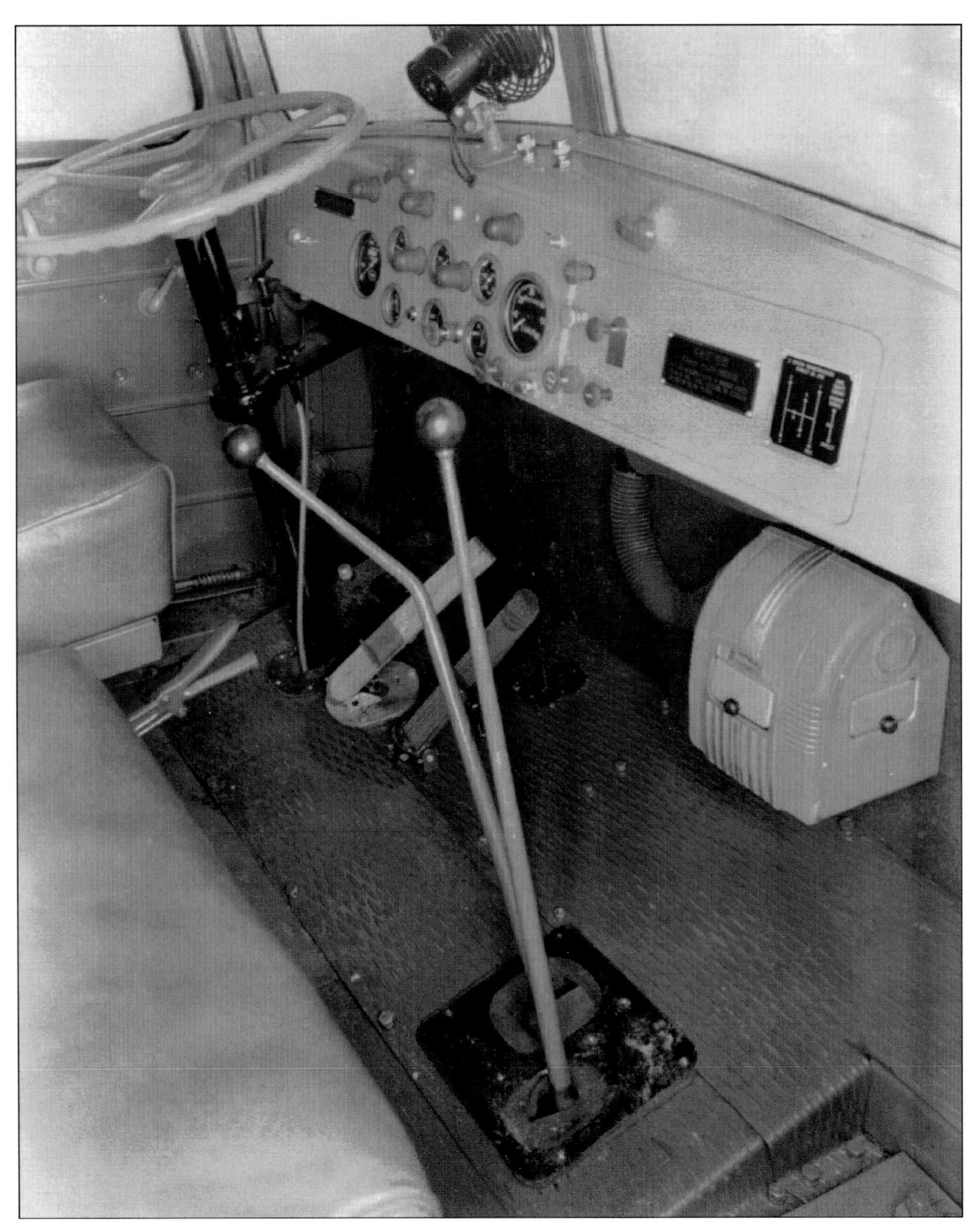

View of the cab fitted to the FCSW chassis built under General Works Order #24. (V7647)

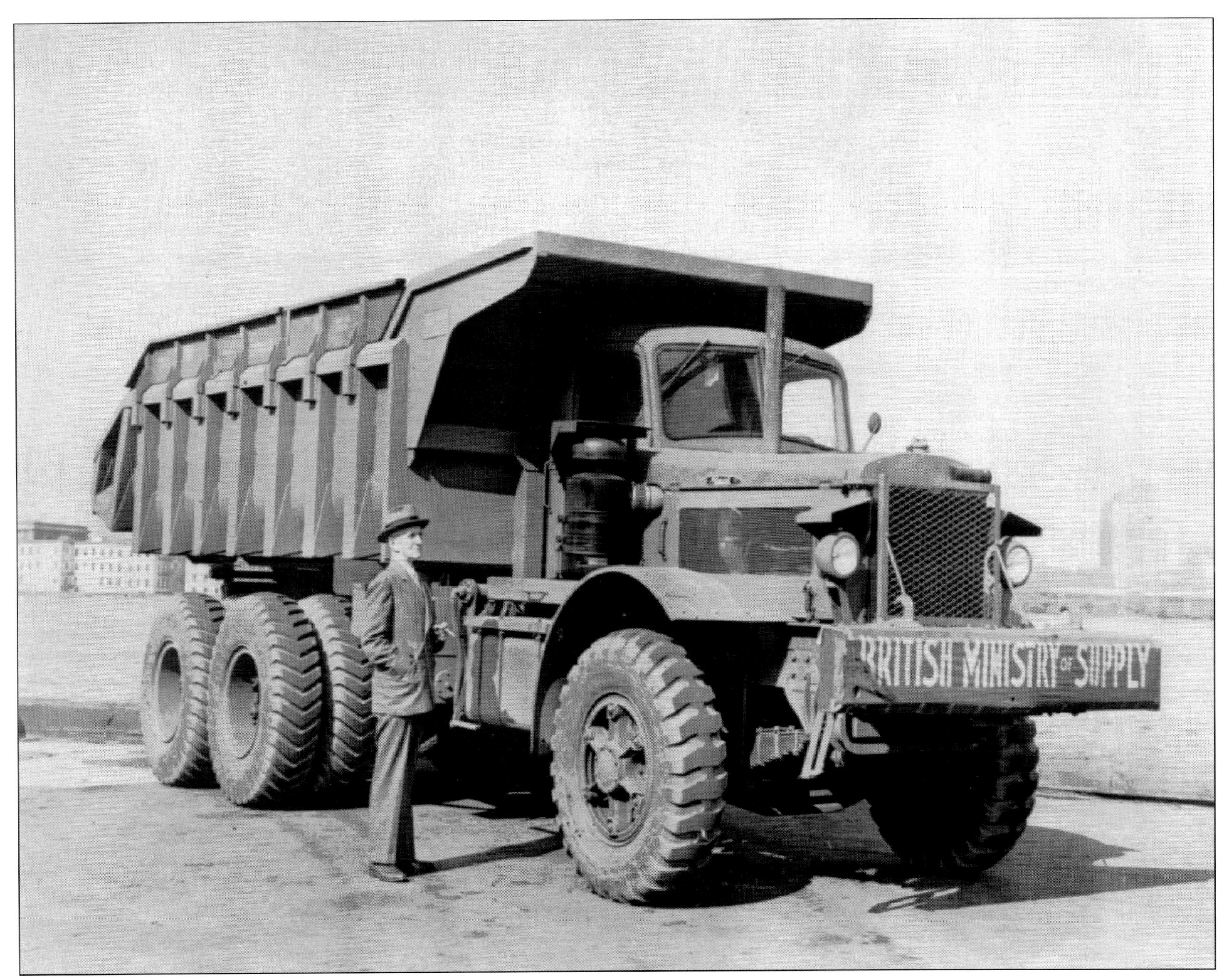

FCSW dump truck shipped to the British Ministry of Supply. October 1944. (M8307)

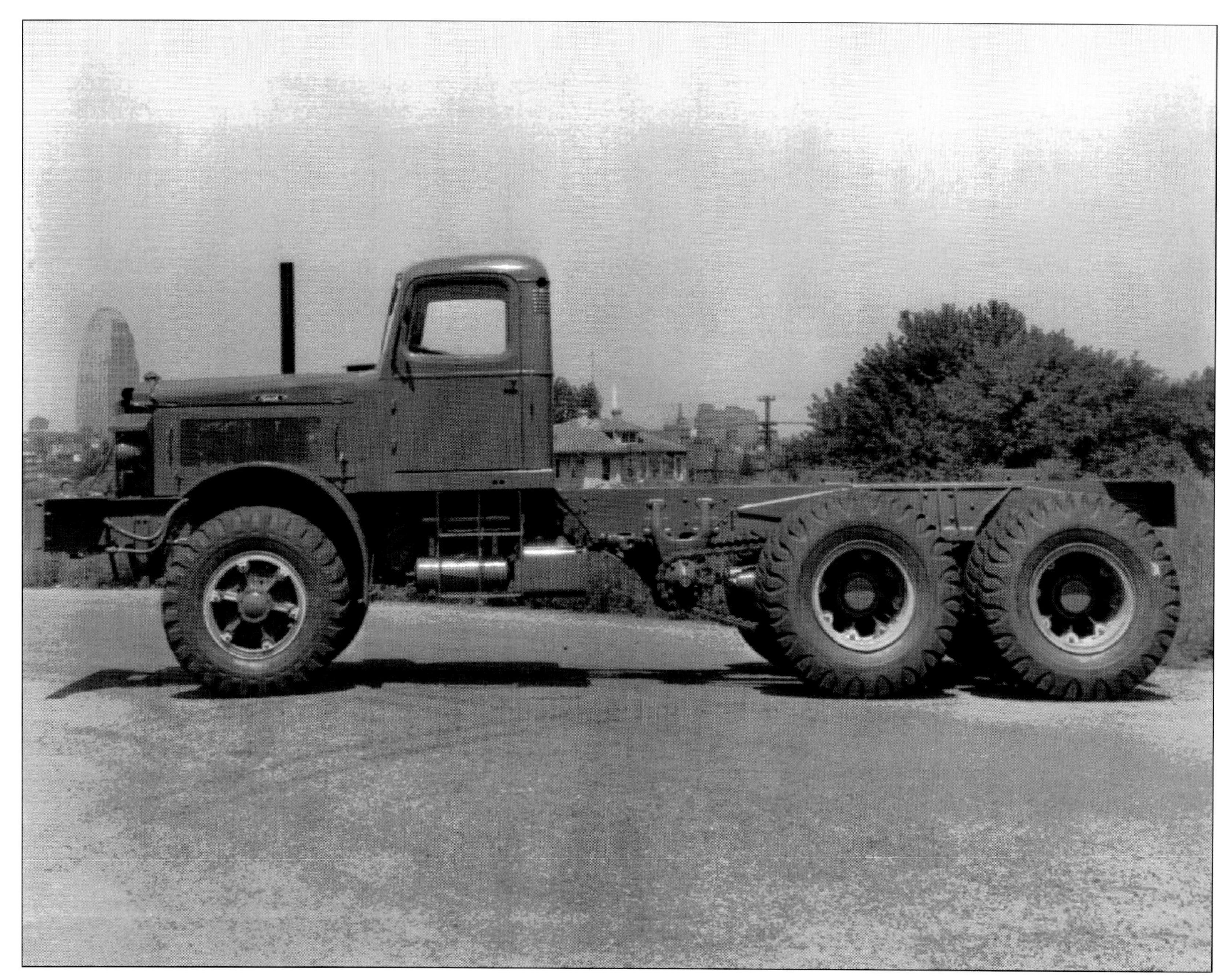

FCSW chassis built under General Works Order #26. August 1944. (V7749)

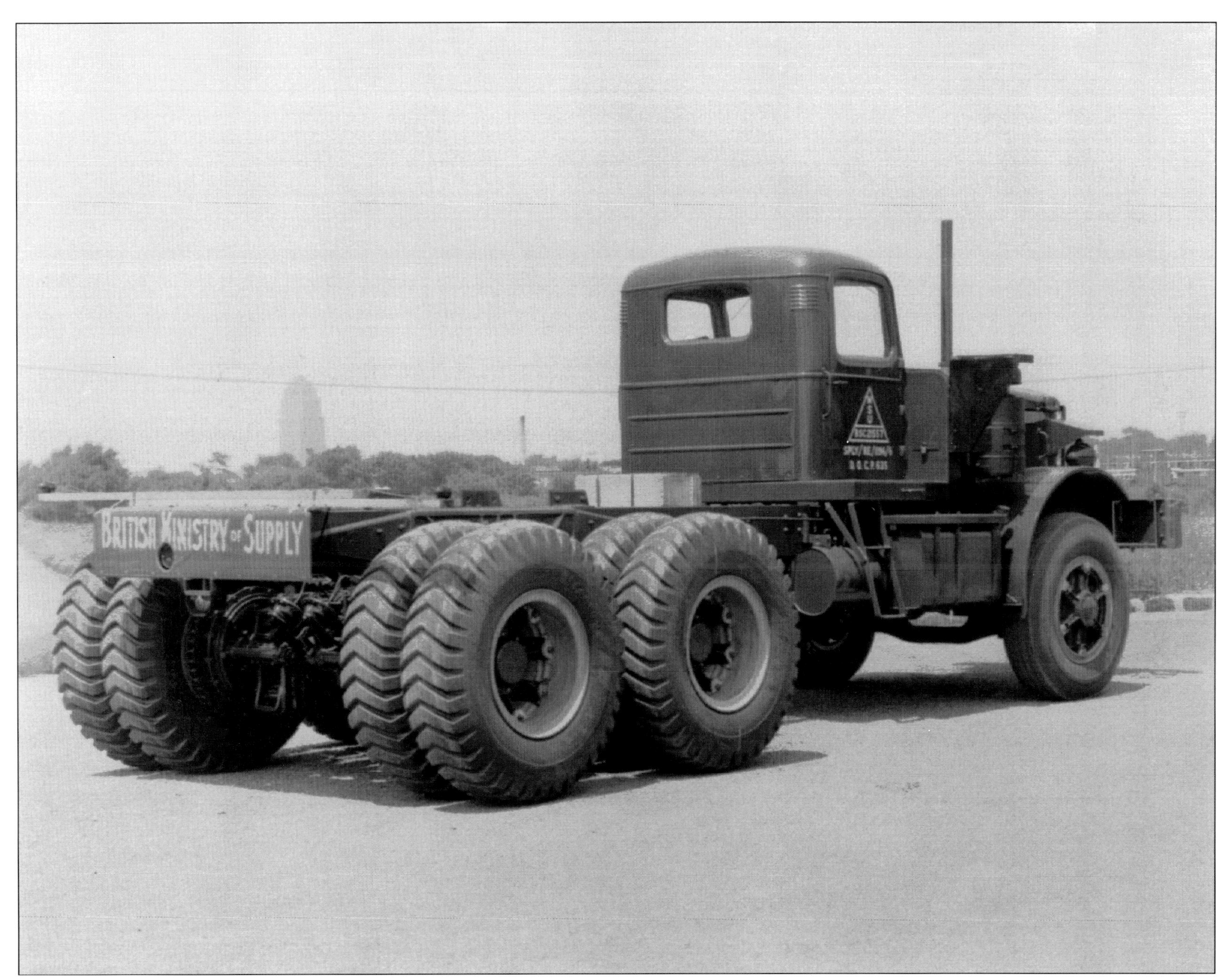

FCSW chassis built under General Works Order #27. (V8052)

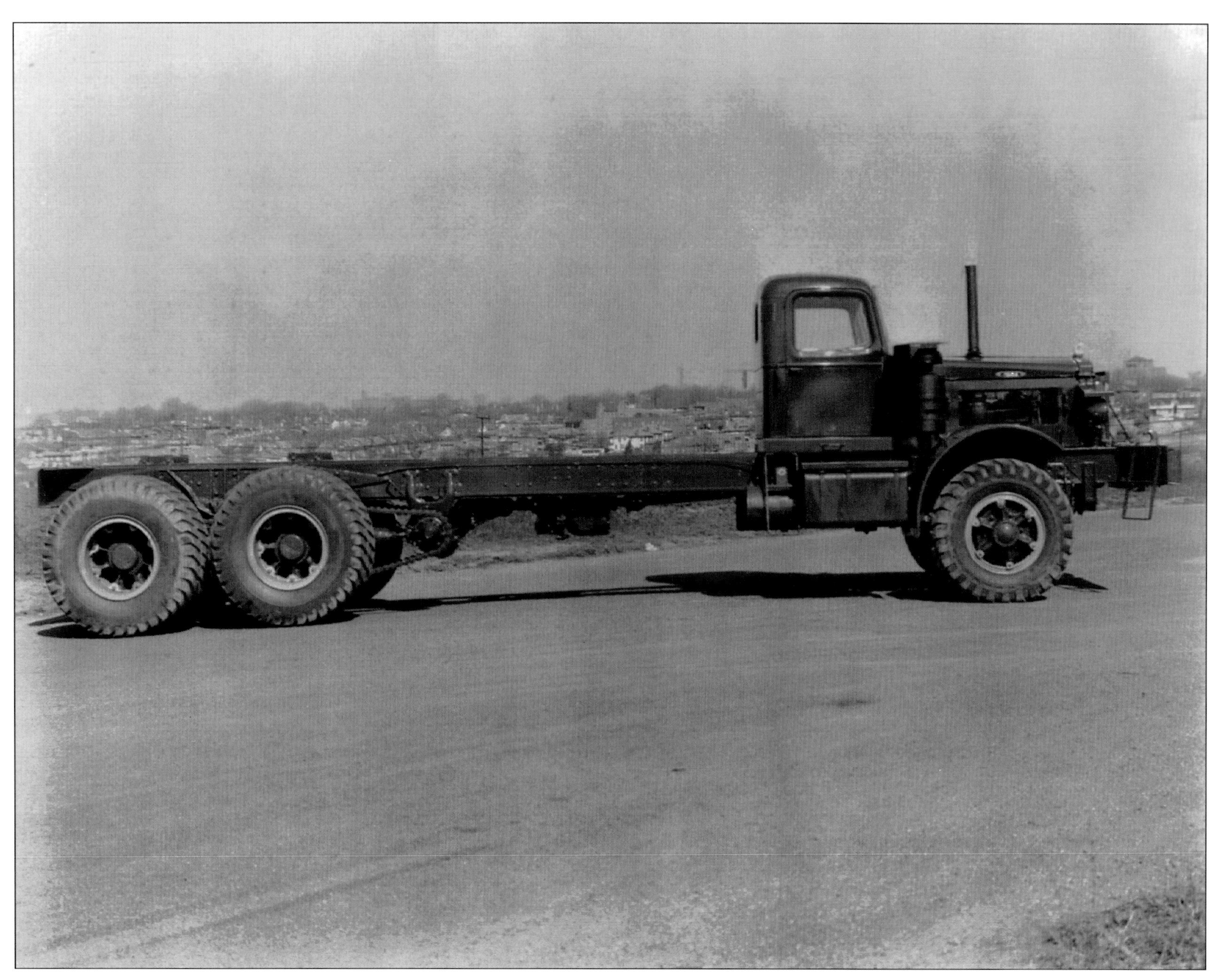

FCSW chassis built under General Works Order #27. (V8052)

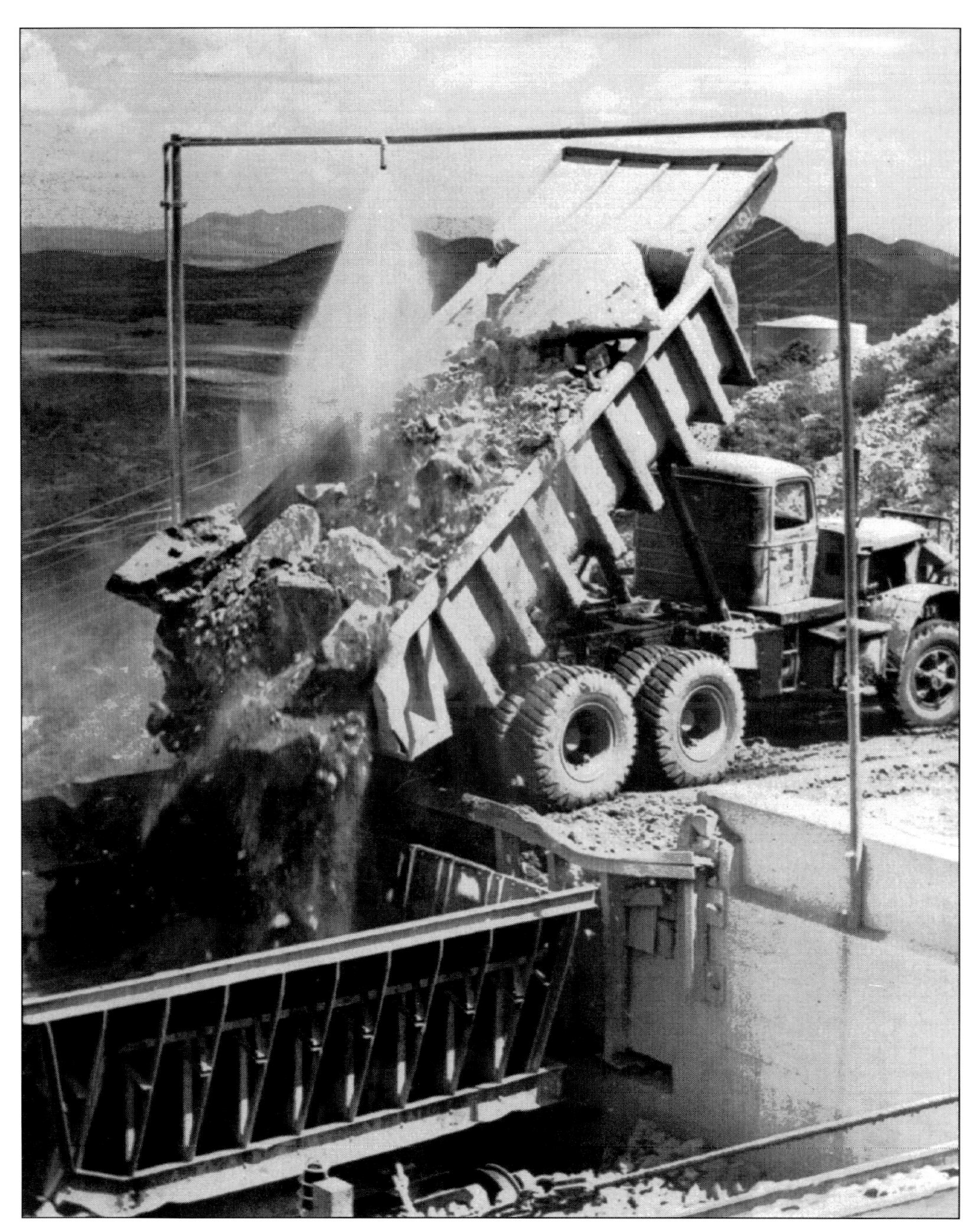

FCSW dump truck operated by Greene Cannea Copper Co., Sonora, Mexico. May 1946. (M9577)

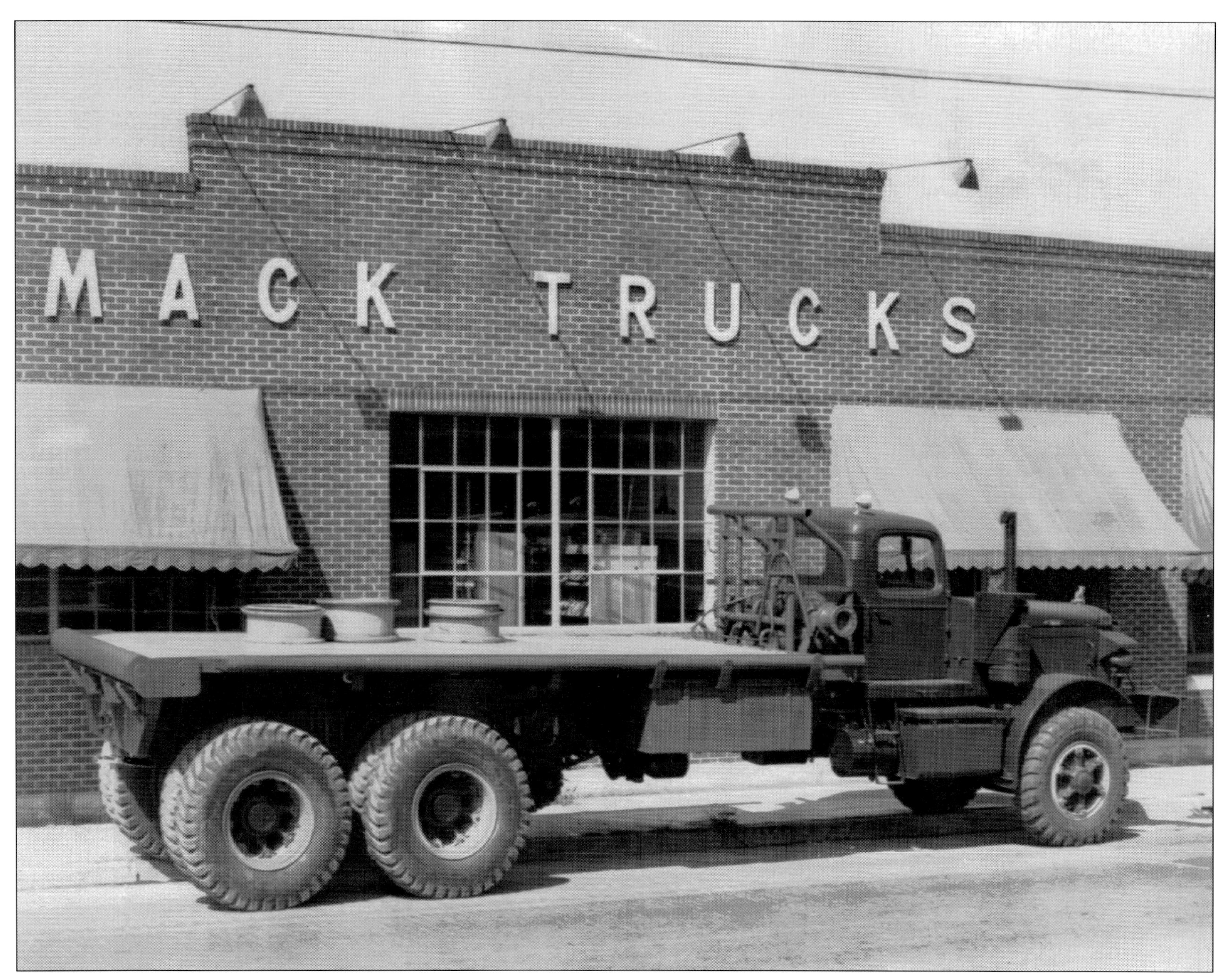

FCSW built for Asiatic Petroleum. July 1945. (M9035)

MACK MODEL NW

The NW was designed specifically for the Third Locks Project of the Panama Canal. Christened "Swamp Dumpers", the NWs featured all-wheel shaft drive, the first heavy-duty Mack trucks that were not chain driven, and Cummins diesel engines.

A total of 16 NWs were built in 1941.

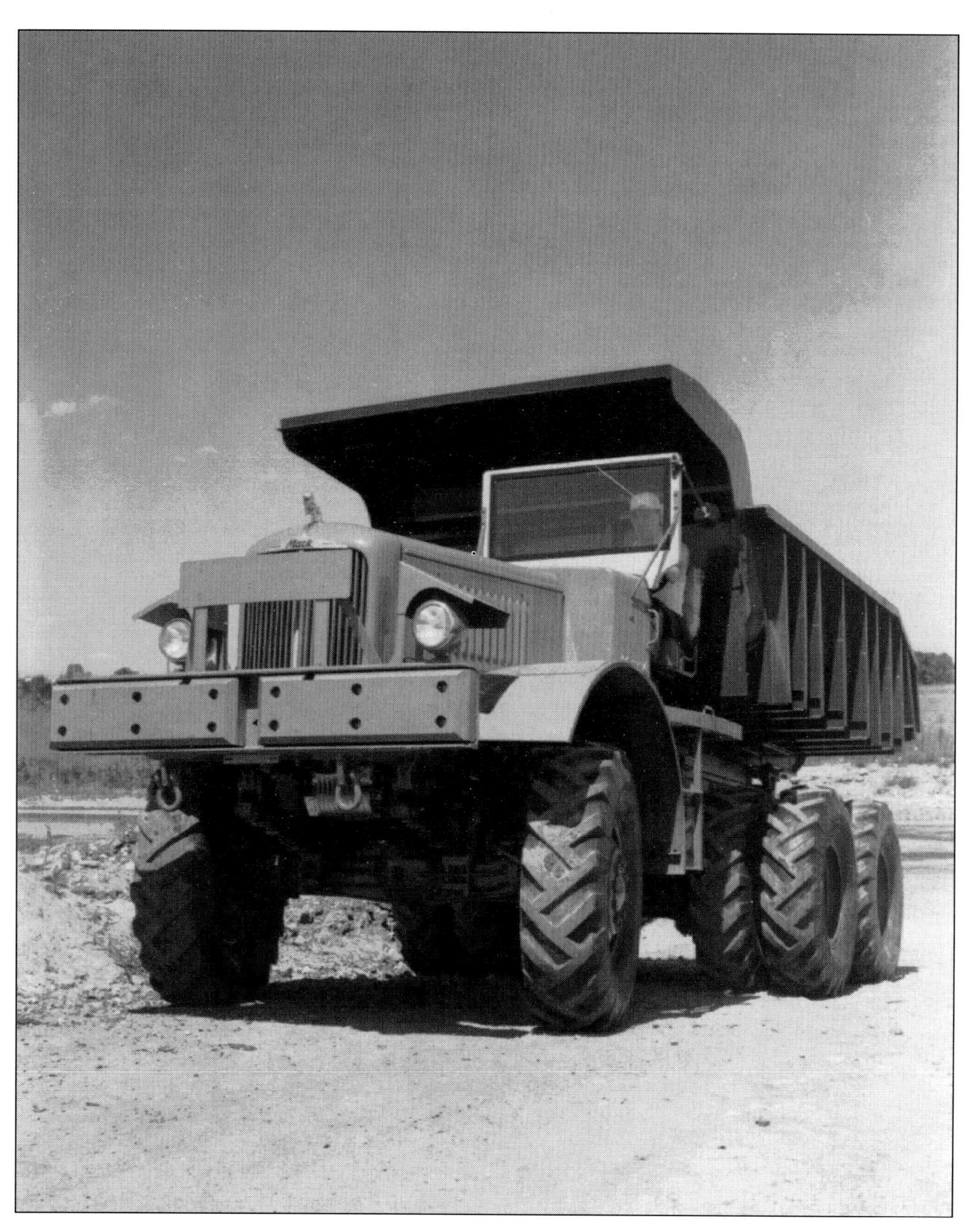

Two views of the Model NW with 12-yard dump body. August 1941. (M5899)

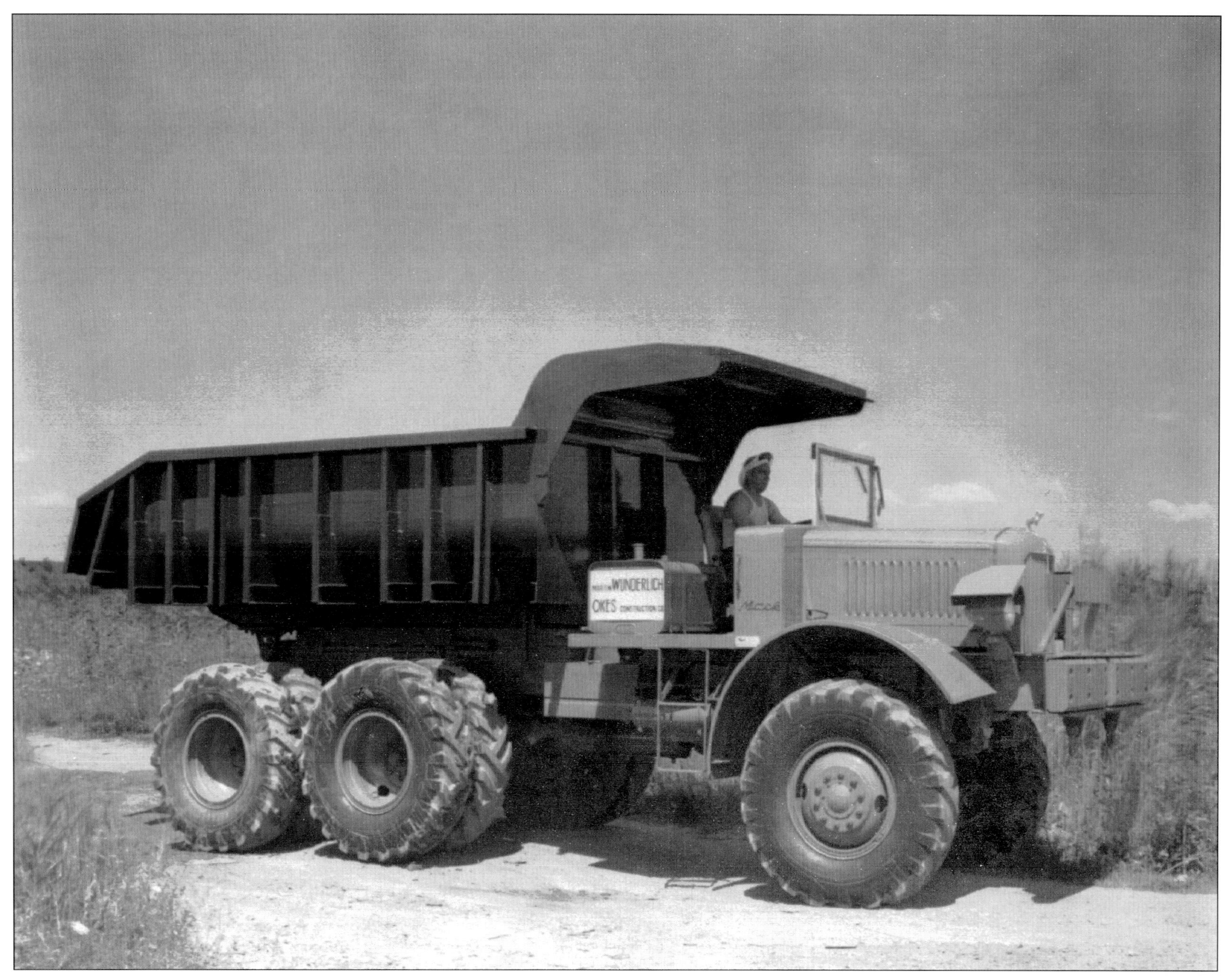

(M5898)

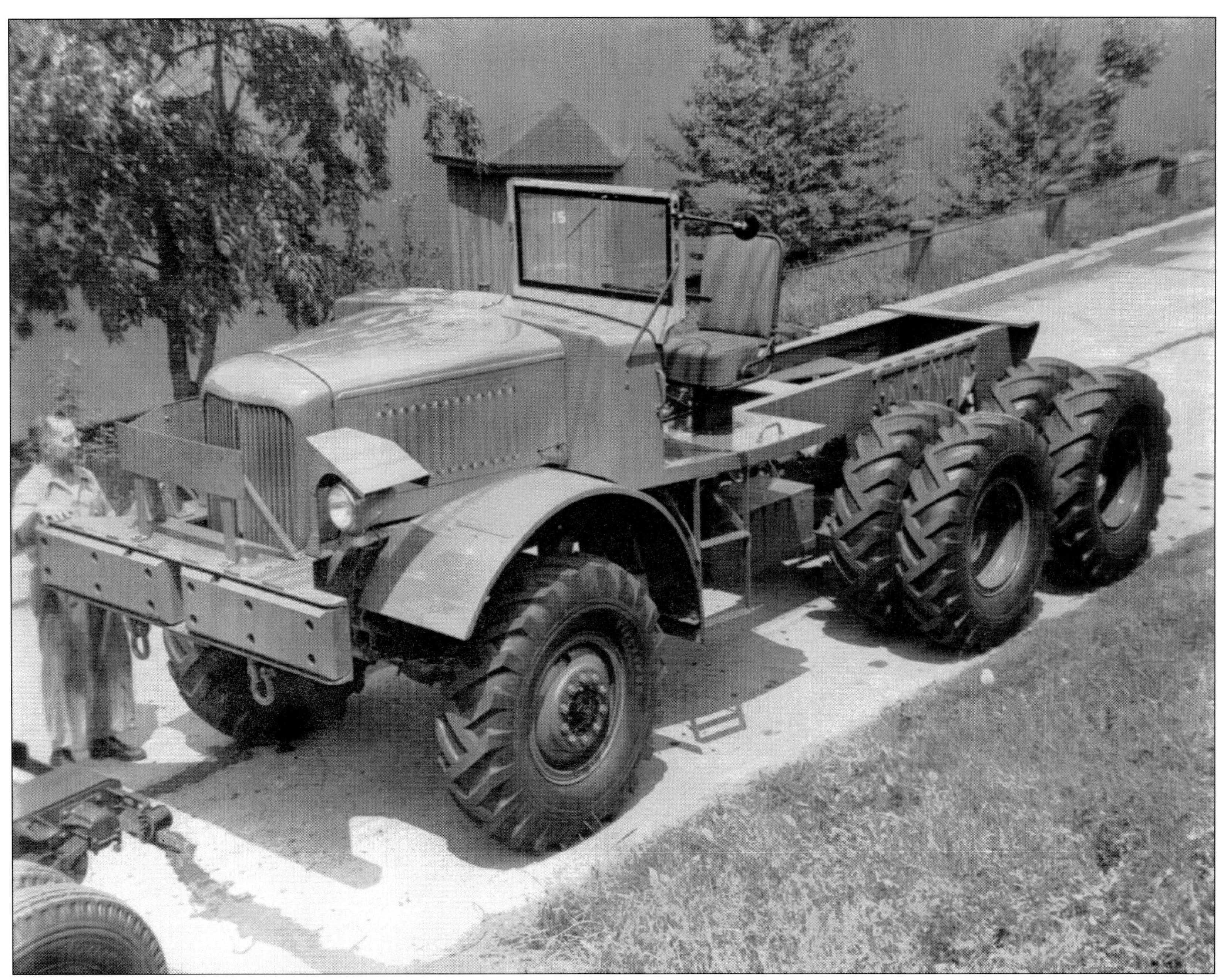

Two views of the NW8D chassis #1002 with open operator platform. (3093)

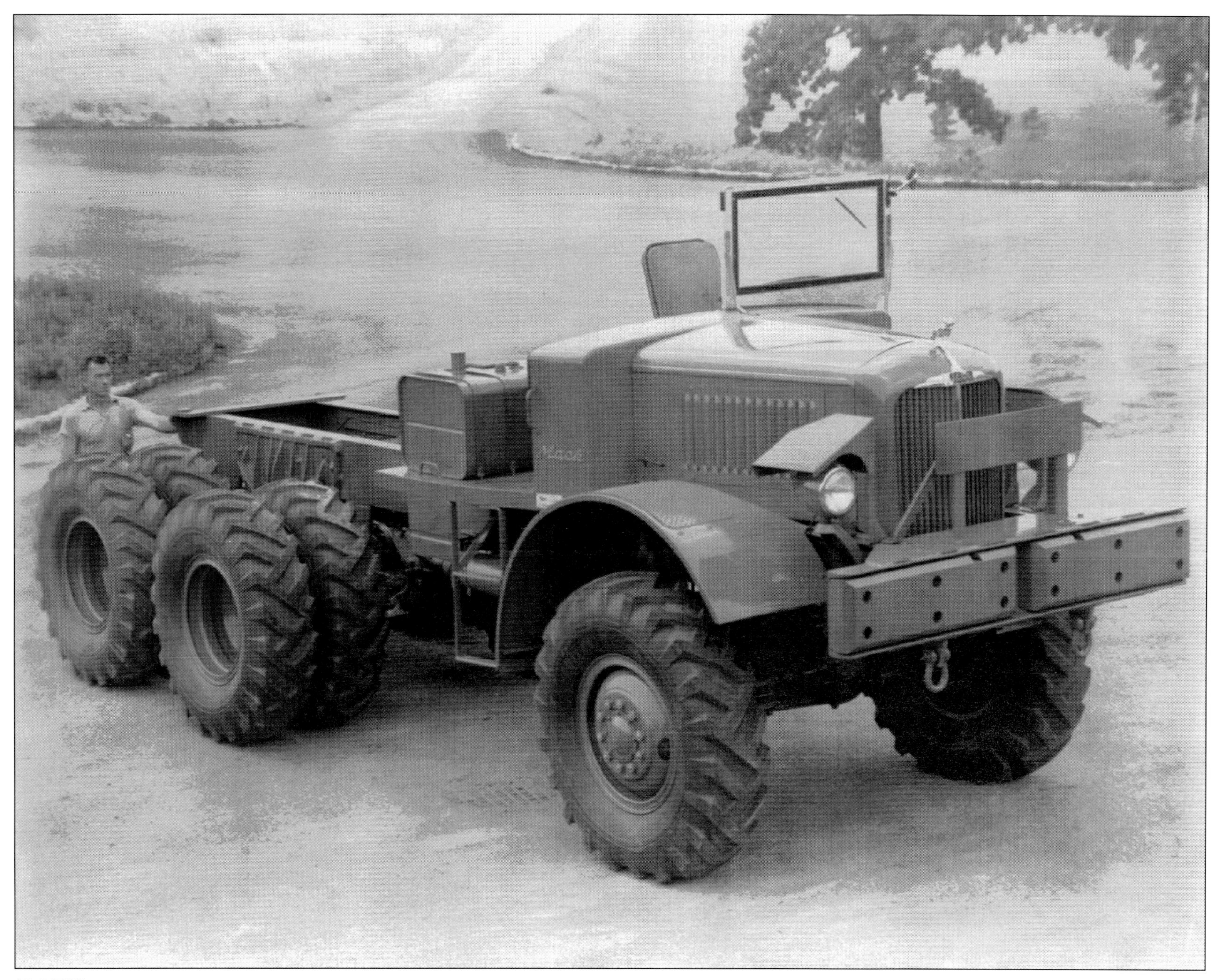

(3170)

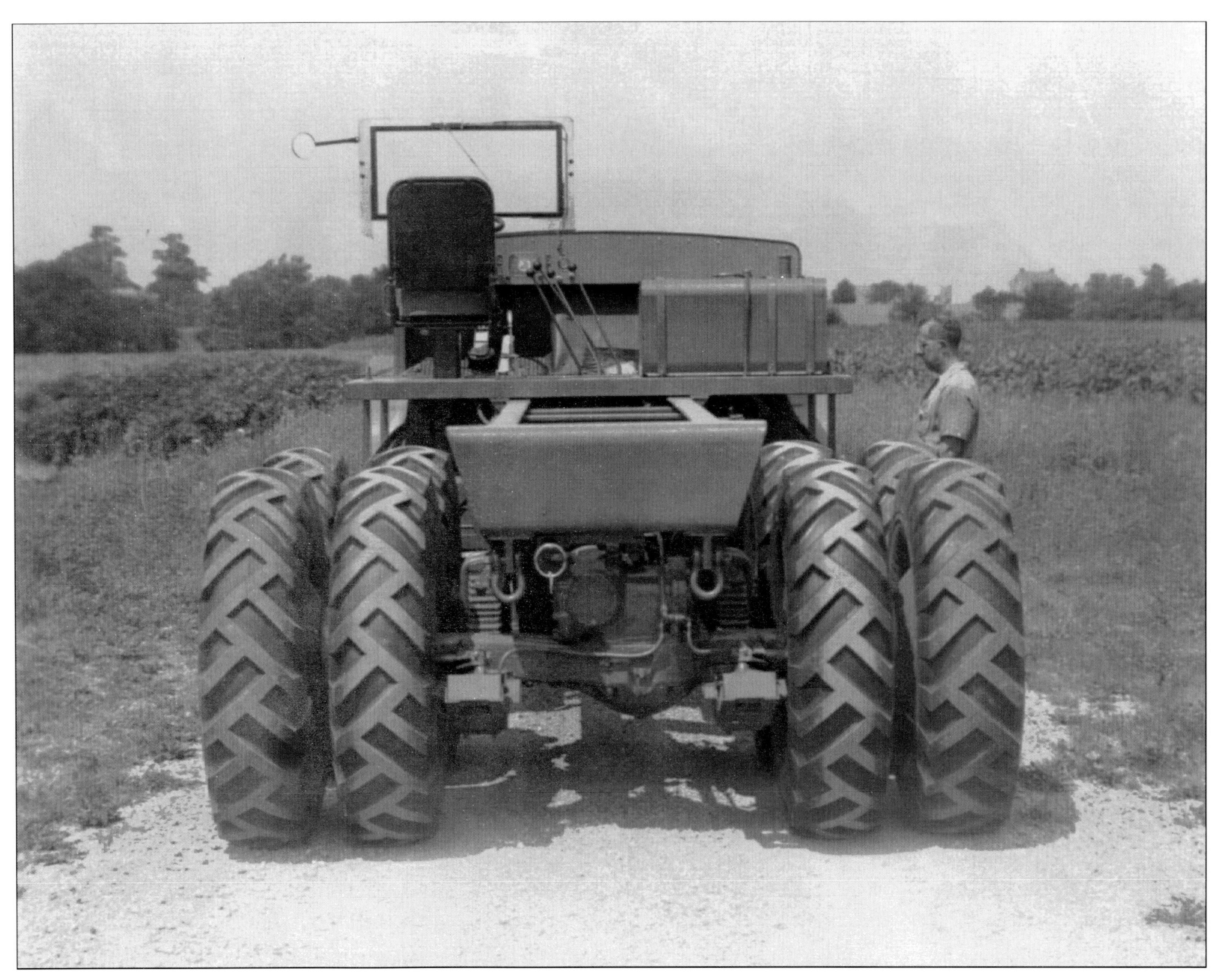

The NW rear tread measured 12 feet. This view shows the driver's position far to the left, which assured him vision to the rear. (V3090)

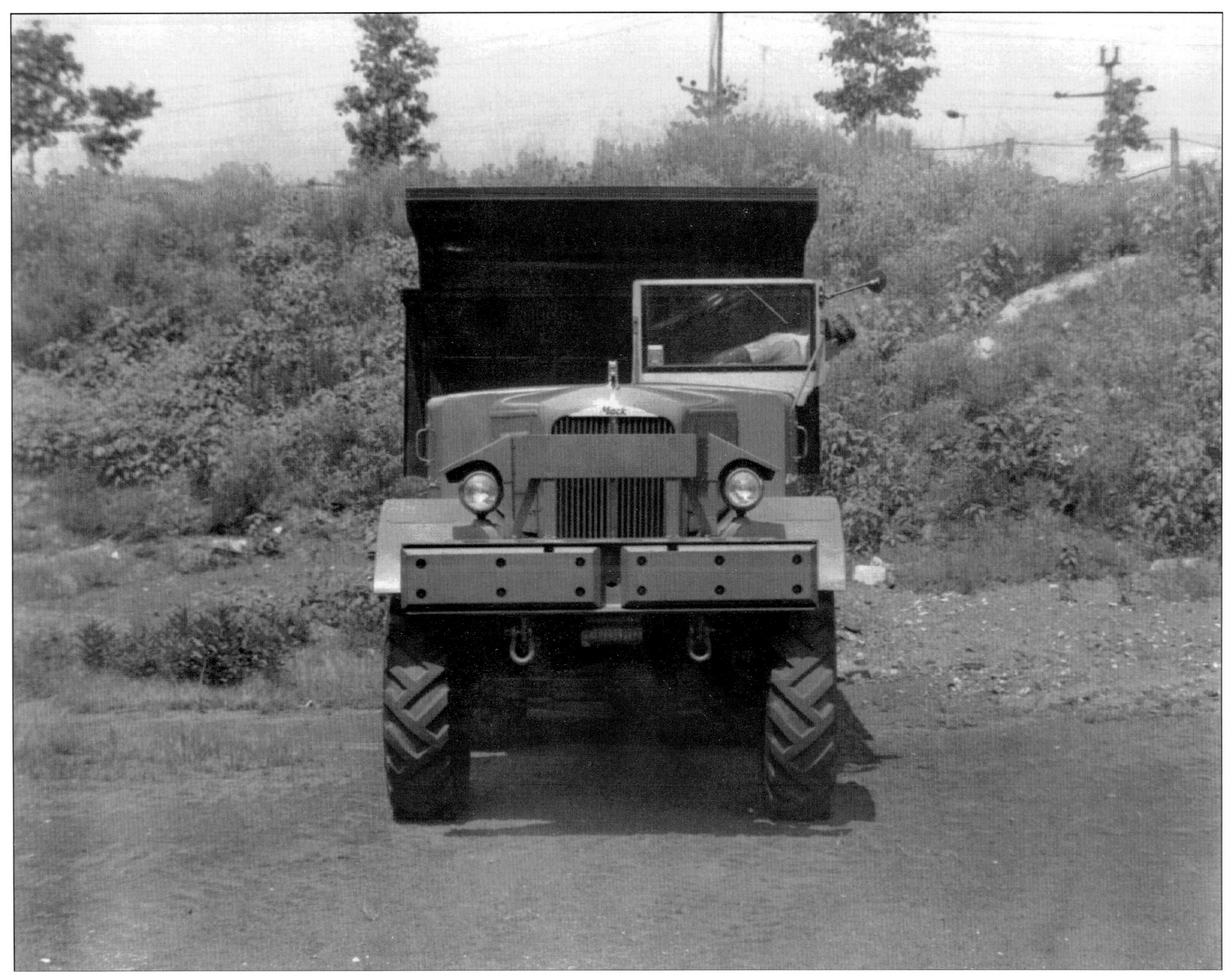

(V3201)

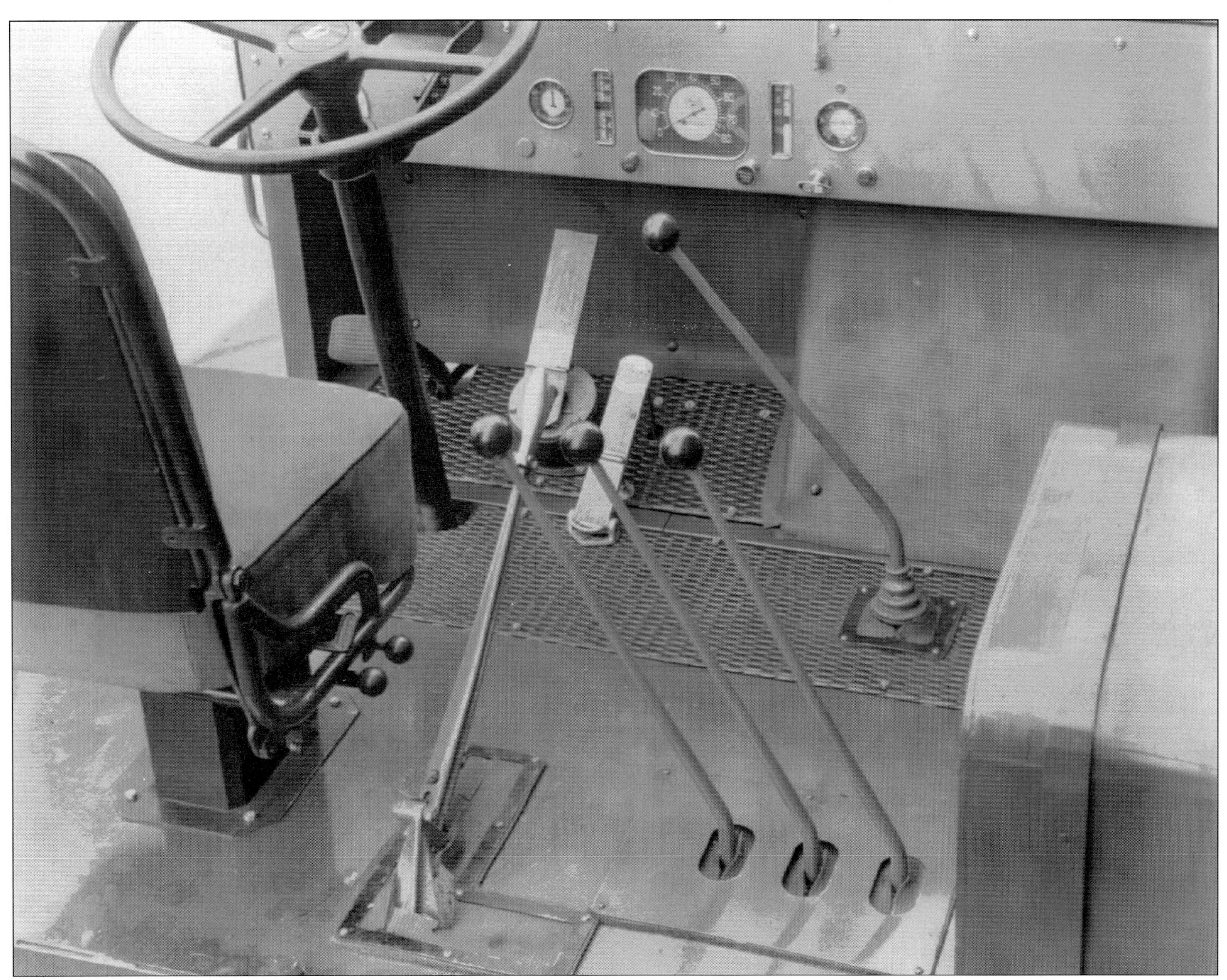

Operator platform of NW8D chassis #1002. (V3087)

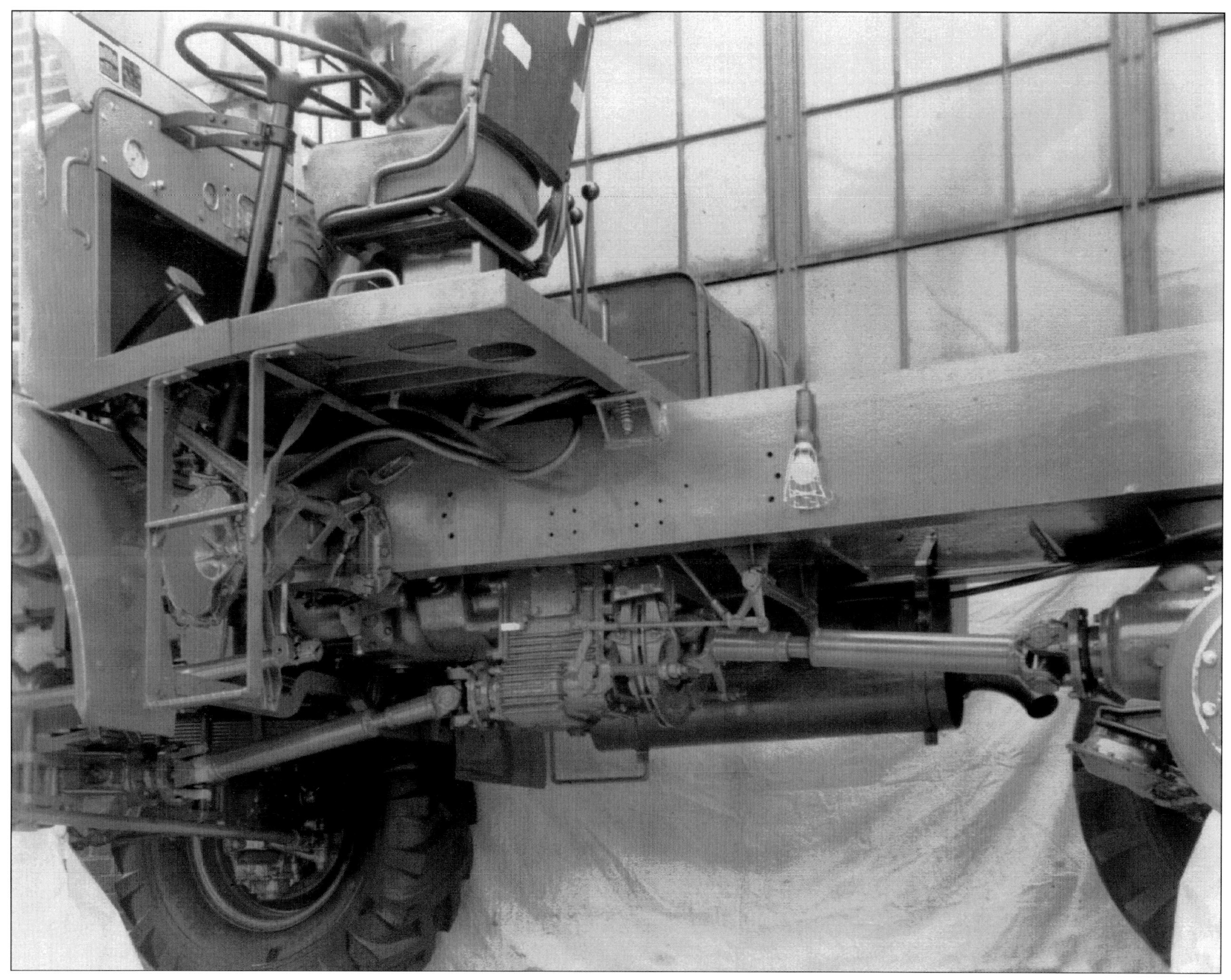

(V3082)

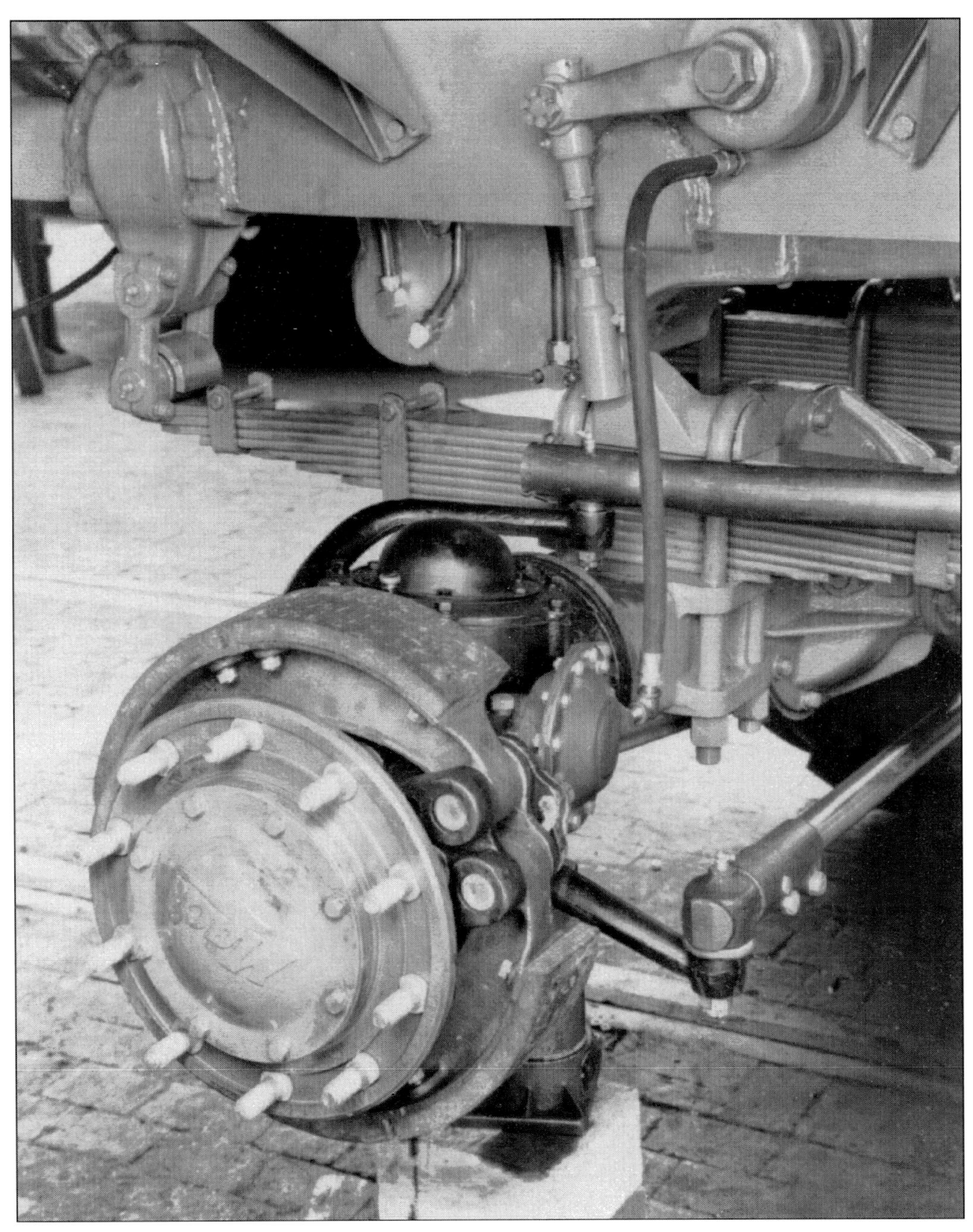

NW left front hub with wheel removed. (V3041)

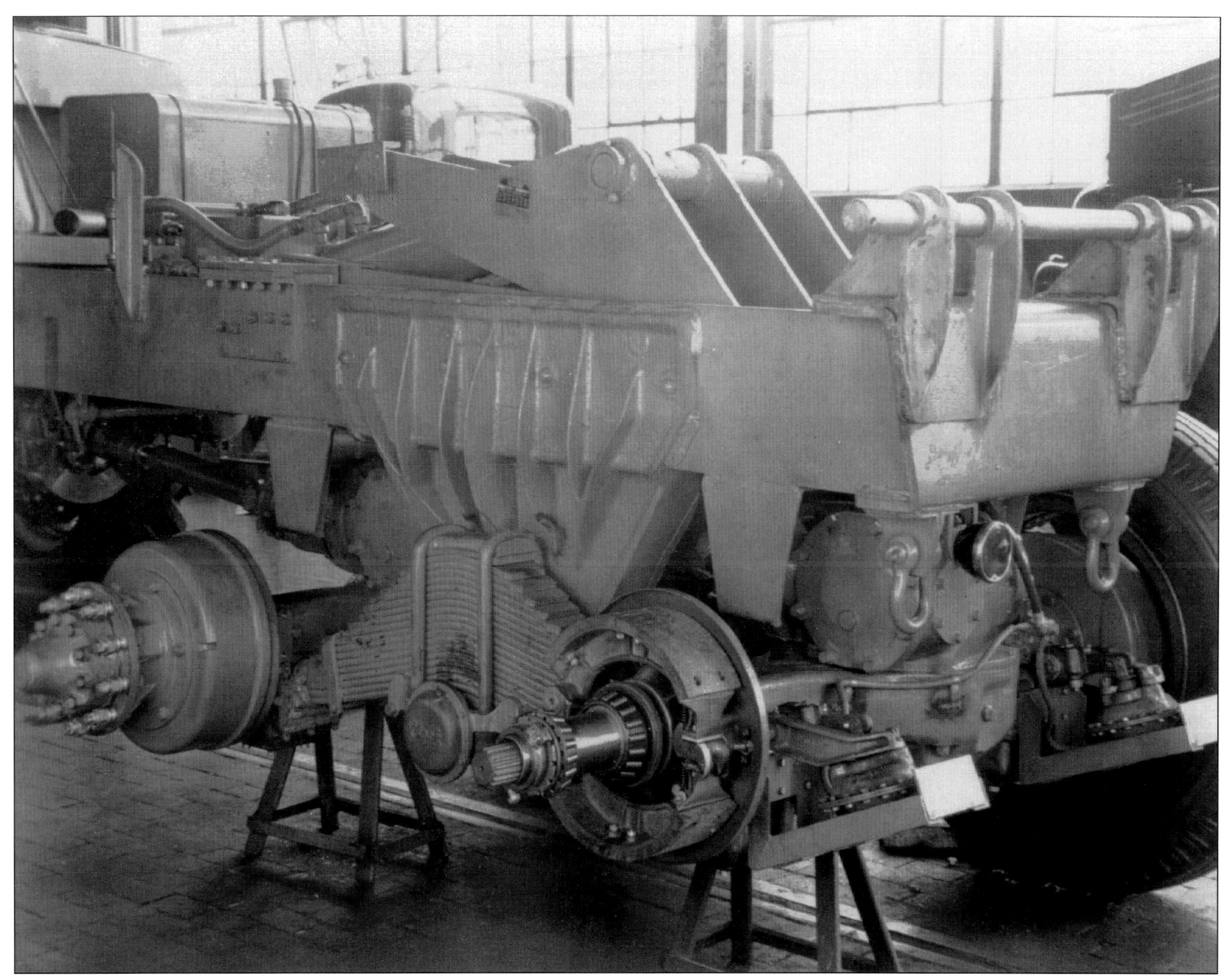

NW8D chassis #1001. November 1941. (V3045)

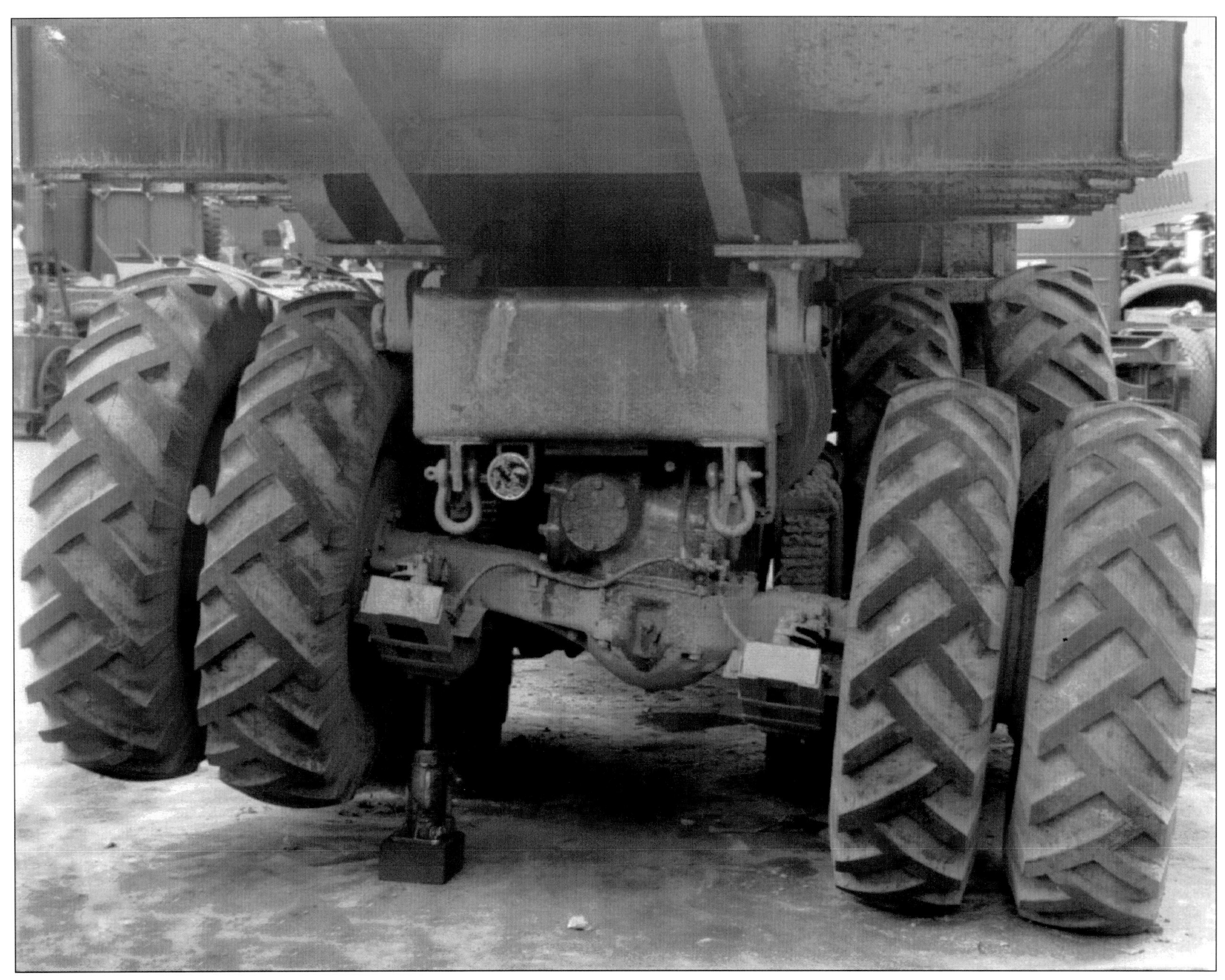

NW8D chssis #1001. (V3071)

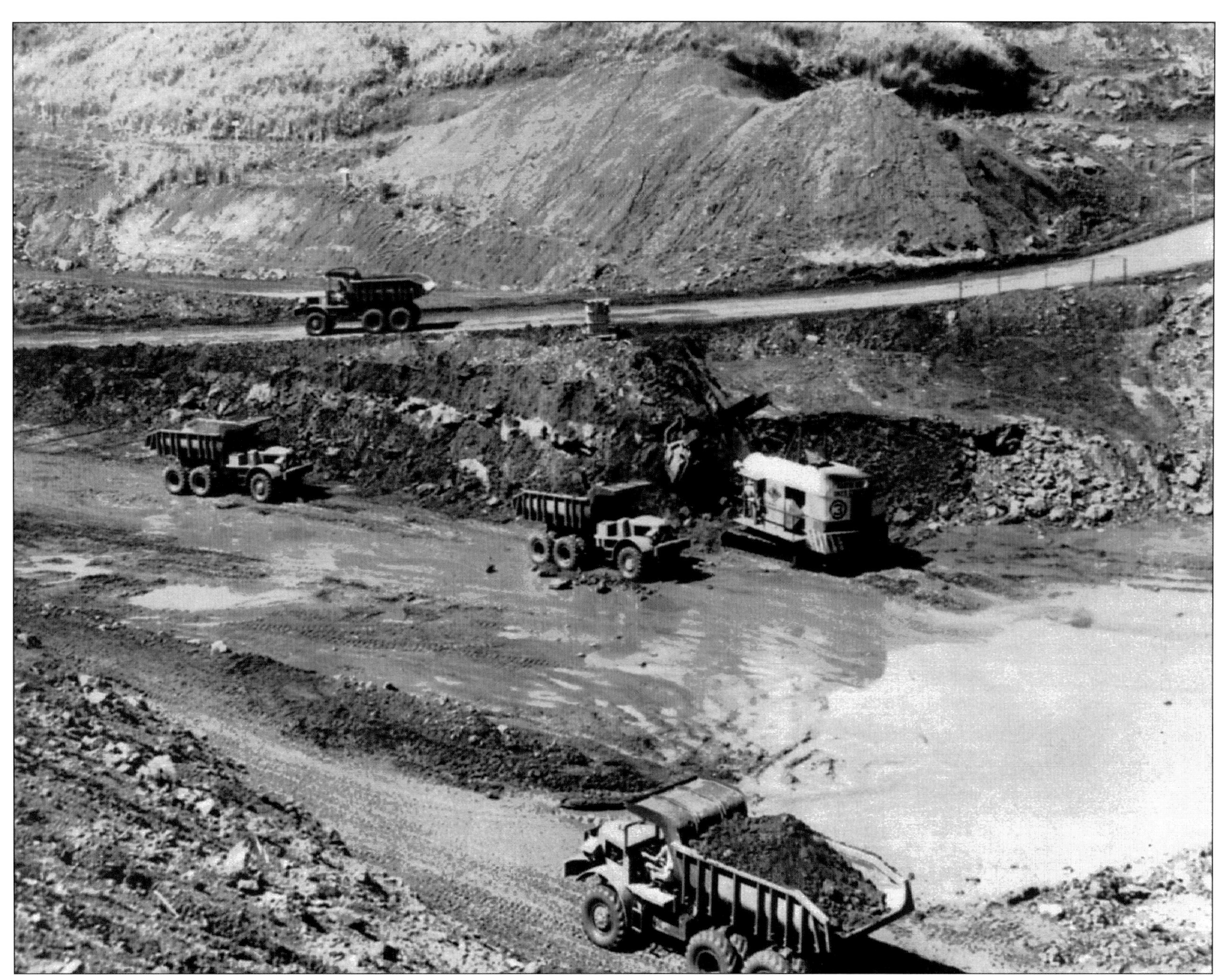

NW dump trucks at work on the Panama Canal Third Locks Project. November 1941. (M6199)

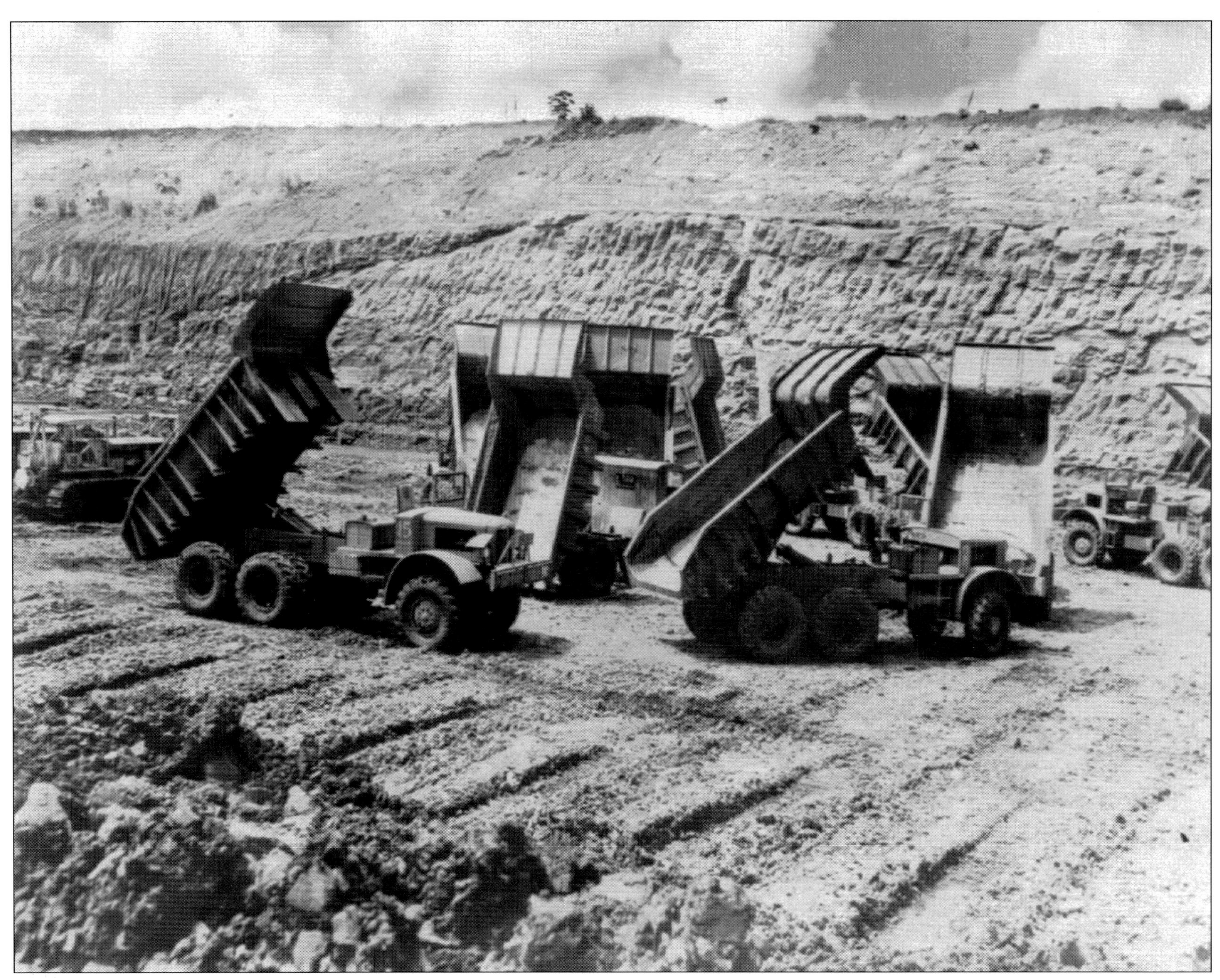

NW dump trucks at work in Panama. (M6152)

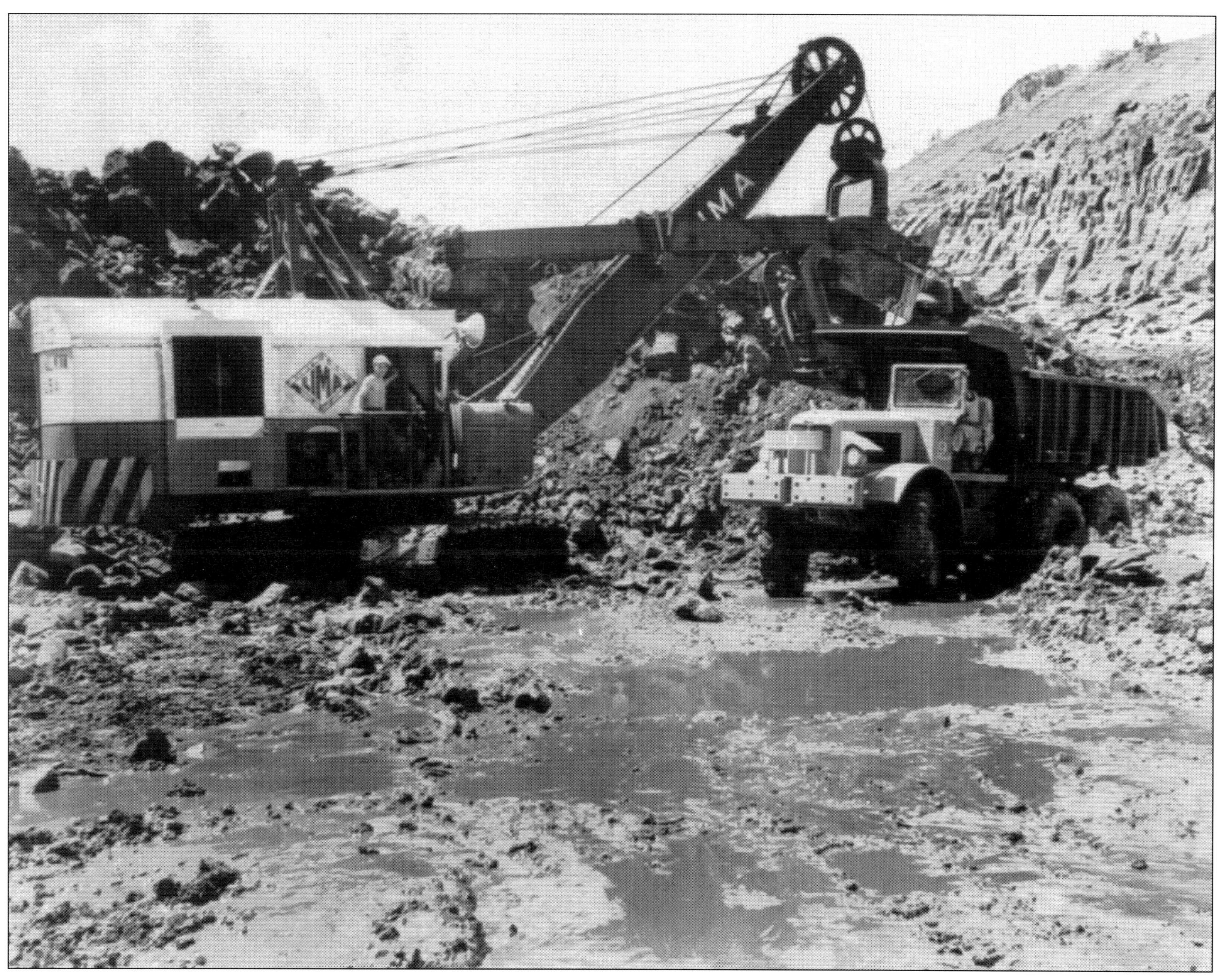

(M6164)

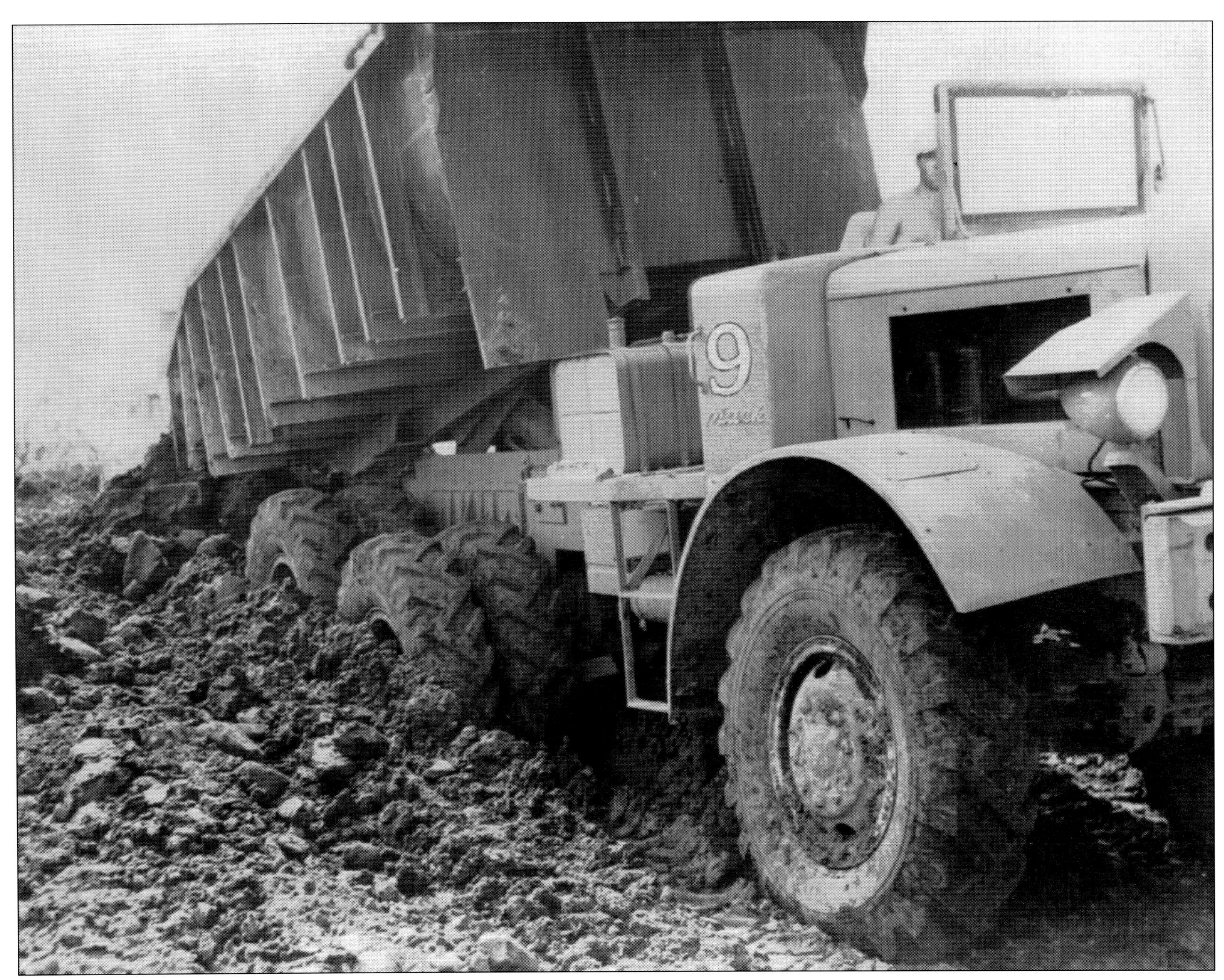

NW dump truck in Panama. (M6148)

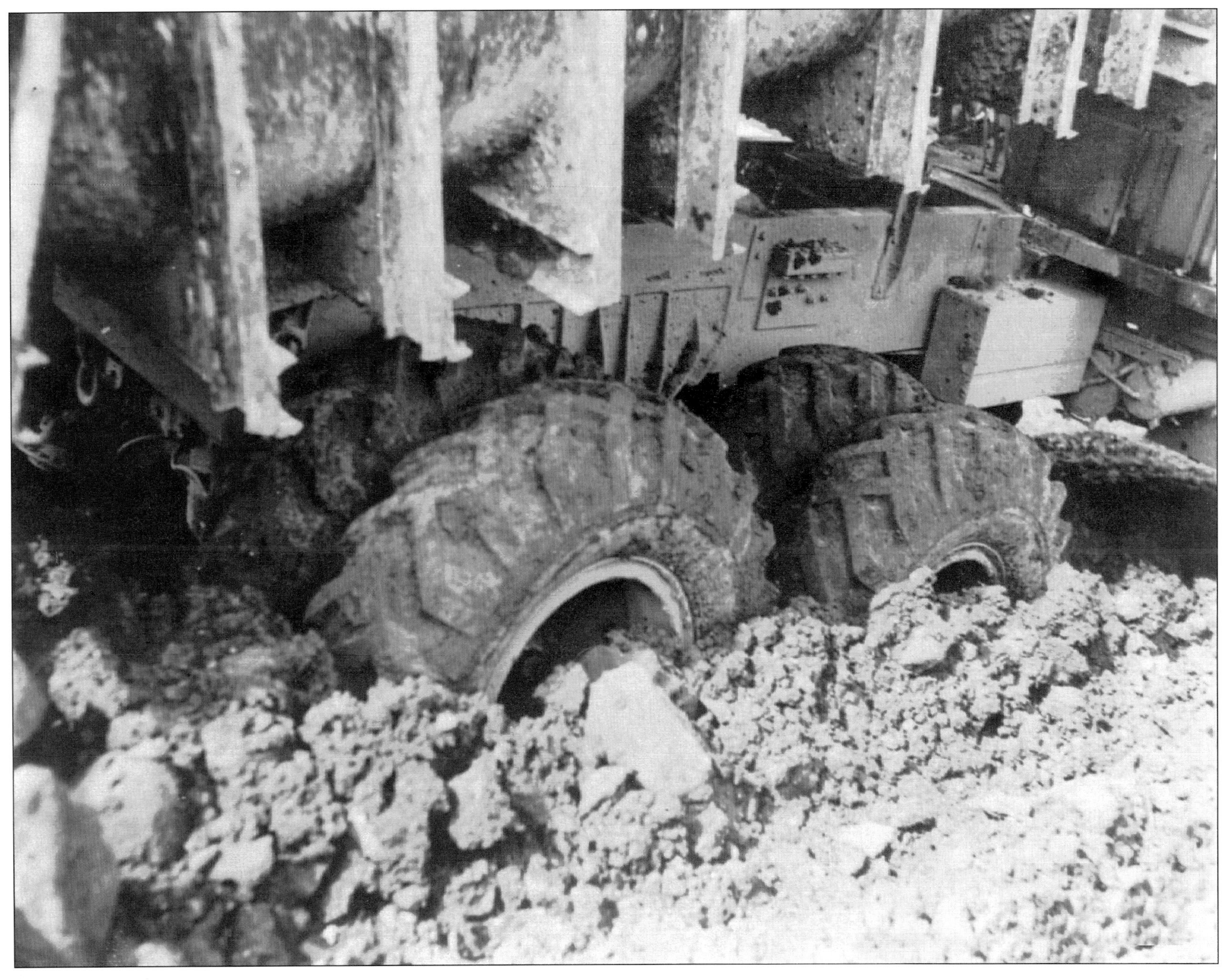

(M6149)

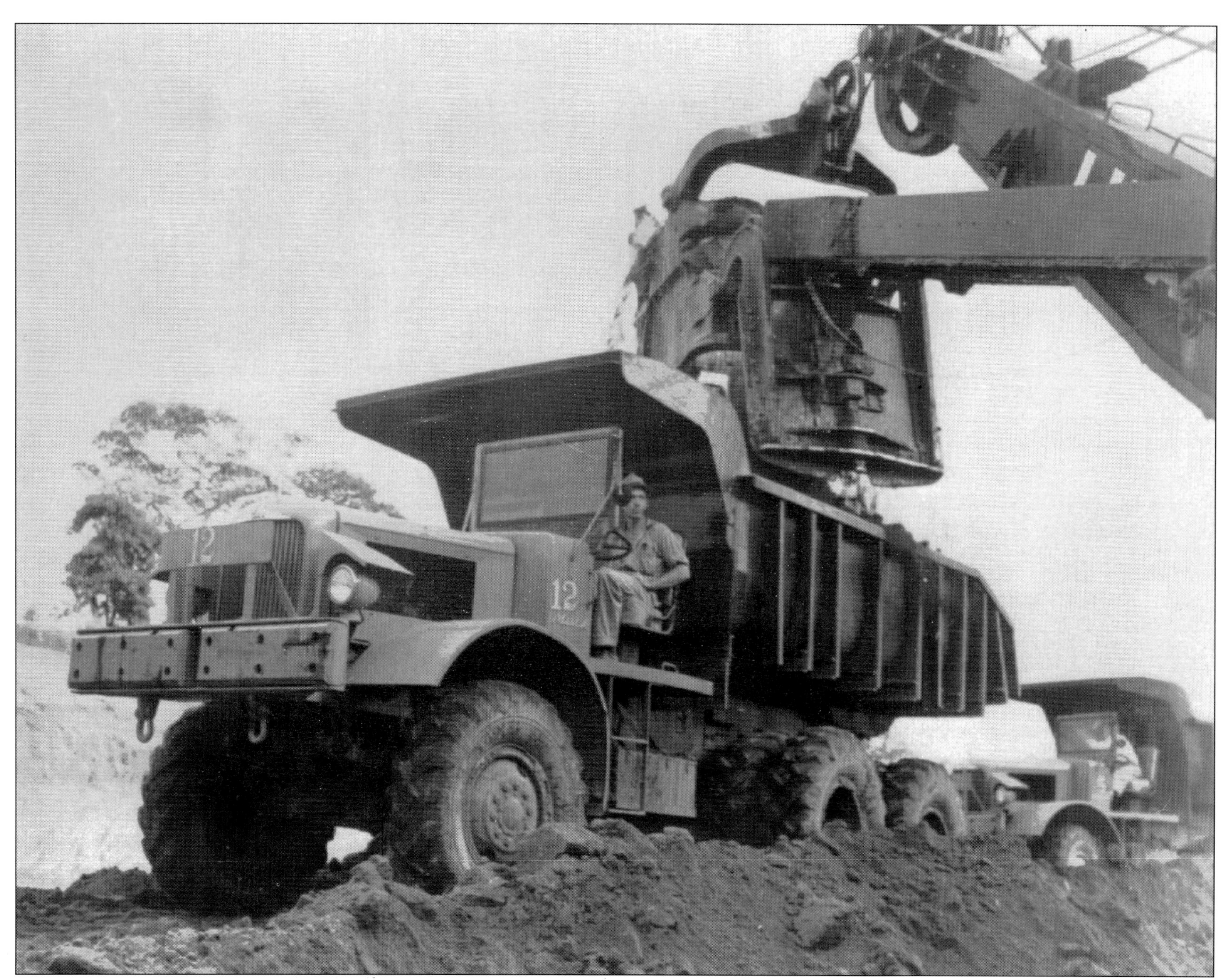

NW dump trucks in Panama. (M6162)

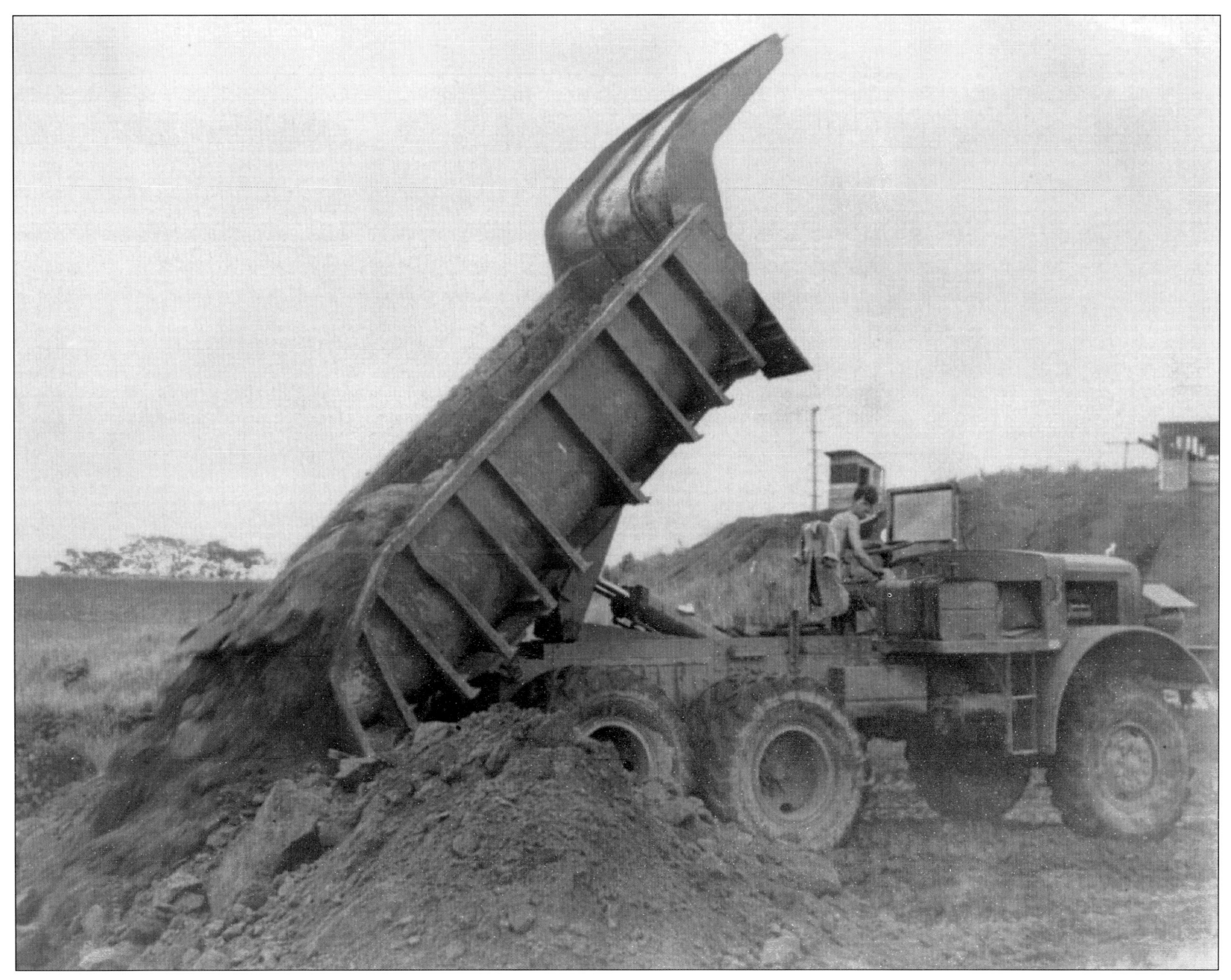

(M6187)

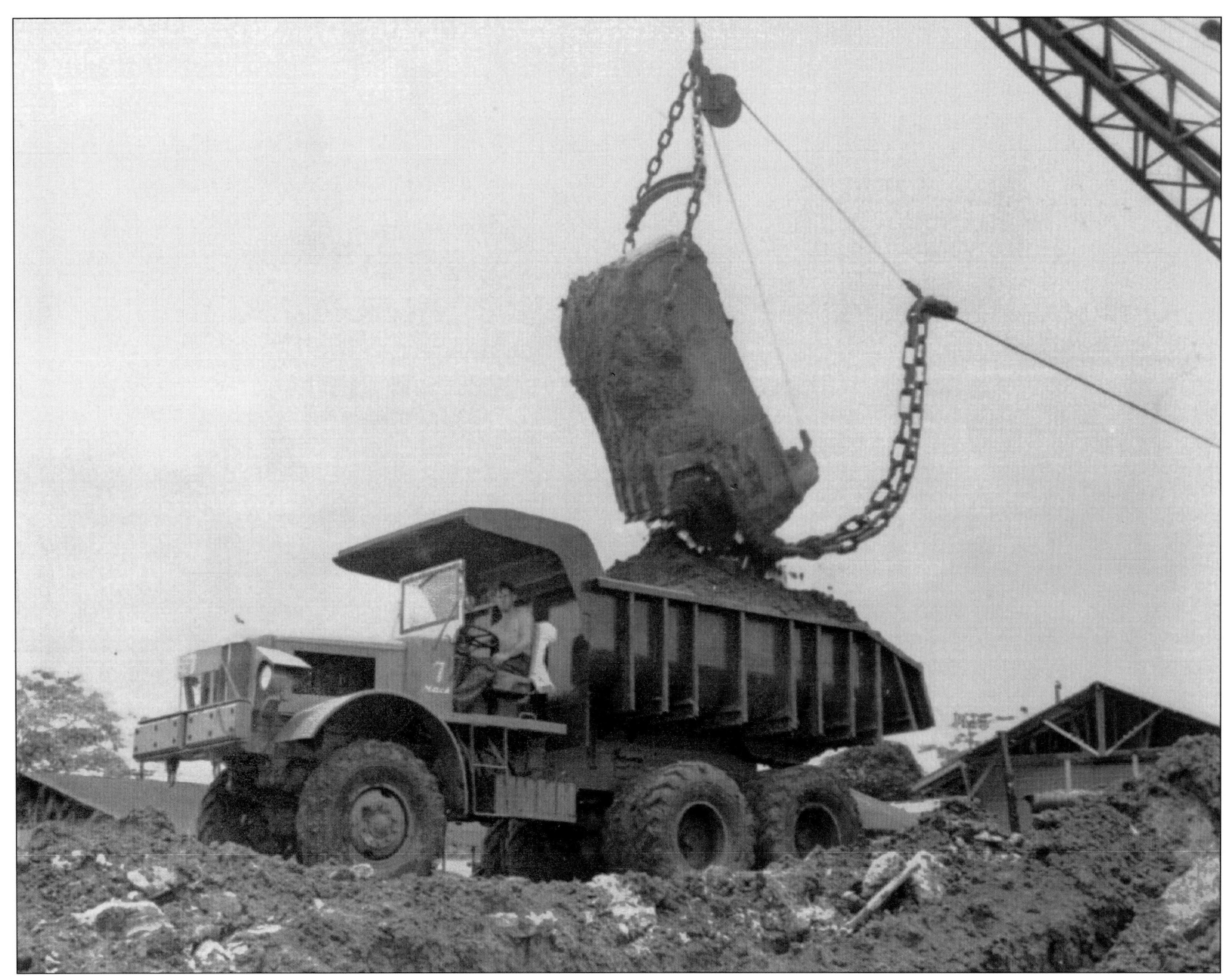

(M5991)

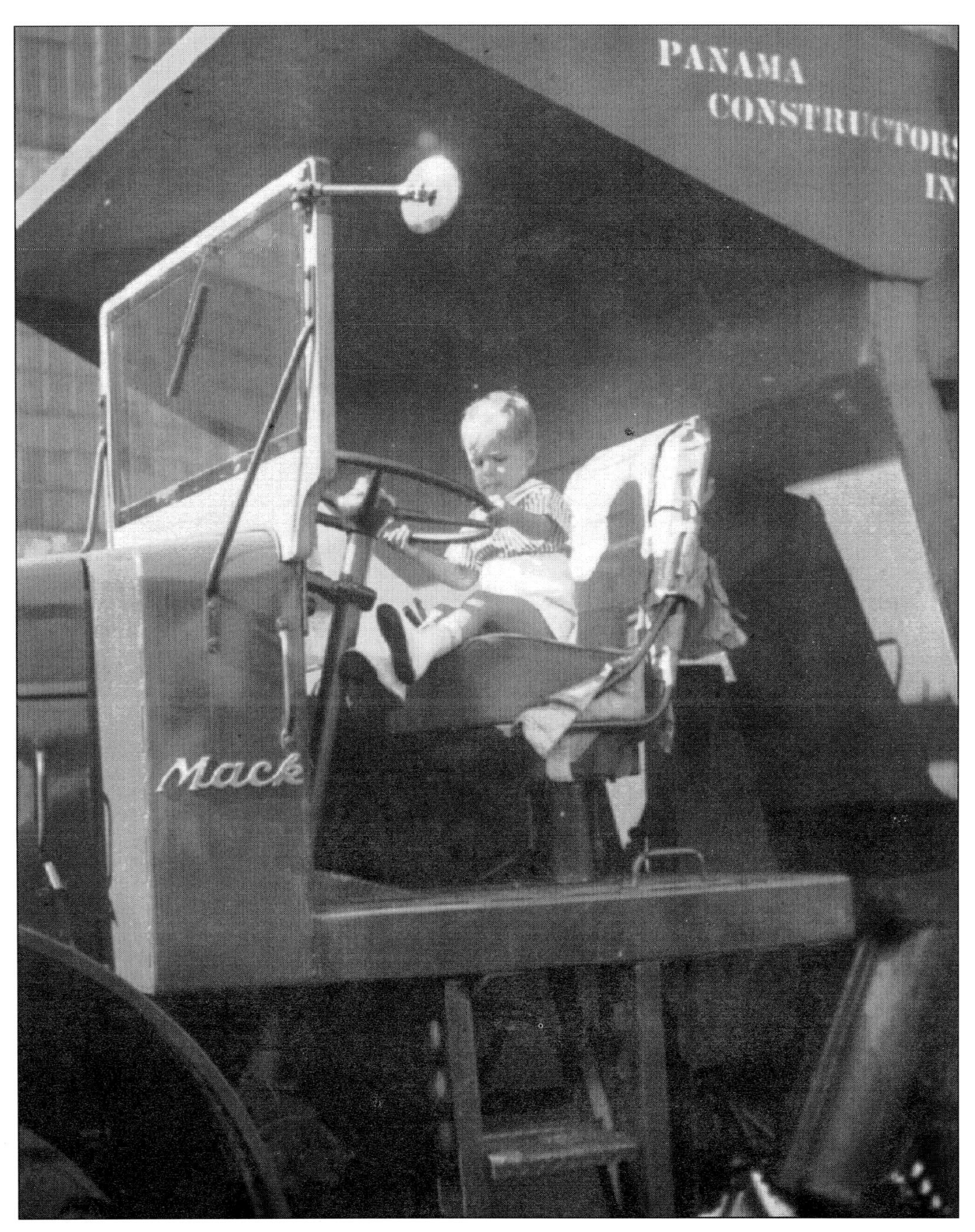

A future operator at the wheel of his Mack NW. December 1941. (M6278)

BIBLIOGRAPHY

Montville, John B., *Mack, Newark, Walter Haessner, Inc., 1973.*

Montville, John B., *Mack, A Living Legend of the Highway,* Tucson, Aztex Corp., 1979.

Rasmussen, Henry, *Mack, Bulldog of the American Highways,* Osceola, Motorbooks International, 1987.

Warth, Thomas E., *Mack Model AB Photo Archive,* Iconografix, Minneapolis, 1994.

Warth, Thomas E., *Mack Model B 1953-1966 Photo Archive,* Iconografix, Minneapolis, 1994.

The Iconografix Photo Archive Series includes:

JOHN DEERE MODEL D Photo Archive	ISBN 1-882256-00-X
JOHN DEERE MODEL A Photo Archive	ISBN 1-882256-12-3
JOHN DEERE MODEL B Photo Archive	ISBN 1-882256-01-8
JOHN DEERE 30 SERIES Photo Archive	ISBN 1-882256-13-1
FARMALL REGULAR Photo Archive	ISBN 1-882256-14-X
FARMALL F-SERIES Photo Archive	ISBN 1-882256-02-6
FARMALL MODEL H Photo Archive	ISBN 1-882256-03-4
FARMALL MODEL M Photo Archive	ISBN 1-882256-15-8
CATERPILLAR THIRTY Photo Archive	ISBN 1-882256-04-2
CATERPILLAR SIXTY Photo Archive	ISBN 1-882256-05-0
CATERPILLAR MILITARY TRACTORS VOLUME 1 Photo Archive	ISBN 1-882256-16-6
CATERPILLAR MILITARY TRACTORS VOLUME 2 Photo Archive	ISBN 1-882256-17-4
TWIN CITY TRACTOR Photo Archive	ISBN 1-882256-06-9
MINNEAPOLIS-MOLINE U-SERIES Photo Archive	ISBN 1-882256-07-7
HART-PARR Photo Archive	ISBN 1-882256-08-5
OLIVER TRACTORS Photo Archive	ISBN 1-882256-09-3
HOLT TRACTORS Photo Archive	ISBN 1-882256-10-7
RUSSELL GRADERS Photo Archive	ISBN 1-882256-11-5
MACK MODEL AB Photo Archive	ISBN 1-882256-18-2
MACK MODEL B 1953-66 Photo Archive	ISBN 1-882256-19-0
LE MANS 1950: THE BRIGGS CUNNINGHAM CAMPAIGN Photo Archive	ISBN 1-882256-21-2
SEBRING 12-HOUR RACE 1970 Photo Archive	ISBN 1-882256-20-4
IMPERIAL 1955-1963 Photo Archive	ISBN 1-882256-22-0
IMPERIAL 1964-1968 Photo Archive Available Early 1995	ISBN 1-882256-23-9
STUDEBAKER 1926-1938 Photo Archive	ISBN 1-882256-24-7
STUDEBAKER 1939-1958 Photo Archive	ISBN 1-882256-25-5
AMERICAN SERVICE STATIONS 1935-1943 Photo Archive	ISBN 1-882256-27-1
MACK FC, FCSW & NW1936-1947 Photo Archive	ISBN 1-882256-28-X
MACK EB, EC, ED, EE, EF, EG & DE 1936-1951 Photo Archive	ISBN 1-882256-29-8
CASE TRACTORS 1912-1959 Photo Archive	ISBN 1-882256-32-8
FORDSON 1917-1928 Photo Archive	ISBN 1-882256-33-6

The Iconografix Photo Archive Series is available from direct mail specialty book dealers and bookstores throughout the world, or can be ordered from the publisher.

For information write to:
Iconografix
P.O. Box 609
Osceola, Wisconsin 54020 USA

Telephone: (715) 294-2792
(800) 289-3504 (USA and Canada)
Fax: (715) 294-3414